HANDBOOK OF LITERARY TERMS

HANDBOOK OF LITERARY TERMS

Literature, Language, Theory

X. J. KENNEDY

DANA GIOIA

MARK BAUERLEIN

PEARSON
Longman

New York   Boston   San Francisco
London   Toronto   Sydney   Tokyo   Singapore   Madrid
Mexico City   Munich   Paris   Cape Town   Hong Kong   Montreal

Vice President and Editor in Chief: Joseph Terry
Executive Marketing Manager: Ann Stypuloski
Senior Supplements Editor: Donna Campion
Production Manager: Joseph Vella
Project Coordination, Text Design, and Electronic Page Makeup: Nesbitt Graphics, Inc.
Design Manager/Cover Designer: John Callahan
Cover: Winslow Homer (1885–1910). *Orange Trees and Gate*. Watercolor, 1885. Private
    Collection. Art Resource, NY.
Manufacturing Buyer: Roy L. Pickering, Jr.
Printer and Binder: Courier Corp.
Cover Printer: The Lehigh Press

For permission to use copyrighted material, grateful acknowledgment is made to the copyright holders on pp. 162–165, which are hereby made part of this copyright page.

Library of Congress Cataloging-in-Publication Data

Kennedy, X. J.
    Handbook of literary terms / X. J. Kennedy, Dana Gioia, Mark Bauerlein
        p. cm.
    ISBN 0-321-20207-4
    1. Literature—Terminology. 2. Criticism—Terminology. I. Gioia, Dana. II.
Bauerlein, Mark. III. Title.
PN44.5.K46 2005
803—dc22

                                        2004006745

Please visit our website at http://www.ablongman.com

ISBN 0-321-20207-4

3 4 5 6 7 8 9 10—CRS—07 06 05 04

Preface

This book is a user-friendly primer of critical terms, aimed at undergraduates getting their first taste of serious literary study. The definitions are concise, the citations pertinent and wide-ranging. All major schools of literary theory are presented clearly and fairly, but we have kept their definitions consistent in purpose and tone with those of other topics—no coy asides on postmodernism or poststructuralism. We present the basic tools of analysis—meter, metonymy, modernism, etc.—straightforwardly, letting the citations from ancient to contemporary literature add the spice of wit and the depth of genius. The goal is to provide students with a practical, instructive, and comprehensive guide to the language of literary study, one neither overly detailed nor facile in its explanations. As they practice the art of interpretation in introductory literature courses, students should regard this volume as a scholastic but accessible aide that eases their engagement with the humanities canon. In short, and on the premise that memory prefers the diverting to the dull, we hope that they absorb the definitions and enjoy the examples.

We understand the dislike many students feel for critical analysis over and above the simple pleasures of reading. We have assembled this little reference book trying not to cancel their joy with unnecessarily dry intellection. Critical terms may seem to them a pointless complication, and they wonder how knowing the meaning of *Bildungsroman* adds to their experience of a novel. They have a point, if the literature in mind is the ordinary product of mass culture, whose conventions are usually so scripted that they merit little attention. But what about the soliloquies of Shakespeare, the ballads of Wordsworth, the jagged metaphors of Emily Dickinson, the stream-of-consciousness of Faulkner? Works of literature with a thick verbal surface and a powerful theme summon a more adept reading knowledge. If they have no critical vocabulary to bring to the work, many readers will miss the refined joys of catching a playful irony, hearing an allusion to Greek myth, or noting a curious change in the sonnet structure.

Learning a critical vocabulary entails much more than knowing the meaning of individual terms. The vocabulary supplies the building materials for what educators call "domain knowledge," namely, the facts, texts, and skills peculiar to a discipline. An older name for it is *humanitas*, the sum of learning and sensibility that distinguishes a cultivated person and orients a liberal arts curriculum. Critical terms are an initial step in the process. Put the terms to use and other talents emerge. As they study the principles of different verse forms, for instance, students begin to acquire a poetic eye and ear, seeing and hearing the customary rhythms of blank verse, heroic couplets, and so on, plus the variations poets make upon them. As they classify narrative voices, a liberating aesthetic distance opens between reader and narrator. As they learn the chronological divisions of literary history, students develop a historical sense, not only appreciating how literary expression has evolved over time, but also perceiving how elements of the past remain alive in the present.

Art historians used to group such talents as connoisseurship. A connoisseur can look at a painting and detail its composition (light, color, foreground and background), identify meaningful icons (a saint, a ruin, a room), and correlate its style and subject with a historical era and region. A connoisseur of literature can do the same, picking out elements of language, structure, and content as formal and historical traits—but only so far as he or she possesses the right vocabulary and the knowledge that goes with it. Such advanced abilities not only improve reading comprehension; they also make reading more meaningful and, usually, more fun.

The combination of joy and discernment isn't as smooth as it sounds, though. In fact, in the humanities it creates what might be called a discipline problem. For students, the humanities can be a perfunctory activity—attending a course, reading books, and writing papers. But behind the classroom lies an entire institution trying to meet two broad, competing demands, and it is important that students understand them.

First, the humanities maintain a public trust. Parents want their tuition dollars to include some exposure to the classics of many cultures, and employers expect college graduates to write clearly and read acutely. Where else but in the humanities curriculum are the great works and deeds of the past preserved and imparted to future generations? Without the ethical examples presented by history and philosophy, most agree, students miss the deeper meanings of humanity, democracy, and modernity. Without the aesthetic challenges posed by art and poetry, their tastes and judgments stagnate. While the society at large slides into coarse entertainments and glib outlooks, the humanities serve as counterweight, allowing individuals a cloistered engagement with beauty, truth, and moral ideals.

Second, in contrast to their public mandate, the humanities aspire to be a scholarly enterprise. In their teaching, humanities professors devise curricula and grade exams, and in their research they observe rules of inquiry and discriminate through peer review. To remain a respectable part of the campus community, they must wield intellectual standards that in their own way appear just as rigorous and sound as those in the sciences. Accountability is everywhere: students to professors, professors to peers, departments to universities, and universities to society. Performance reviews are precisely what keep the humanities creditable as an education plan. Outside the workplace, reading and writing are personal matters, but in the humanities they must become methodical practices and be evaluated on scholastic grounds. Normally, a novel provides a chance for leisure and reflection, but on the syllabus it gathers disciplinary properties (figurative language, plot structure, historical representations) that students are obliged to expound. This is the day-to-day work of the humanities: to systematize literary objects and experiences and grade them accordingly.

These two directives don't easily coalesce. The first asks that humanistic study be accessible to a lay audience, so that any informed person may enter a classroom or open a critical essay and find the discourse there intelligible. The second makes humanistic study answerable to experts, who insist that the discourse satisfy professional standards and protocols. The one treats humanities knowledge as a civic resource for everyone, the other treats it as field material for the initiated. The concerned public likes engaging stories and sensitive commentaries, while the academic community looks for tight arguments and cutting-edge interpretations. How can the humanities please both?

There is no complete scheme to unite accessibility and professionalism, but the best practices manage to bridge the divide, to interest a general readership and clear disciplinary hurdles. One of the instruments for doing so is a book of this kind, a glossary of critical terms. A glossary defines and illustrates a disciplinary vocabulary but reaches out to a nondisciplinary audience. It is a point of transmission drawing lay readers into the semitechnical language of analysis and scholarship. Literary glossaries still cope with the popular vs. academic opposition of the humanities at large, but the opposition takes a specific form. The academic side demands that the definitions be precise and informed, while the popular side demands that they be interesting and manageable. An entry on metaphor that delineates the abstruse musings of theorists on the semantics of analogy may please rhetoric specialists but will turn freshmen off. But then, an entry that defines metaphor merely as "an implicit comparison" and says nothing about its semantic complications gives students a simplistic notion of the term and misrepresents both current and traditional thinking in the field.

Another opposition bears upon the citations. Obviously, a glossary aims first to define terms, and most of the entries have allusions and passages that display the term clearly and directly. Students understand and remember concepts better when they have a vivid illustration at hand, and so we have tried to identify memorable lines of prose, verse, and theory that neatly encapsulate them. But the illustrations also fulfill a secondary task—to convey in bits and pieces a literary tradition. In the general curriculum, the terms provide tools for analysis, while literary history provides material to be analyzed. So, readers should regard the citations not only as fragment-instances of the term, but also as samples from the sweep of world literature. We have chosen quotations from classical, medieval, Renaissance, and modern periods, from European, English, and American authors, and from fiction, poetry, drama, and criticism. In terms of rival demands on the humanities, the challenge is, first, to meet disciplinary needs by selecting passages appropriate to the entry and representative of the canon, and, second, to match popular wants by finding quotations that move and amuse undergraduates. Once again, the choice of citations necessitates a balancing act.

If a glossary is one of the first contacts students have with serious criticism, then to spur further study it should preview the delights and inspirations that serious literature offers. The long-range purpose of humanities teaching and scholarship is to sustain an enlivening heritage and produce knowledgeable, cultivated citizens. Hence, glossaries, along with introduction to literature courses and anthologies, should start the process with vigor and intelligence. We hope this volume is worthy of the two common motives shaping that curricular progress: the natural disposition of young people to learn and the intellectual duty of scholars to judge.

Entries appear in alphabetical order, with cross-references noted at the end of each one and other entry terms printed in bold, except where their mention is perfunctory. Words that students may have difficulty pronouncing are followed by pronounciation guides. Technical terms of rhetoric, prosody, and dramaturgy (**parallelism, box set**) are given quick definitions supplemented with clarifying examples. If they have been the subject of speculations by literary theorists, however, we indicate some of the questions that have been raised. Historical labels and aristic movements (**Augustan Age, Minimalism**) receive longer, descriptive entries that lay out the concerns and styles characterizing them. The passages quoted name some of the leading authors and works and suggest the nature and quality of the literature they produced. Theoretical schools (**deconstruction, cultural studies**) have enjoyed extensive commentary in other glossaries, often out of partisan impulses that forget the educational level of undergraduates. We have pared the discussions down and translated the recondite arguments of theory into basic principles and relevant stakes. We have added philological terms (**Middle English**) to the volume to restore an aspect of literary study often overlooked in introductory courses, namely, the history of the language. The list of entries is not exhaustive, and students will wish to augment this glossary by consulting the more advanced and specialized encyclopedias of poetics, criticism, and literary history. But as an opening document, it will assist both teachers who labor to establish a prevailing critical discourse in the classroom and students not too far removed from high school who struggle to assimilate the mores of higher education.

X. J. KENNEDY
DANA GIOIA
MARK BAUERLEIN

Handbook of Literary Terms

Abecedarius [A–buh–suh–DAR–ee–us] From Latin, "of the alphabet," *a* + *b* + *c* + *d*. A poem arranged on the order of the alphabet, for example, when each successive line or **stanza** starts with a successive letter. Chaucer's "An ABC" (ca. 1365) has an abecedarian stanza arrangement, beginning:

A̲lmighty and al merciable queene . . . (stanza 1)

B̲ountee so fix in thin herte his tente . . . (stanza 2)

C̲omfort is noon but in yow, ladi deere . . . (stanza 3)

to the final stanza:

Z̲acharie you clepeth the open welle . . .

Abstract diction   See Diction.

Accent   An emphasis placed on a syllable in speech. In English, accent usually rests upon the pitch (force of breath) applied, although the duration of the syllable also contributes to the accent. Normal pronunciation of polysyllabic words follows a regular distribution of accented and unaccented sounds. For example, *con*-tract and con-*tract* (or *re*-cord and re-*cord*) are two different words and parts of speech, depending on their accent.

   In literary studies, accent is the basic unit of **prosody** and distinguishes one metrical foot from another. The opening line from John Milton's *Paradise Lost*, Book II (1667), begins with a **trochee** (accented-unaccented), then runs through four **iambs** (unaccented-accented).

High on a *throne* of *royal* *state*, which *far* . . .

Occasionally, the **rhythm** of a line will influence the pronunciation of accent—a process termed "metrical stress"—as in:

Be*fore* high-*piled books*, in *charactery* . . .
(John Keats, "When I Have Fears"; 1818)

The rhythm of the line ensures that *piled* has two distinct syllables, whereas in casual speech the word wavers between one and two syllables. (*See also* **Accentual verse, Meter, Stress.**)

Accentual verse   Verse whose meter is based upon the number of speech stresses per line, not upon the number of syllables. The unstressed syllables may vary, but the rate of accented syllables does not. Much popular poetry, such as

ballads and folk songs in earlier times and **rap** and nursery rhymes today, is written in accentual meter. (*See also* **Accent, Meter**)

Acrostic   A poem in which a vertical order of a letter in each line, when read downward, spells out a word, often the name of a beloved person, or, in the special case of the **abecedarius**, spells out the alphabet. Usually, acrostics highlight the initial letter of each line. Note, for example, what the first letters spell in one of John Davies' *Hymnes to Astraea* (1599) dedicated to Queen Elizabeth:

> Empress of flowers, tell where away
> Lies your sweet Court this merry May,
>   In Greenewich garden allies?
> Since there the heavenly powers do play
> And haunt no other vallies.
>
> Beautie, vertue, maiestie,
> Eloquent Muses, three times, three,
> The new fresh Houres and Graces,
> Have pleasure in this place to be,
>   Above all other places.
> Roses and lilies did them draw,
>   Ere they divine Astraea say;
> Gay flowers they sought for pleasure:
> Instead of gathering crownes of flowers,
>   Now gather they Astraea's dowers,
> And beare to heaven their treasure.

Sometimes, however, acrostics track the final or middle letters in a poem, or even follow a diagonal path, as in Edgar Allan Poe's "A Valentine" (1849). Acrostics date back to the Hebrew Bible and ancient Greek poetry, and may have been used as mnemonic aides in oral performance. (*See also* **Abecedarius.**)

Act   The major structural division in a drama. Further subdivided into **scenes,** acts may include changes of place and time, but they generally function as large-scale segments of the plot. For instance, an opening act may serve to introduce different characters, a second act to raise the prime **complication,** a third act to commence the **rising action,** a fourth act to stage the **climax,** and a fifth act to effect the **resolution.** English Renaissance dramatists, in imitation of Roman playwright Seneca, structured their works into this five-act pattern, whereas nineteenth-century dramatists such as Chekhov and Ibsen preferred a four-act model. Modern playwrights, however, seem to favor a three-act pattern, although experimental works by Samuel Beckett and other *avant garde* artists eliminate acts altogether.

Aestheticism   An artistic movement in Europe in the nineteenth century, aestheticism held that artworks are the highest human achievement and aesthetic responses the most developed human experience. Centered in Paris (major figures: Théophile Gautier, Charles Baudelaire, J. K. Huysmans, Gustave Moreau) and London (Walter Pater, Algernon Swinburne, Oscar Wilde, Aubrey Beardsley), aestheticism argued that art should not be subordinated to external causes such as moral uplift and political platforms, nor should it attempt to follow "nature," as eighteenth-century critics advised. Art should serve only itself. Hence the slogan, "art for art's sake"—that is, art has no other end but beauty. As Wilde put it in the Preface to *The Picture of Dorian Gray* (1891), "There is no such thing as a moral or an immoral book. Books are well-written or badly written. That is all." He added, "All art is quite useless," meaning that art has no practical, worldly aims. It seeks only to please, to provoke, to fascinate.

As a result of their religion of art, aesthetes in their work focused upon manner, style, and artifice, downplaying overt social/political content and psychological depth (although major works such as *Dorian Gray* bear remarkable psychic complexity and moral implications). The mechanisms of form and image and eloquence overrule the putative truth or goodness of the work. To ward off the agenda aspect of art and disavow the norms of nature, aesthetes expanded their theory of art into a mode of life, propagating outlandish dress, drugs, sexual deviance, and antisocial attitudes. Their heroes were figures of intense sensation, such as Edgar Allan Poe and his obsessive narrators, and cultivated absorption, such as Baudelaire's dandies with their exaggerated attention to dress and manner. They declared war on crudeness, vulgarity, philistinism, and bourgeois values, and posed a bohemian sensibility as their antidote. To cultivate beauty in art and life was to escape from unimaginative social mores and conventional thoughts.

As a distinctive movement, aestheticism ended just after the turn of the century. But its influence stretched well into the modern period, finding expression in the defense of high culture by Ezra Pound and T. S. Eliot, the exotic rendering of beauty in Wallace Stevens's poetry, the emphasis on form in **New Criticism**, the brash, antisocial misbehavior of the **Beat Generation**, and the sense of alienation felt by countless writers from James Joyce to Thomas Pynchon. (*See also* **Aesthetics, Symbolist movement**.)

Aesthetics   The philosophical and critical study of beauty. Reflections on the nature of beauty date back to the ancients, but as a formal analysis aesthetics begins in the eighteenth century with critics and thinkers such as Joseph Addison, Edmund Burke (*Philosophical Inquiry into the Origin of Our Ideas of the Sublime and Beautiful*, 1757), and, most importantly, Immanuel Kant (*Critique of Judgment*, 1790). Their goal was to distinguish the moral, intellectual, and emotional elements of the disinterested pleasure we derive from certain objects. In general, aestheticians assert that aesthetic responses are experiences based not upon the material benefits the object provides (money, somatic comforts, etc.), but upon our independent, "pure" appreciation of it. We are drawn to the object not for reasons of advantage, but because of its appeal to the imagination. The object captivates us, pleases by its presence—not on moral grounds (for example, because it illustrates an ethical principle), or on personal grounds (for example, because it reminds us of a happy event in our past), but on artistic grounds, that is, its form, color, shape, treatment, etc. It may have moral and personal benefits, but these are to be distinguished from its aesthetic qualities. Kant went so far as to separate aesthetic virtue entirely from moral and intellectual virtue—we enjoy a painting not because it is good or true, but because it excites our disinterested contemplation.

Aesthetics is important to literary study because most definitions of literature maintain that a work of writing is literary only if its language bears aesthetic traits. Literature is composed of language that doesn't just impart information, but possesses an independent value as language. Practical language, theorists argued, serves only as a means of communication, and once it fulfills its purpose, it disappears. But literary language stands as a form in itself. Something about the sound, arrangement, syntax, diction, metaphors, etc., calls attention to the words and sentences. The words don't just communicate a meaning. They embody a verbal object, and if that object evokes disinterested pleasure in readers and listeners, then it falls under an aesthetic purview. Indeed, many early-twentieth-century theorists argued that without a distinct category of aesthetic language no discipline of literary studies is possible. Instead of being an aesthetic object, literature would be a social, political, historical, or psychological object, and literary studies would be subsumed by sociology, political science, history, and psychology. The aesthetic features of language are, precisely, the subject matter of the literary disciplines. (*See also* **Formalism, Symbolist movement.**)

Alexandrine   [AL–ex–AN–dren] A line of verse composed of twelve syllables, as in Sir Philip Sidney's:

> I sought fit words to paint the blackest face of woe . . .
> (*Astrophel and Stella*; 1591)

The alexandrine is an infrequent verse form in English poetry. Its most customary usage appears in the final line of the **Spenserian stanza**, conceived by Edmund Spenser in *The Faerie Queene* (1590) and imitated by Shelley, Keats, and Tennyson, among others. It is found more commonly in French verse and was the most popular meter in French drama of the seventeenth century (Corneille, Racine, Molière).

Allegory   A narrative in verse or prose in which the literal elements (characters, settings, actions) consistently point to a parallel sequence of ideas, values, realities, virtues, or other recognizable things. Allegory is often used to dramatize moral principles, historical events, religious systems, or political issues, often for didactic or satiric purposes. An allegory has two levels of meaning: a literal level that tells a surface story and a symbolic level in which the abstractions unfold. The names of characters often hint at their allegorical meaning, and the characters' behavior bears them out. For example, in Nathaniel Hawthorne's "Young Goodman Brown" (1835), "Faith" is not only the name of the protagonist's wife but also a token of his religious convictions. The medieval play *Everyman* (ca. 1485) has characters named Good Deeds and Discretion, Aesop's *Fables* present animals acting out specific vices, and portions of Swift's *Gulliver's Travels* (1726) may be read as an allegory of politics in eighteenth-century England. In each case, a concrete element of the narrative is tied to a general idea or thing.

As a literary technique, allegory isn't bound to genre or form. Allegories appear in prose and verse, comedy and tragedy, and may be as short as a two-paragraph **fable** or as long as a Renaissance **epic**. They borrow materials from the worlds of politics, art, religion, psychology, and philosophy, and put them to critical, patriotic, devotional, or ironic uses. The only requirement for an allegory is that two or more levels of meaning be sustained consistently and that the abstract meaning be, more or less, conventional.

Since the **Romantic Period**, writers have often treated allegory as an inferior creation. Allegory, they maintain, involves a mechanical conversion of pre-existing materials—for instance, a political situation—into fanciful narratives. Samuel Taylor Coleridge called it "a translation of abstract notions into a picture-language" (*The Statesman's Manual*, 1816), a "proxy" for established beliefs and conditions. The abstract meaning—for instance, a moral precept—exists independently of the work, the latter being a mere illustration of it. A higher art is to exercise the imagination upon reality and produce a new vision of things, not just a figurative version of them. (*See also* **Fable, Parable, Symbol.**)

Alliteration   The repetition of a consonant sound. Strictly speaking, alliteration marks the beginning of words ("cool cats"—initial alliteration), but the term is often applied to sounds and syllables within them ("In *k*itchen *c*ups *c*on*c*upiscent *c*urds"—a combination of initial and internal alliteration). Alliteration was a structural rule of Anglo-Saxon poetry, in which lines were broken in the middle by a **caesura** and the initial stressed syllable in the second part alliterated with stresses in the first part. Middle English poets continued the practice, as in the line from *Sir Gawain and the Green Knight* (ca. 1375–1400):

Falles upon faire flat, flowres there schewen . . . (l. 507)

During the course of **Middle English** the line pattern disappeared, and since then alliteration rarely serves as a structuring device. But it remains an essential feature of the music of verse, serving to accentuate different meanings and effects. Sometimes, alliteration highlights a comic mood, as in John Gay's "A New Song of New Similes" (1727):

> *Plump* as a *p*artridge was I known,
>   And *s*oft as *s*ilk my *s*kin,
> My cheeks as fat as butter *g*rown;
>   But as a *g*roat now thin!

Or, it can emphasize ideas:

> I have always a*sp*ired to a more *sp*acious form . . .
>   (Czeslaw Milosz, "Ars Poetica"; 1969)

As an essential constituent of literary language, alliteration often has but an incidental value in poetry and prose. But in such cases when a repetition of sounds distinguishes a meaning or an atmosphere, alliteration is more than gratuitous—it contributes to the overall significance of the work. (*See also* **Assonance, Consonance.**)

Allusion   A brief, sometimes indirect reference in a text to a person, place, thing, or prior text, be it fictitious or actual. An allusion may appear in a literary work as an initial quotation, as a passing mention of a name, or as a phrase borrowed from another writer, bringing with it the meanings and implications of the original. Allusions imply a common knowledge between reader and writer and operate as a literary shorthand to enrich the meaning of a text. Usually, allusions are simple and clear, easily understood if one is familiar with the pertinent literary or historical context. The interpretative difficulty lies in determining how the material alluded to fits in here, in the new work's setting. Other times, however, allusions may be dense and complex, and unraveling them is part of the interpretation of the work as a whole. The opening lines of T. S. Eliot's *The Waste Land* (1922) are a rich example:

> April is the cruelest month, breeding
> Lilacs out of the dead land . . .

The lines echo the opening of Chaucer's *Canterbury Tales* (1386–1400):

> Whan the April with his showres soote . . .

and perhaps also Walt Whitman's "When Lilacs Last in the Dooryard Bloom'd" (1866), which mourns the assassination of Lincoln (killed in April 1865). Such allusions imply an intimate relation to tradition, and demand that readers adopt the same.

Critics categorize allusions into many kinds, the most prominent being: (1) topical—references to specific real events and issues; (2) personal—references to circumstances in the author's life; (3) metaphorical—references to prior works that, inserted into the new work, endow the latter with another layer of significance; and (4) imitative—reference to another work by imitating its rhetoric, genre, or phrases.

Ambiguity   The basic definition of "ambiguity" is, simply, "a quality or state of indistinctness, equivocation, or duality"—in ordinary discourse a pejorative trait. But in literary contexts, ambiguity is an important and sophisticated feature of language. Poetic discourse often works by suggestion, by connotation and nuance, or by the condensation of multiple, contradictory attitudes and feelings. Ambiguity is their verbal counterpart. Instead of marking deficiencies of style, ambiguity (well-handled) in literature signifies rich, copious expressions and provocative viewpoints. The fact that many ambiguities are perpetual—that is, not resolveable into single implications—only heightens their effect. For example, Sylvia Plath's "Lady Lazarus" (1966) documents in bizarre terms, including Holocaust and carnival freak show allusions, Plath's previous brushes with suicide. But it ends with a frightening image of voracious female destruction:

> Out of the ash
> I rise with my red hair
> And I eat men like air.

The import is ambiguous. The "ash" alludes to the Phoenix legend, which correlates with the death-resurrection motif (Lazarus) in the poem. But the conversion of the Phoenix into a devourer of men is inscrutable. The basic sense is clear, but the implications (and Plath's intentions) remain murky, and the murkiness contributes to the baneful atmosphere of the poem. (*See also* **Connotation, Denotation.**)

American Renaissance   A term coined by critic F. O. Matthiessen to name the outpouring of major literature in the northeastern United States in the decades before the Civil War. Its main figures include Ralph Waldo Emerson, Nathaniel Hawthorne, Herman Melville, Henry David Thoreau, and Walt Whitman. Major works include Emerson's *Nature* (1836), "Self-Reliance" (1841), and "The American Scholar" (1837); Hawthorne's *The Scarlet Letter* (1850) and *Twice-Told Tales* (1837); Melville's *Moby-Dick* (1851); Thoreau's *Walden* (1854); and the first edition of Whitman's *Leaves of Grass* (1855). The epoch is important not just because of the talent of the individual writers, but also because it marked the first full-scale flowering of a national literature. If we add writers Emily Dickinson, Frederick Douglass, Margaret Fuller, Edgar Allan Poe, and others to the movement (Matthiessen and later Americanists have been faulted for the restrictiveness of their list of authors), we have a corpus that rivals the productions of any national tradition in the world. Before the American Renaissance, only a few writers such as Washington Irving and James Fenimore Cooper enjoyed a wide audience and an international reputation. Most American literature, critics said, was derivative and "Europeanized." As Emerson put it in "The Poet" (1842), "We have yet had no genius in America." At the same time, however, writers began searching the American scene for fitting literary subjects—Hawthorne's Salem, Thoreau's Concord woods,

Whitman's Manhattan—and writing about them in innovative ways, for example, Whitman's free verse and Melville's metaphysical drama. Today, such works are essential American readings, the first major collective literary expression of the United States.

Anapest [AN–uh–pest] A metrical foot in verse in which two unstressed syllables are followed by a stressed syllable, as in "on a *boat*" or "in a *slump*." In Edgar Allan Poe's "Annabel Lee" (1849), several lines are strictly anapestic:

> But our love it was stronger by far than the love . . . (l. 27)

> For the moon never beams without bringing me dreams . . .
> (l. 34)

> And the stars never rise but I see the bright eyes . . . (l. 36)

(*See also* **Meter.**)

Anaphora [an–AA(as in "cat")–for–uh] The repetition of the same word at the beginning of lines of verse, sentences, or parts of sentences. For example,

> Mine – by the Right of the White Election!
> Mine – by the Royal Seal!
> Mine – by the Sign in the Scarlet prison–
> Bars – cannot conceal!
> > (Emily Dickinson, "Mine – by the Right of the White
> > Election!"; ca. 1862)

Anecdote A short narrative usually consisting of a single incident or episode. Often humorous, anecdotes can be real or fictional. When they appear within a larger context, as an author's digression or a brief story told by one character to another, they tend to reveal something meaningful to the work as a whole.

Antagonist The thing that opposes the **protagonist** in a narrative or drama. The antagonist may be another character, society itself, a force of nature, or even a conflicting impulse within the protagonist. For example, in Sophocles' *Antigone* (ca. 450 B.C.E.), Antigone (who wishes to bury her dead brother) is the protagonist and Creon (who forbids the burial) the antagonist. In Mark Twain's *Huckleberry Finn* (1884), we might say that Huck is the protagonist and his own conscience (which, ironically, tells him not to help the slave Jim escape) the antagonist. The conflict between such forces is what drives the plot and maintains the reader's interest.

Anticlimax An unsatisfying and trivial turn of events in a literary work that occurs in place of a genuine **climax**. An anticlimax often involves a surprising shift in tone from the lofty or serious to the petty or ridiculous. The term is used negatively to denote a feeble moment in a **plot** in which an author fails to create an intended effect. The term can also be applied positively, however, to denote a clever dramatic device when a writer implements it skillfully for humorous or ironic effect. For example, John Dryden's mock-heroic poem "MacFlecknoe" (1682) ends just as its hero, the bard Prince Flecknoe, is about to anoint his successor, a moment calling for high eloquence. But before he can do so, his underlings open a trap door,

> And down they sent the yet declaiming bard.
> Sinking he left his drugget robe behind,
> Borne upwards by a subterranean wind.

The anticlimax has a satiric thrust, that is, to deflate Thomas Shadwell (the talentless "MacFlecknoe"), a rival of Dryden's who pretended to literary greatness. (*See also* **Bathos**.)

Antihero   A **protagonist** who lacks one or more of the conventional qualities attributed to a **hero**. Instead of being dignified, brave, idealistic, or purposeful, the antihero may be cowardly, self-interested, alienated, or weak. Although instances of the antihero are sprinkled throughout literature since ancient times—for instance, Cervantes' *Don Quixote* (1605) and Byron's *Don Juan* (1819–24)—the antihero in the current sense is essentially a twentieth-century character. Their antiheroism tends to reflect the spiritual or social afflictions of modern man and woman—atheism, loneliness, mistrust of authority, disillusionment with Western ideals. Posing a satiric or frank contrast to traditional portrayals of idealized heroes and heroines, antiheroes are figures of moral and psychological waywardness, and also of social and ethical criticism. Their oppositional nature stems not simply from within, but from the interaction of self and society; hence, their failings point to themselves and to the worlds they inhabit. Modern examples range from Arthur Miller's Willy Loman in *Death of a Salesman* (1949) to the sex-crazed Jewish adolescent in Philip Roth's *Portnoy's Complaint* (1969).

Antithesis   Words, phrases, clauses, or sentences set in deliberate contrast to one another. A species of **parallellism**, antithesis balances opposing ideas, feelings, tones, or structures, giving crisp expression to their pairing and heightening its effect. Alexander Pope was a master of antithesis in verse, as in the final lines of Epistle I of *Essay on Man* (1733):

> All Nature is but art, unknown to thee;
> All chance, direction, which thou canst not see;
> All discord, harmony not understood;
> All partial evil, universal good:
> And, spite of pride, in erring reason's spite,
> One truth is clear, Whatever is, is RIGHT.

(*See also* **Chiasmus**.)

Apostrophe A direct address to an absent person or thing as if it were present and sentient. In poetry an apostrophe often hails an entity not ordinarily spoken to, as when Shakespeare announces, "No! Time, thou shalt not boast that I do change" (Sonnet 123, 1609). Some apostrophes are mere conventions, such as the epic poet's invocation to the muse; but in skillful hands, an apostrophe can serve powerful dramatic purposes. In issuing apostrophes to inanimate objects, dead or absent persons, abstract things, or spirits, the speaker often is given the opportunity to articulate thoughts aloud, to say to idealized entities what cannot be said to other characters. The opening of John Donne's "The Sun Rising" (1633) has an apostrophe to the sun that allows Donne to express his frustration at having to depart his beloved's bed:

> Busy old fool, unruly sun,
> Why dost thou thus,
> Through windows and through curtains call on us?
> Must to thy motions lovers' seasons run?

(*See also* **Invocation**.)

Apprenticeship novel *See* **Bildungsroman.**

Archaism A word or phrase that is obsolete. Used consistently, archaic elements—such as the verb stem *-eth* (*sheweth*, *rejoiceth*) and pronouns *ye* and *thou*—amount to a poetic style, often recalling Biblical or Medieval traditions. Writers insert archaisms into their works for various reasons—for instance, to evoke past settings, to express nostalgia for a prior period, or to foment a revival of earlier tastes and beliefs. In William Morris's "Rapunzel" (1858), the lines:

> *Mary, maid withouten wen* [blemish],
> *Keep me!* I am lone, I wis [know]. . .
>   (163-64)

contain two archaisms that contribute to the fairy tale atmosphere of the story of Rapunzel. In "Sunday Morning" (1915), Wallace Stevens alludes to ancient myths of paradise and inserts a sharp archaism for support:

> There is not any haunt of prophecy,
> Nor any old chimera of the grave,
> Neither the golden underground nor isle
> Melodious, where spirits *gat* them home . . .

Archetype [AR–keh–type] A recurring symbol, character, landscape, or event found in myth and literature across different cultures and eras. In terms of structure, an archetype merely serves as a model from which writers create different versions and copies. But in literary criticism, archetypes have a primal character, an occult significance rooted in human psychology and the prehistoric past. For an image, symbol, etc., to qualify as an archetype, it must have a long history and an existence across cultures and peoples—archetypes are not social constructs or political inventions. The modern idea of the archetype derives from early anthropologists such as Sir James Frazer, who combed myths from various cultures for repeated patterns and figures, and from the Swiss psychologist Carl Jung, who believed that all individuals share a "collective unconscious," a set of fundamental memories common to the human race. To archetypal thinkers, a pattern or figure repeated in myth and literature is an index of profound human fears and longings, of deep structures of experience, of cosmic beliefs. An example of an archetypal character is the devil-figure, which often appears in pure mythic form (as in Milton's *Paradise Lost*, 1667), but in modern literature occurs often in disguise, like Fagin in Charles Dickens's *Oliver Twist* (1837–38) and Abner Snopes in William Faulkner's "Barn Burning" (1938). (*See also* **Mythological criticism.**)

Arena theater   A modern, nontraditional performance space in which the audience surrounds the stage on four sides. The stage can be circular, square, rectangular, or ellipsoidal. In contrast to the **picture-frame stage**, with its privileged single point of view from the center of the orchestra seats, arena staging favors no one portion of the audience. In addition to its democratic openness, arena staging offers intimate seating arrangements combined with a larger seating capacity. (*See also* **Theater in the round.**)

Aside   In drama a few words or a short passage spoken in an undertone or to the audience. By convention, other characters onstage are deaf to the aside. For example, in *Hamlet* (1601), in response to Polonius's proverbial "with devotion's visage / And pious action we do sugar o'er / The devil himself," the guilty Claudius admits in an aside:

> O, 'tis too true!
> How smart a lash that speech doth give my conscience!
> The harlot's cheek, beautied with plastering art,
> Is not more ugly to the thing that helps it
> Than is my deed to my most painted word.
> O heavy burden!
> (III.i. 47–55)

Assonance   [AS–sow–nuntz] The repetition of two or more vowel sounds in successive words, which creates a kind of rhyme. Like alliteration, the assonance may occur initially ("*a*ll the *a*wful *au*guries") or internally ("wh*i*te l*i*lacs"). Assonance focuses attention on key feelings or concepts, and makes a phrase more musical and memorable. For example, at the beginning of *Song of Myself* (1855–92), Walt Whitman clusters three strong vowels:

> I l*oa*f and invite my s*ou*l,
> I lean and l*oa*f at my *ea*se . . .
> (ll. 4–5)

Atmosphere   The dominant mood or feeling that pervades all or part of a literary work. Atmosphere is the total effect conveyed by the author's use of language, images, and physical setting, and often foreshadows the ultimate **climax** in a narrative. For instance, the opening lines of Carson McCuller's *The Ballad of the Sad Cafe* (1943) set a decisive atmosphere for the rest of the story:

> The town itself is dreary; not much is there except the cotton mill, the two-room houses where the workers live, a few peach trees, a church with two colored windows, and a miserable main street only a hundred yards long.

When pathetic characters and sordid events follow this description, we aren't surprised. However, atmosphere is an imprecise element in literature, based as much upon **connotation** and suggestion as upon explicit statements in the work. The relation between atmosphere and **theme**, **plot**, **character**, and other elements is usually fuzzy, and to try to make atmosphere more distinct and clear-cut is sometimes to distort its atmospheric nature. (*See also* **Tone**.)

Auditory imagery   A word or sequence of words that refers to the sense of hearing. For example, in "Goblin Market" (1862) by Christina Rossetti, goblin-men offer fruits to a young woman:

> The whisk-tailed merchant bade her taste
> In tones as smooth as honey,
> The cat-faced purr'd,
> The rat-paced spoke a word
> Of welcome, and the snail-paced even was heard.
> One parrot-voiced and jolly
> Cried "Pretty Goblin" still for "Pretty Polly";
> One whistled like a bird.
> (ll. 107–14)

(*See also* **Imagery**.)

Augustan Age   This term has two related meanings. First, it refers to the greatest epoch of Roman literature, coincident with the Emperor Augustus (27 B.C.E.–14 C.E.), in which Virgil, Horace, and Ovid wrote. Second, it refers to the early-eighteenth century in British literature, a neoclassical period of political activity, with Tories battling Whigs for power, and literary flowering, with commercial writers competing with serious talents for patronage and readership. Both societies had endured civil wars in preceding years, and both also created a social and political world in which writers were prominent voices. In London, writers enjoyed a rising middle-class reading and theater-going public and a patronage system in which aristocrats and politicians courted them for their talents. Hundreds of poets, dramatists, and hack writers vied for influence, but Joseph Addison, Richard Steele, William Congreve,

Alexander Pope, and Jonathan Swift dominated the field. These British Augustans emulated the Roman writers as the highest literary models, favoring their concern with social reality and human virtues (or, more often, vices), as well as their insistence on well-crafted compositions. In explicit imitation of Roman Augustan discourse, Augustan verse and prose in England were characteristically formal in structure and diction, and sophisticated in theme and character. Addison and Steele made the periodical essay into a polished medium of social commentary. Congreve's comedies are beloved to this day. Pope is one of the great versifiers in English literature, and works such as *The Rape of the Lock* (1714) remain models of urbane satire composed in arresting heroic couplets. Swift regarded humanity as fraught with pride, pretense, vanity, and ignorance, and imagined bitter tales to expose the flaws. None of them claimed originality for their ideas and forms—the ancients always anticipated them. Each believed that, for example, Horace's satires upon Roman society applied equally well to their own.

The Augustan movement lasted well into the eighteenth century, until a new generation of writers (William Collins, Laurence Sterne, William Cowper, William Blake) judged their aesthetic artificial and their vision of humanity pessimistic. Their criticisms paved the way for the **Romantic Period**, whose leaders defined art and truth explicitly against the urbanity and satire of the neoclassical outlook. (*See also* **Romantic Period, Satire**.)

Authorial intrusion   *See* **Editorial point of view**.

Avant garde   [Ah–vawn gahrd] From the French "advance guard," the term signifies any group of artists and thinkers that conceives new and experimental forms and theories in the arts and culture. The *avant garde* arose as a social phenomenon in the mid-nineteenth century, as artists and intellectuals in Europe began to feel alienated from the spreading bourgeois society of the time. The middle-class world, they observed, is commercial and conventional, valuing artworks the same way it values any other commodity—as a source of profit, security, status, or escapism. It wants artworks to satisfy customary expectations, to match the norms of popular audiences. *Avant garde* figures envision a different activity for art: that is, to test the limits of their craft, to turn the medium to other, more aesthetic and conceptual uses, to break up solidified social and aesthetic attitudes and forge new, and temporary, alternatives. Operating on principles such as Ezra Pound's "Make it new," they challenge audience expectations. Painters such as Paul Cézanne and Georges Braque break up visual space into cubic surfaces; poets such as William Carlos Williams and E. E. Cummings dismantle words and letters and scatter them around the page; sculptors such as Carl Andre and Dan Flavin work in ready-made materials such as bricks and fluorescent lights. Out of their experiments come new aesthetic conventions. But as they are articulated in works of art, *avant garde* principles have an ironic consequence: as an artist succeeds in his or her craft and an artist's or movement's style and concerns are adopted by mainstream culture, they become, by definition, the targets of future *avant garde* practice. (*See also* **Mass culture.**)

Ballad   In its simplest sense, a ballad is a song or song-like poem that tells a story; but in the history of English and European literature, the ballad has features of style, content, and social context that distinguish it. Common among semi-literate or illiterate cultures and of unknown authorship, originally ballads were instances of folk art sung or recited and transmitted from performer to performer without being written down. They form a yeoman literature shaped by popular tastes and sensational topics, and sometimes the expression of a troubled community such as the Scottish border lands in the fifteenth and sixteenth centuries. Narrated in a straightforward third-person voice, they highlight **plot** and downplay the complexities of **character**, the action related in swift and direct description. In their compressed and emotional exposition are documented the labors of rural life and the drama of local legends, portraying outlaws, peasant heroes, and ill-fated lovers in action. Bearing the hallmarks of oral composition, they invoke formulaic expressions, follow a regular stanza pattern, slip smoothly into dialogue, and contain numerous refrains.

Impressed with the simplicity and immediacy of ballads, serious poets began to imitate the form—first, in the Renaissance and, then, at the end of the eighteenth century. Imitators such as William Wordsworth (*Lyrical Ballads*, 1798) prized them for the rustic portrayals of rural life, imparting the gentle pleasures of the countryside and dropping the sensationalistic plots. In terms of form, there are many variations of ballad verse, but most consist of quatrains made up of lines of three or four metrical feet in a simple alternating rhyme scheme. The stanzas in Wordsworth's "The Tables Turned" are strict examples:

> Up, up! my friend, and quit your books,
> Or surely you'll grow double;
> Up, up! my friend, and clear your looks;
> Why all this toil and trouble?

> The sun, above the mountain's head,
> A freshening luster mellow
> Through all the long green fields has spread,
> His first sweet evening yellow.

(*See also* **Ballad stanza** *and* **Broadside ballad.**)

Ballad stanza   The most common pattern of the ballad consists of four lines rhymed *abcb* or *abab*, in which the first and third lines have four metrical feet and the second and fourth lines have three feet.

> Ah! Well-a-day! what evil looks
> Had I from old and young!

Instead of the cross, the Albatross
About my neck was hung.

> (Samuel Taylor Coleridge, "The Rime of the Ancient
> Mariner," ll. 139–42; 1798)

Baroque   A movement of art, architecture, and, to a lesser extent, literature that thrived during the seventeenth century, roughly between the Renaissance and the Enlightenment. In terms of content, it may be considered a counterpart to the explosion of scientific learning and political theory at the time, and many such subjects are to be found in Baroque artworks. Abraham Cowley wrote poems on political philosopher Thomas Hobbes and on the Royal Society, and Andrew Marvell sprinkled his lyrics with astronomical references. In terms of form, the Baroque is characterized by energetic and lavish shapes and images, and it involves the viewer or reader in an active relationship. Artists try to capture motion and power at crucial moments, as when the sculptor Gianlorenzo Bernini selects dynamic subjects such as Daphne at the instant of her metamorphosis into a laurel tree, just before her ravishment by Apollo. As viewers witness the scene, their apprehension of the artwork becomes a dynamic experience in itself. To appreciate Bernini's Daphne, viewers must see her from all sides, in a sense participating in the representation as their different angles present a different aspect of the whole. Literary examples are less striking, but still bear the energy and force of Baroque visual art. For instance, John Donne composes poems filled with extravagant metaphors, such as the injunctions "Goe, and catch a falling starre, / Get with child a mandrake root" ("Song," 1633); and Richard Crashaw takes the story of St. Teresa of Avila being pierced by an angel's shaft and remakes her into the agent of God's power, not the recipient ("The Flaming Heart," 1652). Such odd metaphors and intense conceits draw readers into the dramatic scene, enticing them to share the complexity of characters in the midst of intense experience.

Bathos   [BAY–thos] In literature, an unintentional lapse from the sublime to the ridiculous or trivial, first formulated by Alexander Pope in *Treatise on the Art of Sinking in Poetry* (1727). Bathos differs from **anticlimax** in that the latter sometimes is a deliberate effect, intended for humor or contrast, whereas bathos occurs through failure. An attempt to capture the grand and profound comes off as inflated and fatuous. For example, in "Passage to India" (1871), Walt Whitman announces:

> Not you alone proud truths of the world,
> Nor you alone ye facts of modern science,
> But myths and fables of eld . . .

Striving to echo the depths of past and present, Whitman fails to elevate the references into a heightened subject. The language—especially *ye* and *eld*—sounds artificial and falls flat; and the phrase "proud truths of the world" is too abstract and the "facts of modern science" too prosaic to bear the amplitude Whitman demands.

Beat Generation   A group of American writers from the 1950s who made anti-Establishment, countercultural stances into a short-lived, but influential aesthetic movement. Regarding post–World War II U.S. culture as conformist, consumerist, and repressive, they advocated a life of experimentation and rebelliousness, combining religious mysticism, drugs, sexual liberation, and wayfaring into a "beat" sensibility. Though their freewheeling lives often resulted in dysfunction and despair, the writings they produced brought them fame and notoriety, and the Beats became established icons in the social landscape of the Fifties. Their members included Jack Kerouac, William Burroughs, and Allen Ginsburg; leading Beat works are the novel *On the Road* (1957) and the **free verse** poem *Howl* (1956). The opening lines of *Howl* impart the intense experiential attitude, as well as the effusive rhetoric, of Beat expression:

> I saw the best minds of my generation destroyed by
> madness, starving hysterical naked,
> dragging themselves through the negro streets at dawn
> looking for an angry fix,
> angelheaded hipsters burning for the ancient heavenly
> connection to the starry dynamo in the machinery of night, . . .

Bildungsroman   [BIL–dungs–ROW–mawn] German for "novel of growth and development," the *Bildungsroman* is a subgenre that originated in eighteenth-century German fiction and spread across Europe and the United States. Sometimes called an **apprenticeship novel**, it depicts a youth who struggles toward maturity, forming a worldview or philosophy of life and leaving behind the concerns of adolescence. The development of the protagonist gives the *bildungsroman* a coherent plot structure, and each character encountered and action undertaken proves a formative step in the youth's course toward adulthood. Dickens's *David Copperfield* (1849–50) and Joyce's *Portrait of the Artist as a Young Man* (1916) are classic examples of the *bildungsroman* in English.

Biographical criticism   The practice of using the author's life to derive interpretations of the work. Although the work is understood as an independent creation, the biography of the author provides the material to underscore subtle but important meanings. Learning that Jorge Luis Borges was a librarian or that Mary Shelley's parents were two of the leading radicals of their era prompts readers to be sensitive to certain aspects of their work that they might otherwise miss or undervalue. Although literary theorists have assailed biographical criticism on methodological grounds, the biographical approach to literature has endured, mainly because of its advantages in illuminating literary works.

It is important to distinguish between biography and biographical criticism. **Biography** is a branch of historical scholarship. It yields a written account of a person's life. To establish and interpret the facts of an author's life, a biographer uses all the available evidence—not just personal documents such as letters and diaries, but also the stories and poems for the light they shed on the personal record. Biographical criticism, however, is not concerned with recreating the course of an author's life. It focuses on explicating the literary work by compiling relevant materials from the life.

Readers must use biographical interpretations cautiously. To treat the work solely as a reflection of the life is to reduce the multiple meanings and values of a work to one historical reality, the author's experience. Moreover, readers must examine biographical materials with a critical eye. Writers are notorious for revising the facts of their own lives. They often delete embarrassments and invent accomplishments, trading the truth for a preferred image. Family and friends cooperate and destroy or distort biographical materials after the author's death. John Cheever frequently told reporters about his sunny, privileged youth. After Cheever's death, biographer Scott Donaldson discovered a childhood scarred by a distant mother, a failed, alcoholic father, and nagging economic uncertainty. Once these facts came out, critics regarded Cheever's work in a different light.

An added danger, especially in the case of a famous writer such as F. Scott Fitzgerald, is that the life can overwhelm the work, leading critics to draw simple connections between this element in the work and that event in the life, with the latter taking priority. The texts are complicated and mystifying, but the real life events are (putatively) not, and so critics are tempted to invoke the latter to resolve the former. A savvy biographical critic remembers to base an interpretation on what is in the text itself. Biographical data should amplify the meaning of the text, not cover it with life episodes.

Biography   A factual account of a person's life, examining all available information and texts relevant to the subject. (*See also* **Biographical criticism**.)

Black Box theater   *See* **Flexible theater**.

Blank verse   The most common meter of unrhymed poetry in English, introduced by Henry Howard, Earl of Surrey, in the mid-sixteenth century in a translation of *The Aeneid*. The form is simple: five iambic feet per line (decasyllabic verse) and no rhymes (*blank* means "unrhymed.") Lacking stanza form and rhyme, blank verse is well-fitted to complex, lengthy subjects and many literary works of epic scope have been written in it, including John Milton's *Paradise Lost* (1667) and William Wordsworth's *The Prelude* (1850). The form also suits dramatic dialogue. Shakespeare's plays are written primarily in blank verse, as are Ben Jonson's. In other poetic forms involving meditative subjects, poets have used blank verse to ruminate informally upon personal and philosophical matters—as in Samuel Taylor Coleridge's **conversation poem** "This Lime-Tree Bower My Prison" (1797)—the unrhymed pentameter line allowing for casual, extemporaneous reflection. The modern era is considered a period of formal experimentation, but many canonical modernist works appear in blank verse, such as Wallace Stevens's *Notes toward a Supreme Fiction* (1942), much of Hart Crane's *The Bridge* (1930), and Robert Frost's "Mending Wall" (1914). (*See also* **Iambic pentameter.**)

Blues   A type of folk music developed in the nineteenth century by African Americans in the South, often addressing suffering and loss. Blues lyrics traditionally consist of three-line stanzas in which two identical lines are followed by a third concluding, rhyming line. Strict formal models of the blues follow a set chord progression and stick to a pentameter verse length. For example:

> I hate to see the evening sun go down,
> I hate to see the evening sun go down,
> 'Cause when it does my baby's not aroun'.

The influence of the blues is fundamental in virtually all styles of popular American music—jazz, **rap,** rock, gospel, country, and rhythm and blues. In literature it has enjoyed wide influence among African American writers such as Langston Hughes, Ralph Ellison, and Gwendolyn Brooks.

Box set   The illusion of scenic realism for interior rooms was achieved in the early-nineteenth century with the development of the box set, consisting of three walls that joined in two corners and a ceiling that tilted as if seen in perspective. The "fourth wall," invisible, ran parallel to the proscenium arch. By the middle of the nineteenth century, the addition of realistic props and furnishings made it possible for actors to behave onstage as if they inhabited private space, oblivious to the presence of an audience, even turning their backs to the audience while speaking if the dramatic situation required it. Audiences recognized the rooms on stage as more or less like their own, and understood their viewing as a window into real lives. Realist and naturalist dramatists such as Henrik Ibsen and Maxim Gorki favored the box set as a faithful representation of actual settings, a less artificial and theatrical staging of action. (*See also* **Naturalism, Realism.**)

Broadside ballads   Poems printed on a single sheet of paper, often set to traditional tunes. Most broadside ballads, which originated in the late-sixteenth century, were an early form of verse journalism, cheap to print and widely circulated. Anonymous and crude—except in literary adaptations of them—broadside ballads formed a kind of street discourse, ranging from base entertainment to sensational accounts of crime and punishment to irreverent sallies on religious and political practices. Printers sold them at fairs and markets and on street corners, though critics called them hackwork and authorities monitored their political content (the English Parliament banned broadside ballads in 1649).

Burlesque   In general, a burlesque is any entertainment containing ribald humor and antic situations. But in literary studies, burlesque is something more specific: a comic genre in which a serious style or topic is coupled with, respectively, a ridiculously discrepant topic or style. In burlesque works, a minor incident such as the clipping of a lock of hair may be treated as an epic matter (as in Alexander Pope's *The Rape of the Lock*, 1714), or a character's trivial, vain feelings may be handled as earth-shaking phenomena. The style and subject matter don't match—a grandiose style broaches a trivial subject, or a grand subject is represented in a low style (as in **doggerel** verse). Thomas Gray's "Ode on the Death of a Favorite Cat" (1748) invokes the elevated language of the **ode** to recount a "tabby" drowning in a fishbowl:

> 'Twas on a lofty vase's side,
> Where China's gayest art had dyed
> The azure flowers, that blow;
> Demurest of the tabby kind,
> The pensive Selima reclined,
> Gazed on the lake below.

Because burlesque relies on literary conventions of what is high and what is low, it changes over time. What is capable of being burlesqued at one time isn't at another. On the nineteenth-century English stage, for example, a popular form of burlesque was a broad caricature, **parody**, travesty, or send-up of musical plays and opera. Gilbert and Sullivan's Victorian operettas burlesqued grand opera, taking the latter's high passion and theatrical action and putting it to comic uses. But because of the decline of opera's popularity today, it is no longer an effective target for humor. (*See also* **Comedy**, **Satire**.)

Cacophony [Keh–KAW–fuh–nee] A harsh, discordant sound (Greek: *kakos* "bad" + *phone* "sound"), often mirroring the meaning of the object to which it refers, for example, "Grate on the scrannel pipes of wretched straw" (John Milton, "Lycidas," 1637.) The opposite of cacophony is **euphony**.

Caesura, cesura [Say–ZHU–rah] A pause within a line of verse. Traditionally, caesuras appear near the middle of a line, but their placement may be varied to create expressive rhythmic effects. The five successive caesuras in Tennyson's "Ulysses" (1842), for example, rhythmically impart the frustration of the hero after his return to Ithaca:

> How dull it is to pause, to make an end,
> To rest unburnished, not to shine in use!
> As though to breathe were life! Life piled on life
> Were all too little, and of one to me
> Little remains . . .
>   (ll. 23–26)

Captivity narrative   A popular prose genre in the United States and Canada in the late-eighteenth and nineteenth centuries. Captivity narratives take place on the frontier, where white settlers and native peoples conduct trade, socialize, and sometimes erupt into violence. In the standard captivity plot, a white woman is kidnapped and held among the tribe, often after seeing her husband and brothers slaughtered. Trapped in Native American society, the captive undergoes forced marriages, forced labor, itinerance, and pagan ritual. Her shocking experiences are recounted in sensationalistic detail for American and Canadian readers, as Christianity is put to the test, as well as the white woman's strength and virtue. Native American stereotypes abound, although some narratives manage to grant human qualities to the captors and express the complex motivations behind the Native American response to incursions on their lands.

Carpe diem   [KAR–pay DEE–um] Latin for "seize the day." Originally spoken in Horace's *Odes* I (11 C.E.), the phrase has become a thematic label for lyric poetry concerned with human striving and the passing of time. It often appears as an argument made by a lover seducing his beloved, as in Andrew Marvell's "To His Coy Mistress" (1681), which opens: "Had we but World enough, and Time / This coyness Lady were no crime." The *carpe diem* injunction, then, encapsulates a local situation—a man exhorting a woman to "make much of time"—and a hedonistic vision of life as fleeting and pleasure as shadowed by mortality.

Catharsis   [keh–THAR–sus] Literally, in ancient Greek, a "cleansing" or "purging." Aristotle made the term into a technical feature of tragedy in his treatise *Poetics*. After Plato objected to poetry because it "fed and watered the passions" and led audiences into irrational behavior, Aristotle countered that superior drama evokes the passions but in a governed, structured way. In a well-constructed tragedy, he argued, passions are aroused but then purged through the course of the drama. Audiences are enthralled by the spectacle and fascinated by the characters, but as the action proceeds the passions are steered toward rational directions and an acceptance of the characters' destiny. The drama touches the deepest chords in the human psyche, then harmonizes them with each other and with the fated conditions of life. Better to give passions a regulated release through structured representations, Aristotle implied, than to try to suppress them and the poetry that excites them. The ensuing release of passion isn't just an emotional experience. It is accompanied by an intellectual clarification, so that instead of simply identifying with characters and reacting to events in the plot, viewers are led to reflect upon them from a distance.

Central intelligence   The sensibility or mentality through which a story is told. Henry James conceived this term to describe a **narrator**—not the author—whose perceptions shape the way a story unfolds, colors the presentation of characters, and determines the **atmosphere**. The narrator is more than just an observer; he or she is an "intelligence," a developed mind processing what it takes in. To James, the central intelligence gives the action a dramatic quality, a layer of human perspective that is discerning and somewhat detached, but not altogether impartial and unemotional. (*See also* **Narrator, Point of view.**)

Character   A person represented in a narrative or drama. By convention, characters have moral, intellectual, and emotional qualities sufficiently developed to make them recognizable individuals. This isn't to say that characters are equivalent to real persons, but only that they bear plausible human traits, and that their speech and actions are attributable to human motives. A character may be as one-dimensional as the **stock characters** of Medieval drama and as complex as the interiorized narrators in the **stream-of-consciousness** novel. Writers may fill their works with three-dimensional figures—as in the novels of Fyodor Dostoevsky—or they may focus on one fully-formed character and surround him or her with a cast of types, as in the hard-boiled detective story (corrupt cop, gun-toting thug, *femme fatale*, etc.). Analyzing the nature of characters and the dynamic between them is an essential part of the interpretation of literature.

One can also examine characters outside the context of the works in which they appear. Some characters fit archetypal patterns to the point that they may be compared with characters of similar profile, though they originate in other cultures and times. Or, they may be applied to their creators, as when Sigmund Freud analyzes Hamlet and his relation to mother, father, and uncle as a reflection of Shakespeare's own Oedipal situation. Such interpretations are risky and speculative, and they strengthen when they gather copious examples for support. But given the power characters exert over readers' imagination, one can't resist taking them as meaningful bearers of human experience. Changes in character over time signal innovations in literary tradition (for instance, the advent of the **novel**) and shifts in broad notions of human psychology. In naturalist fiction, characters tend to be represented as driven by two forces that lie outside the ego: one, primal, irrational instincts that the characters neither control nor apprehend; and two, social settings that determine the characters' world view and consequent fate. In a world in which human beings are defined by the condition of their soul, fictional characters tend to talk and act as soul-based agents, whereas in a Marxist world characters often evolve as an illustration of class struggle and worker alienation. In other words, characters in fiction and drama serve as an index of the philosophical conception of men and women at a given time. (*See also* **Archetype, Dynamic character, Flat character.**)

Character development   The process by which a character is introduced, revealed, and changed in a story. While **static characters** undergo little development, **dynamic characters** experience a meaningful transformation over the course of the narrative. Character development depends upon a host of narrative factors: (1) does the character undergoing development appear in the first-person or the third-person **point of view**, or through another character's perspective?; (2) if third-person or another character, what relation does the narrator or other character have to the developing character?; (3) are the character's thoughts and feelings rendered directly or indirectly?; and (4) what is the nature of the character's development (moral, intellectual, spiritual, etc.)?

Chiasmus [Kai–AZ–mus] A syntactical pattern in which the words or parts of speech in one part of a sentence are reversed in the other part. The reverse-order pattern makes for a balanced, condensed phrase that yields popular truisms such as "When the going gets tough, the tough get going." In more sophisticated contexts, it can be a conclusive-sounding rhetorical device signaling important reversals. For instance, in his *Narrative of the Life of an American Slave* (1845), Frederick Douglass describes his months with a cruel overseer, singling out a crucial moment when he decided to fight back against the outrages. He introduces his decision with a memorable chiasmus: "You have seen how a man was made a slave; you shall see how a slave was made a man."

Child ballads In the late-nineteenth century, Harvard professor Francis J. Child compiled over three hundred authentic **ballads** and published them in *The English and Scottish Popular Ballads* (1882–1898). The creations of oral folk culture—these so-called "Child ballads"—focus on supernatural and sensational events, with characters taken from notorious love affairs, Robin Hood legends, and English-Scottish border disputes in the fifteenth and sixteenth centuries.

Chorus In classical drama, the chorus is a group of characters placed on stage to comment upon the action and express traditional wisdom. The chorus originates in ancient Greece, probably developing out of religious ritual, and as the oldest manifestation of stage playing it may have been instrumental in the evolution of drama as a discrete art form. By the time of Aeschylus it has been incorporated into drama as a conventional element, serving as a kind of intermediary between the actors and the audience. Numbering usually around a dozen masked characters chanting and dancing in unison, the chorus stands as witness to the events represented in the play, judging them often through the filter of beliefs sacred to or widespread in the society at large. This gives the chorus an unstable position in the drama— both part of the play and the interpretation of it—and sophisticated dramatists such as Euripides use it to heighten the play's tension (say, between the hero's tragic fate and the collective beliefs represented by the chorus). Generally, in older plays the chorus' opinion is trustworthy, as if it rendered the conclusive external judgment of the events on stage. But as Athenian drama evolved, the chorus came to have either (1) more of an ornamental role in the presentation, orating choral odes that are only tangentially related to the action; or (2) more of an internal dramatic role, its opinions placed into counterpoint with the other characters.

Clerihew   [CLAIR–uh–hew] A comic verse form named for its inventor, Edmund Clerihew Bentley. A clerihew begins with the name of a person and consists of two metrically awkward, rhymed couplets. Humorous and often insulting, clerihews serve as ridiculous minibiographies, usually of famous people. An anonymous example:

> Spinoza
> Collected curiosa:
> Bawdy belles-lettres,
> Etc.

Climax   The moment of greatest intensity in a story or drama, which almost always occurs toward the end of the work. The nature of the climax varies. It can take the form of a final confrontation between the protagonist and antagonist, as when in *The Iliad* Achilles finally fights and kills Hector; or it may involve not a major action but simply a piece of information that reorients the dynamics of the characters—for instance, the revelation in Henry Fielding's novel *Tom Jones* (1749) that Tom is Squire Allworthy's illegitimate nephew; or it may stem from a character's fundamental change of heart, as in Percy Shelley's *Prometheus Unbound* (1819), when Prometheus, initially "eyeless in hate" (l. 9), declares near the beginning:

> Grief for awhile is blind, and so was mine.
> I wish no living thing to suffer pain.
>   (ll. 304–05)

In each case, the central conflict of the story peaks, and the plot begins to wind down. In a conventional story, the climax is followed by the **resolution**, in which the effects of the climactic action are settled. When applied to drama, climax has a slightly more technical meaning—that is, the structural component of the play that comes after the characters have been introduced and the central conflict established, and the action has led matters to a critical juncture. In a traditional five-act play, the climax follows the introduction and rising action, and after the climax comes the **falling action**, and *dénouement*. (*See also* **Anticlimax, Rising action**.)

Close reading   A method of analysis involving careful step-by-step explication of a poem in order to understand how various elements work together. A common practice of **formalist criticism** in the study of a text, close reading assumes that literature is a dense, multifaceted discourse that contains ambiguous, connotative, metaphorical language, and that only a detailed inventory of its verbal features can account for its full significance. Broaching lines of verse or a passage of prose, close reading begins with the verbal surface, identifying the **diction**, grammar, **figures of speech**, and images. Then, it builds those elements into larger judgments about the work—its themes, motifs, ironies, etc.—taking care to reach no generalization without ample evidence provided by the close reading.

Closed couplet Two rhymed lines that contain an independent and complete thought or statement. The closed couplet usually pauses lightly at the end of the first line; the second is more heavily end-stopped, or "closed":

> I should have been a pair of ragged claws
> Scuttling across the floors of silent seas.
> > (T. S. Eliot, "The Love Song of J. Alfred Prufrock," ll. 73–74; 1915)

Closed couplets that rhyme and are written in rhymed iambic pentameter are called **heroic couplets:**

> My life has been the poem I would have writ,
> But I could not both live and utter it.
> > (Henry David Thoreau, "My life has been . . ."; 1849)

(*See also* **Couplet.**)

Closed *dénouement* [DAY–new–mawn] One of two types of conventional *dénouement* or resolution in a narrative or drama. In closed *dénouement*, the author ties everything up at the end of the story so that little is left unresolved. The central conflict fueling the action has ceased, and although what has transpired in the work may be memorable and disturbing, no mystery remains, no happenings are unexplained. In *Oedipus*, for example, the action climaxes in the revelation of Oedipus's identity, with the attendant horror of his having killed his father and married his mother. Despite the suffering that ensues, the operative questions have been answered. We know the cause of the plague in Thebes, we know who Oedipus is, and we accept his fall. (*See also* **Open *dénouement*, Plot.**)

Closed form A generic term that describes poetry written in an established pattern of **meter, rhyme**, line, and/or **stanza**. A closed form adheres to a set structure as in the **triolet**, with a predetermined rhyme scheme and line length. Poets approach the form as a container in which they must fit a content—a restriction that many contemporary poets reject. Other closed forms include the **sonnet, sestina, villanelle**, and **ballad**. (*See also* **New Formalism.**)

Closet drama A play or dramatic poem designed to be read aloud rather than performed. Many post-Renaissance verse dramas are examples of closet drama, such as John Milton's *Samson Agonistes* (1671), Lord Byron's *Manfred* (1817), and Percy Bysshe Shelley's *Prometheus Unbound* (1819).

Colloquial English The casual, informal language of ordinary native speakers. Sometimes defined against proper English, colloquial English loosens grammatical rules and incorporates regional expressions, conversational styles, and familiar addresses. Although not as "low" as slang, colloquial English is not as "high" as traditionally conceived literary language. However, colloquial speech has often worked its way into literary works, and the difference in register between the two discourses has been used to skillful effect. The rural and laborer-class characters in Shakespeare's plays speak colloquially and contrast with the more refined speech of the central characters. Eighteenth-century **picaresque** novels by Defoe and others contain a host of characters mouthing colloquial phrases that indicate their social and geographical place. In the Romantic Era, Wordsworth introduced colloquialism into his *Lyrical Ballads* (1798) as a programmatic gesture, challenging the priority of formal language in verse and calling for the poet to become "a man speaking to men." Nineteenth-century regionalists such as Mark Twain not only had their characters speak colloquially, but their narrators as well, so that the entire work was a colloquial document. In such cases, colloquial language is a natural mode of expression, and its diction, grammar, figures of speech, etc., constitute an index of a way of life. (*See also* **Diction, Levels of diction, Regionalism.**)

Comedy   In the most common sense, comedy is any work aimed at amusing an audience. In literary studies, though, comedy has a more complex and varied meaning, and over time, the definition of comedy has changed significantly. In ancient Greece and Rome, comedy tended to be populated with low characters doing low things—Aristotle: "Comedy is . . . an imitation of characters of a lower type" (*Poetics*)—sometimes satirizing human nature and social norms, other times simply indulging a taste for the ridiculous and vulgar. In the **Medieval** and **early-Renaissance Periods**, comedy was defined as a movement of the plot from complication and difficulty to clarity and contentment. Thus Dante's *Divine Comedy* (1314-21), a decidedly unfunny work, counts as comedy because, Dante once explained, "at the beginning it is horrible and fetid, for it is hell; and in the end it is prosperous, desirable, and gracious, for it is paradise." By Shakespeare's and Ben Jonson's time, the plot direction lingers but the demands of humor take priority, and the action centers on social matters such as the capricious travails of young lovers. With the advent of Restoration comedy and **Sentimental comedy** in the late-seventeenth and eighteenth centuries, the genre is dominated by urbane portrayals of human foibles, while lesser comic forms such as *commedia dell'arte* and **farce** continue as popular entertainments. Since then, however, the structural and generic distinctions of traditional comedy have broken down, and just about anything that amuses falls under the category.

   In examining a tradition of comedy, one must also recognize that comic situations and characters arise in genres outside comedy, even in tragedy (for example, the gravediggers in *Hamlet*, 1601). Indeed, given the presence of comedy in all cultures, one must search for the source of comedy outside literary contexts, in cross-cultural behaviors, social settings, and psyches. Hence, anthropologists and psychologists, as well as literary scholars, have formed theories about comedy as part of a general understanding of human nature. Anthropologists have linked comedy to carnivals, festivals, rituals of misrule, and other events in which social and rational conventions are loosened. Early-twentieth-century classicists who were influenced by anthropology traced ancient comedy to primitive rituals of combat, death, resurrection, and sacred marriage, for example, the reenactment of a boasting pretender coming to a sacred site and being exposed by a priest or king. As the religious significance of the rites faded, the performance developed into a social/emotional experience, whereby instinctual energies otherwise controlled are released in a comic milieu and observers laugh at the misbehavior. Comedy becomes the representation of riotous human impulses, treated not as menacing but as an inevitable part of the human condition. The humor masks a deep response to life—a smile in the face of catastrophe, the joy at witnessing a villain brought to ruin by his own machinations—and has just as much significance as the suffering of tragedy. Philosopher Suzanne Langer once wrote, "Tragedy is the image of Fate, as comedy is of Fortune."

Psychologists take a more individualized approach and relate comedy to the curious phenomenon of laughter. The laughter evoked by comic scenes, they claim, indicates deep attitudes and traits in the human psyche. Noting the fact that laughter seems to originate in observations of or stories about others— it's funny when you see someone slip on a banana peel; it's not funny when you slip on a banana peel—psychologists assume that laughter entails a social relationship between the laugher and the object laughed at. Some tie it to a sense of superiority, as when we laugh at others' mistakes, especially when that other at first appeared superior to everyone else. The laughter marks an emotional escape from the insecurity the other person aroused in us, which has now passed. Others tie laughter to a disruption of normal relations, as when people of different classes, ages, or cultures exchange identities, and misunderstandings follow. The situation allows for a momentary suspension of social bonds, and characters move freely in roles otherwise denied to them. Here, the laughter it evokes comes from the discordance of, say, a peasant playing a king. In one scene in Richard Sheridan's play *A School for Scandal* (1777), a wealthy older man visits his nephew in disguise, having heard the youth is spending the family money on trifles. He pretends to be a money lender, and the nephew offers him several family portraits for sale. As they survey each one, the nephew describes the forebears in mocking terms, while the uncle grows more and more irritated and dismayed, intending to cut off the young man's inheritance. The comedy of the scene stems from the inherent tension between the generations, which the situation expresses by having the younger, powerless man express his frustration at the elders who want him to curb his youthful sports. What happens at the end of the scene prevents our laughter from turning bitter: they arrive at the portrait of the uncle himself, and the young man refuses to sell it, admitting that the uncle had always treated him well. The uncle recognizes his nephew's good nature and changes his mind. Here, the playwright lets audiences have it both ways. Youth is allowed to mock age, power, and money—but not so much as to invert the familial order. The uncle is still in control, and the nephew still respects him.

Such cases are witty and fun, yet, with only a slight adjustment, they could be the stuff of misery. The same situations could be played for tears as well as laughter—someone slipping on a banana peel could really be hurt! Indeed, in some modern versions of tragicomedy, such as in the plays of Anton Chekhov, one sometimes cannot tell whether what appears on stage is sad or whimsical. The nearness of comedy to tragedy suggests deeper sources for the comic impulse than mere entertainment. (*See also* **Burlesque, Comedy of manners, Parody, Romantic comedy, Satire, Slapstick.**)

Comedy of manners   A realistic form of comic drama that flourished with the seventeenth-century French playwright Molière and the English Restoration dramatists. In the typical comedy of manners situation, the playwright portrays the social relations and sexual intrigues of privileged and intelligent men and women, whose verbal fencing and witty repartee produce the principal comic effects. Stereotyped characters from contemporary life (jealous husbands, conniving rivals, country bumpkins, and effeminate fops) reveal by their deviations from the norm the decorum and conventional behaviors expected in polite society. In their world, reputation, status, and deportment are paramount, and the virtues of sincerity, earnestness, and purity are as often the sign of dullness as of goodness. In the more cynical versions of comedy of manners, such as Sir George Etherege's *The Man of Mode* (1676) and William Wycherley's *The Country Wife* (1672), social traits are held up for scrutiny and moral parameters are shaken. In the latter play, a renowned seducer returns to London and lets it be rumored (falsely) that a venereal disease has rendered him impotent, thus encouraging possessive husbands to trust their wives in his company. The ensuing complications allow for a reflection upon shifting marital customs, city ways and rural manners (one of his conquests comes from the countryside), and the fragility of trust. Milder versions, such as Oscar Wilde's *The Importance of Being Earnest* (1895), soften the satire, but still ridicule prevailing social codes. Both kinds offer a microcosm of civilized society, letting bemused audiences witness the competitions for love and prestige, be they whimsical or bitter. Modern practitioners include G. B. Shaw (*Arms and the Man*, 1898), Noel Coward (*Private Lives*, 1930), and Tom Stoppard (*Arcadia*, 1993). (*See also* **Comedy.**)

Comic relief   The appearance of a comic situation or character in the midst of a serious action. Comic relief usually serves merely to lighten an atmosphere and balance the somber with the entertaining. But sometimes, though ostensibly playful and trivial, comic relief introduces a sharp contrast in mood that can have important thematic significance. In Christopher Marlowe's *Dr. Faustus* (ca. 1590), just after Faust has bargained with Mephistophilis, trading his soul for absolute knowledge, Faust's servant and a clown enter the scene and banter in puns. When the clown mocks the servant, the latter calls upon two devils to threaten him and force him into the servant's control. The ludicrous horseplay calls Faust's own motives into question and makes his heroic-seeming strivings a matter of vain pride. In Shakespeare's *Macbeth* (1605), just after the murder of King Duncan, a knock sounds at the gate and a drunken porter appears, his blundering not only providing comic relief but intensifying the horror of Macbeth's regicide. As Thomas De Quincey described the scene in a famous essay, once the deed is done and the audience is enraptured by the horror, the ordinary world must return: "the re-establishment of the goings-on of the world in which we live first makes us profoundly sensible of the awful parenthesis [the murder] that has suspended them."

Coming-of-age story   *See* **Initiation story**.

Commedia dell'arte   [ko–MAY–dee–uh del AR–tay] A rollicking mode of comic performance enacted by traveling groups of Italian players in the mid-sixteenth century. Plots revolved around a few **stock characters** placed in familiar situations taken partly from ancient sources, partly from **folk tales**. *Commedia* performers, some masked, improvised their lines after a given scenario (a brief outline marking entrances of characters and the main course of action), a flexible outline that allowed them to adjust the performance to local preferences. The acting included not only standard dialogue but **mime**, dance, and song. Amidst the entertainment and clownishness may run a plot line such as a pair of young lovers, aided by a clever servant, foiling older masked characters who oppose their union. Characters include Pantaloon (a skinny, aged man), the Captain, the Doctor, Inamorato (male lover) and Inamorata (female lover), the servants Harlequin and Scapino, the singer Cantarina, and the dancer Ballerina. Aspects of *commedia dell' arte* cropped up in some of the comedies of Shakespeare, Ben Jonson, and Molière, and they survive today in puppet shows and children's stories.

Common meter   A popular verse form made of quatrains whose lines alternate between four and three feet and rhyme *abab* or *abcb*, with a heavy pause after the second line. "Amazing Grace" and many other hymns are in common meter, and they influenced many poets who followed the hymnal tradition, such as George Herbert and Emily Dickinson. William Wordsworth's brief "A Slumber Did My Spirit Seal" (1800) falls into common meter:

> A slumber did my spirit seal,
>   I had no human fears;
> She seemed a thing that could not feel
>   The touch of earthly years.

No motion has she now, no force;
　She neither hears nor sees;
Rolled round in earth's diurnal course,
　With rocks, and stones, and trees.

(*See also* **Ballad stanza**.)

Complication　The introduction of a significant development in the central conflict between characters (or between a character and his or her circumstances) in a drama or narrative. Aristotle (*Poetics*) says that a complication initiates the **rising action** of a story's plot. Dramatic oppositions (motivation versus obstacle) resulting from the complication are the force that drives the **plot** from action to action. A character's goal or want may be confronted by several kinds of obstacles, such as another character, an aspect of society, a cosmic force such as fate or "the gods," or competing inner impulses. Complications may be external or internal or a combination of the two. A fateful blow, such as an illness or an accident that affects a character, is a typical example of an external complication—a problem the characters cannot turn away from. An internal complication, in contrast, springs from within the character—for example, a moral confusion or a tainted past—and might not be immediately apparent. In Herman Melville's famous short story "Bartleby the Scrivener" (1853), the complication starts when Bartleby, a copyist in a law office, responds to his boss's request that he examine a document with, "I would prefer not to." The lawyer is stupefied, and the rest of the plot concerns how he handles an employee whom he pities but who won't follow orders.

Conceit　Common in Renaissance and seventeenth-century love poetry, a conceit is a far-flung metaphor comparing dissimilar things. Most notably used by the Italian poet Petrarch in praise of his beloved Laura, *conceit* comes from the Italian *concetto*, "concept" or "idea," and has just as much an intellectual aspect as an emotional one. In "Hymne to My God, in My Sicknesse" (1635), for example, John Donne casts his doctors as cosmographers and his body as their map, an unusual comparison designed to entertain as much by its eccentricity as by its pathos. The Petrarchan conceit is intended to convey the paradoxes and extremes of love, the lover's wild metaphors paralleling his seething emotions. Thus Thomas Wyatt the Elder, in an adaptation of Petrarch, compares his condition to a ship in a storm, tossed by winds (his sighs) and a "rain of tears," with "every oar a thought" and no stars to guide him to port ("My galley charged with forgetfulness," 1557). The so-called "metaphysical conceit," associated with Donne and early-seventeenth-century English poets, is a more discursive expression, invoking scientific, religious, and mechanical learning in hyperbolic comparisons. Metaphysical conceits are often striking, as when George Herbert casts himself as an impoverished tenant asking his landlord (God) for a "new small-rented lease" ("Redemption," 1633). In a notorious attack on metaphysical conceits, eighteenth-century man of letters Samuel Johnson condemned them for their plundering artificiality: "The most heterogeneous ideas are yoked by violence together; nature and art are ransacked for illustrations, comparisons, allusions" (*Lives of the Poets*; 1779). (*See also* **Metaphor**.)

Conclusion   In plotting, the end or outcome of a drama or narrative, shortly following the **climax**. In its simplest function, the conclusion merely amounts to the final actions and descriptions in the work, but in literary criticism and theory the conclusion usually involves a more logical or determinate relationship to the preceding sections and the **plot** as a whole. Specifically, the conclusion completes the "working out" or "working through" of the central conflicts. The ingredients that have come together to produce a **dramatic situation** are given their final form, the interest generated by the events and personages developed and settled. When conclusions take a "logical" ending form, they mark a **resolution** or *dénouement* ("the untying of the knot"), whereby the plot complications that grew during the **rising action** are disentangled and no further complications can enter. Protagonists have succeeded or failed, antagonists are dispatched, the mystery is solved, misunderstandings are dispelled. In unified plots—that is, plots that have (according to Aristotle) a clear beginning, middle, and end—the conclusion is the necessary and final outcome of the preceding events (**closed** *dénouement*). In an **open** *dénouement*, the conclusion is ambiguous; at the climax of the story the major characters meet their fate and the major action terminates, but the conclusion allows different possibilities for what that outcome is or means. (*See also* **Plot**.)

Concrete diction   *See* **Diction**.

Concrete poetry   A visual poetry in which the printed words and letters both spell out a meaning and compose a visual image on the page. Thus, the poem represents a meaning and an image, and readers both take in the words and apprehend the picture the words form by their arrangement. Visual poetry dates back to ancient works (sometimes called "pattern poems"), and it has enjoyed vogues throughout Western literary history. Twentieth-century poets have adopted the genre as a mode of poetic experimentation. For example, E. E. Cummings's "l(a" (1958) spells "loneliness," with the phrase "a leaf falls" interjected between *l* and *o*; and it also represents the falling in the shape of the verse (with some visual puns along the way);

l(a

le
af
fa

ll

s)
one
l

iness

In the 1950s and 1960s, European and Brazilian poets refined the genre, trying to avoid the simple mimesis of objects or ideas through the layout of typeface (as, for instance, George Herbert's "The Altar," 1633, whose words appear in the shape of an altar). Later poets began mixing words with photography and other visual media, forging a hybrid discourse of verbal and pictorial signs. The variations have made the term *concrete poetry* a loose one, applying to any poem that represents something by its material shape as well as by the meaning of its words.

Confederation poets   A group of Canadian poets (centered in Ottawa) writing in the 1880s and 1890s, whose works are considered the first distinctly Canadian voice in literary history. Led by Charles G. D. Roberts, Bliss Carman, Archibald Lampman, and Duncan Campbell Scott, they set out to forge a national, transcontinental identity in verse. As Roberts advised, "We must forget to ask of a work whether it is Nova Scotian or British Columbian, of Ontario or of New Brunswick, until we have inquired if it be broadly and truly Canadian." The aim expresses the spirit of Dominion, that is, the independence and nationalism of late-nineteenth-century Canadian civil life; and some Confederation poets worked as civil servants in the government (Lampman was a clerk in the Post Office Department, Scott was head of the Department of Indian Affairs). However, in their poems, it is not Canadian politics that stand out, but the Canadian wilderness. Strongly influenced by Romantic nature poetry, especially William Wordsworth and John Keats, they pictured landscapes from the Maritime Provinces to the Pacific Coast, peopling them with Iroquois Indians, solitary woodcutters, pioneer settlers, struggling farm workers, and the poets' own probing subjectivity. Nature is a mighty presence, sometimes violent and sometimes ethereal, ever touching the soul of the poet:

> Here in the midnight, where the dark mainland and island
> Shadows mingle in shadow deeper, profounder,
> Sing we the hymns of the churches, while the dead water
>   Whispers before us.
>
> Thunder is traveling slow on the path of the lightning:
> One after one the stars and the beaming planets
> Look serene in the lake from the edge of the storm-cloud,
>   Then they have vanished.
>   (Scott, "Night-Hymns on Lake Nipigon"; 1905)

Coupling their nature meditations with sonorous language and unusual rhythms and stanza forms, the Confederation poets established, for a time, the definitive moods and *topoi* for Canadian poetry. While much of their poems have disappeared with time and have only a historical interest, a significant corpus remains central to the Canadian canon and is highly regarded as a momentous application of Romantic aesthetics and attitudes to the newly-formed Canadian nation.

Confessional poetry   Emerging in the 1950s and 1960s, confessional poetry aims for a frank exposure of the poet's personal life. More concerned with the private aspects of life (along with the guilts and embarrassments) than is standard autobiography, confessional poetry reveals aspects of experience kept hidden in normal social intercourse. As Anne Sexton, whose psychiatrist advised her to work through her problems in verse, put it:

> My friend, my friend, I was born
> doing reference work in sin, and born
> confessing it. This is what poems are . . .
> ("With Mercy for the Greedy"; 1962)

For these writers, poetry is a treatment of personal conflict, the very act of confessing being part of the poem's content. Robert Lowell's collection *Life Studies* (1959) included poems about the death of his mother and his seclusion in the locked ward of a psychiatric hospital, leading one critic to observe, "It is hard not to think of *Life Studies* as a series of personal confidences, rather shameful, that one is honor bound not to reveal" (M. L. Rosenthal). As a result, confessional poetry intensifies the reading process, drawing readers into private dramas and clouding their moral and aesthetic judgment with uncomfortable disclosures—the suicide of a father, nursing one's infant, etc. Should readers interpret the poem as verbal artwork or as personal confession? Both, of course, but it is hard to manage them simultaneously. Furthermore, even if they appreciate the artistry of confessional poems, readers may not share the poets' absorption in their own experience. Many efforts come off as maudlin, pointless, self-indulgent, as if they existed only to aggrandize the details of an unhappy life. The amorphous verse forms confessional poets prefer appears to many simply as careless practice. Although the best confessional work—by Lowell, Sexton, John Berryman, W. D. Snodgrass, and Sylvia Plath—unites intimate circumstance with artistic control, later generations of poets eschewed confessionalism as discounting poetic form and relying on a naive conception of self-expression. (*See also* **Language poetry, New Formalism.**)

Conflict   The central struggle between two or more forces in a literary work. Conflict generally occurs when some person or thing prevents the **protagonist** from achieving his or her intended goal. Opposition can arise from another character, external events, preexisting situations, fate, or even some aspect of the character's personality. The conflict in F. Scott Fitzgerald's *The Great*

Gatsby (1925), for instance, is an external one between Gatsby's idealized love for Daisy and the social circumstances of her present life. In Robert Browning's **dramatic monologue** "Andrea del Sarto" (1855), the conflict is an internal one between Andrea's commitment to his art and his hapless love for his straying wife, showing that conflict need not occur only within narratives. Without conflict, a **plot** has no *raison d'être*. It is what holds readers' attention and makes them interested in the outcome. (*See also* **Antagonist, Character, Complication, Rising action.**)

Connotation   An association or additional meaning that a word, image, or phrase may carry, beyond its literal reference or dictionary definition. Whereas denotative meanings signify a thing with precision (even vague things are denoted without vagueness), connotative meanings belong to feelings, attitudes, valuations, and biases, and are often fuzzy and variable, changing from one situation to another. A word may have connotations locally (that is, within the context of the work) or traditionally (that is, from all the uses to which it has been put in the past, in literature and in history). A rose in literature is not only the literal flower. It also carries associations attached to it, both from the many poems treating roses as metaphors for love, time, etc., and from historical events, such as the War of the Roses in late-medieval England. Hence, when William Carlos Williams begins a poem "The rose is obsolete" (1923), he invokes all the traditional associations as well, then pronounces judgment:

> The rose carried the weight of love,
> but love is at an end—of roses
>
> It is at the edge of the
> petal that love waits . . .

In twentieth-century theories of literary language and poetic meaning, connotation has assumed an essential place. Philosopher/critic I. A. Richards and, after him, advocates of **New Criticism** defined poetic language squarely against denotative, reference-oriented statements. Richards distinguished four kinds of meaning—*sense, feeling, tone,* and *intention*—and singled out *feeling* as the characteristic meaning of poetry, while New Critic Cleanth Brooks spoke of poetic structure as "balancing and harmonizing connotations, attitudes, and meanings." Whereas the significance of, say, a scientific paper lies in the strict referential meaning of the words and data (metaphors have no place in clinical reports), the significance of a poem rests upon the figures of speech, suggestions, nuances, tones, echoes, and subtexts—in general, that is, the connotations that the words bring to the poem and that the poem itself creates in the course of its unfolding. In James Joyce's story "The Dead" (1914), for example, as dinner guests enjoy a holiday party, snow drifts down in the Dublin streets and covers the landscape. Joyce's various citations of the word *snow* import the standard connotations of winter, cold, gloom, and also merriment. But by the end of the story, especially with the final paragraph describing snow falling all across Ireland upon "the living and the dead," the deathly connotation of *snow* intensifies such that to mention *snow* is to invoke mortality. These accruals of connotative meaning, whereby words are turned and shifted to other senses, are a cornerstone of verbal art, and the best writers manage to create fresh connotations in striking, clever ways. Sometimes, their usage is adopted in ordinary discourse. For students and scholars of literature, although the analysis of connotations is a less exact process than the catalogue of denotations, it is a fundamental element is literary criticism. (*See also* **Denotation, Figure of speech, Semantics.**)

Consonance [KON–suh–nuntz] Consonance has been defined strictly as either the repetition of consonant sounds at the end of stressed syllables (*prove-love*), or the repetition of two or more consonant sounds in stressed syllables having different vowels (*door-dare*). More loosely, it names any repetition of consonants not located at the beginning of the words. Thus, it differs from **alliteration** in the placement and, sometimes, number of consonants. Word-pairs such as *reason/raisin* and *mink/monk* are both alliterative and consonant. Because consonance occurs in final stressed syllables, it may be considered a form of internal rhyme, and many poets have used it to musical effect. In Gerard Manley Hopkins' "The Wreck of the Deutschland" (1916), the lines mingle alliteration and consonance into a profusion of *w, s, d, l, b,* and *ns* echoes:

> W*orld*'*s* stran*d*, sway of the sea;
> L*ord* of living and dea*d*;
> Thou hast bound bo*nes* and vei*ns* in me . . .

(See also **Assonance, Rhyme.**)

Convention Any established feature or rule in literature that is commonly understood by authors and readers. Conventions bear a cultural authority, not an individual one, and are generally agreed to be appropriate for customary uses, such as the sonnet form for a love poem or the opening "Once upon a time" for a **fairy tale**. Indeed, without conventions some genres could not function, for it is only convention that allows an Elizabethan stage to represent a battlefield (as in Shakespeare's history plays) or a fictional narrator to speak as if he or she were a real person. Authors rely on them to frame the imaginary universe of the work, and audiences accept them as part of aesthetic experience.

Conventions include formal traits, such as the turn after the ninth line in an **Italian sonnet** and the **aside** in drama; material traits, such as the realistic props in the **box set** and the dedications following the title page in books; and subject matters, such as **stock characters** and **recognition** scenes. In other words, virtually any pattern, technique, and topic may become a convention if it is repeated often enough and accepted habitually by a readership. Mastering literary conventions is essential to artistic training, and handling them in novel ways is harder than first appears. Furthermore, because conventions are inclined to overuse, innovative writers sometimes work against them (and their social implications). Experimental poets violate conventions of form, as when William Carlos Williams incorporates a title into the first line:

> The Yachts
>
> contend in a sea which the land partly encloses . . .
>   (1935)

Satirical writers often invoke conventions only to mock them, as when Lord Byron begins Canto III of *Don Juan* (1819–24) with a humorous deflation of the customary epic invocation to the Muses:

> Hail Muse! *et cetera.*—We left Juan sleeping . . .

Such unconventional uses point to an impatience with the prevailing habits, as if the old conventions are no longer credible. Hence, while conventions may seem at first to be handy instruments that facilitate, but are not essential to the work, in truth they stand as a subtle index of literary practice; and the course of their uses and abuses forms an important literary history in itself.

Conventional symbols   Symbols that, because of their frequent use, have acquired a standard significance. They may range from complex metaphysical images, such as those of Christian saints in Gothic art, to social customs, such as a young bride in a white dress. Romantic and Symbolist poets and theorists defined the symbol as a unique and mysterious manifestation of a supersensual reality, brought into being by the genius of the artist, but conventional symbols reappear frequently and have a broad cultural grounding. Social, political, and religious rituals call upon them routinely, and the meanings they impart are recognizable and stable. (*See also* **Convention, Symbol.**)

Conversation poem   A casual, reflective poem whose discourse is meant to resemble informal conversation. Often composed in **blank verse**, conversation poems seem to issue from an extemporaneous situation and to proceed without strict design. The poem unfolds according to the meditations of the poet. In one of the first instances of the subgenre, Samuel Taylor Coleridge's "This Lime-Tree Bower My Prison" (1797), Coleridge sits among some linden trees nursing an injured foot while his friends hike across the countryside.

> Well, they are gone, and here must I remain,
> This lime-tree bower my prison!

The occasion is a chance one, and Coleridge speaks as if the reader were an acquaintance sitting beside him. He imagines what his friends will observe on their walk, follows them as "they wander on / In gladness all." He names one of them "gentle-hearted Charles" (Charles Lamb) and hopes his views bring on apprehensions of "the Almighty Spirit," then he experiences a spontaneous joy: "A delight / Comes sudden on my heart." The easeful ruminations culminate in solicitations of Nature and Beauty, as Coleridge's thoughts meander from his immediate circumstances to lofty recognitions. Other famous conversation poems include Coleridge's "The Eolian Harp" (1796) and "Frost at Midnight" (1798), and William Wordsworth's "Tintern Abbey" (1798). (*See also* **Dramatic monologue**.)

Cosmic irony Related to **irony of fate**, cosmic irony names the discrepancy that falls between a character's aspiration and the treatment he or she receives in the world. As opposed to **verbal irony**, which marks a semantic difference between literal meaning and intended meaning, cosmic irony involves a relation between human beings and the workings of time, chance, and fate. It may apply to actual persons as well as to fictional characters, if the persons' lives follow an ironic pattern. Consequences count as ironic because it seems that circumstances play unexpectedly upon a person's motives, for instance, when a character desires something and fate helps him or her realize it, only to have it turn out to be the worst thing that he or she could achieve. Hopes are raised, then dashed, expectations are toyed with, assumptions are shown to be blind. In the Old Testament Book of Esther, the conniving Prince Haman prepares a fifty-cubit high scaffold on which to hang Mordecai, but when Haman makes the error of praising Mordecai to the king (thinking he is praising himself), Haman ends up being the one hanged. In retrospect, such outcomes appear to have a design working behind them, as if God or Nature were mocking human ends, both villainous and virtuous. (*See also* **Irony**.)

Cothurni [Kuh–THUR–nigh] High, thick-soled, laced boots worn by Greek and Roman tragic actors in late classical times to make them appear taller than ordinary men and lend dignity to the production. Earlier, in the fifth-century Athenian theater, actors wore soft shoes or boots or went barefoot.

Couplet A verse unit of two lines, usually rhymed and of equal length. Sometimes couplets stand alone, as in the typical **epigram** and in the two-line stanzas in John Greenleaf Whittier's "Barbara Frietchie" (1863) and Wallace Stevens's "The Man with the Blue Guitar" (1937). Usually, though, couplets are integrated into larger verse forms—for example, in Jonathan Swift's "Stella's Birthday" (1727), which begins:

> This day, whate'er the fates decree,
> Shall still be kept with joy by me . . .

They are also in **English sonnets**, whose final two lines form a rhymed couplet, as do those of the *ottava rima* stanza. When placed in terminating positions, as in the latter two cases, the couplet tends to form a complete thought, with the statement's meaning extending or contrasting the preceding lines' content and structure. In his sonnets (published 1609), Shakespeare usually runs through twelve lines exploring a single theme or thought, delaying the "turn" until the thirteenth line. At that point, the couplet sums up the preceding with a general comment, a motto, a promise, etc.:

So long as men can breathe, or eyes can see,
So long lives this [the poem], and this gives life to thee.
(Sonnet 18)

But if the while I think on thee, dear friend,
All losses are restored and sorrows end.
(Sonnet 30)

For sweetest things turn sourest by their deeds;
Lilies that fester smell far worse than weeds.
(Sonnet 94)

However, when couplets appear as the basic verse form of longer poems, they must function not only as complete units, but also as steps in a narrative or lyric flow. In the seventeenth century, French dramatists Racine, Molière, and Corneille perfected the **alexandrine** couplet into a standard convention of dialogue. In England, during the **Neoclassical Period**, John Dryden and Alexander Pope made the **heroic couplet** the reigning verse of the time, the former translating *The Aeneid*, the latter *The Iliad*, into polished, harmonious couplets that are sometimes end-stopped, sometimes enjambed. The following lines from Dryden's "Absalom and Achitophel" (1681), which describe a young prince eager for the throne appealing to the populace for support, display the couplet as a flexible medium of narrative:

Surrounded thus with friends of every sort,
Deluded Absalom forsakes the court:
Impatient of high hopes, urged with renown,
And fired with near possession of the crown.
The admiring crowd are dazzled with surprise,
And on his goodly person feed their eyes:
His joy concealed, he sets himself to show,
On each side bowing popularly low;
His looks, his gestures, and his words he frames,
And with familiar ease repeats their names.
Thus formed by nature, furnished out with arts,
He glides unfelt into their secret hearts . . .
(ll. 682-93)

Over the course of the eighteenth century, the heroic couplet declined, and by the **Romantic Period** it had gained the reputation of being artificial and mechanical. In twentieth-century British and American poetry, couplets appear infrequently and have the same unremarkable status as other traditional verse forms. (*See also* **Closed couplet.**)

Cowboy poetry   A genre of folk poetry written by people with firsthand experience in the life of horse, trail, and ranch. Cowboy poetry dates back to the mid-nineteenth century, but remains popular today. Plainspoken and often humorous, it is usually composed in songlike verse, such as **ballad stanzas,** and is meant to be recited aloud. One of the earliest and best known is "The Cowboy's Lament" (ca. 1880), attributed to Frances Henry "Frank" Maynard, whose opening stanzas exemplify the mood and prosody of the genre:

> As I walked out in the streets of Laredo,
> As I walked out in Laredo one day,
> I spied a poor cowboy wrapped up in white linen,
> Wrapped up in white linen as cold as the clay.

> "Oh beat the drum slowly and play the fife lowly,
> Play the dead march as you carry me along;
> Take me to the green valley, there lay the sod o'er me,
> For I'm a young cowboy, and I know I've done wrong."

> "I see by your outfit that you are a cowboy"—
> These words he did say as I boldly stepped by.
> "Come sit down beside me and hear my sad story;
> I am shot in the breast and I know I must die."

Crisis   From the Greek word *krisis*, meaning "decision," a crisis marks the moment in a **plot** at which a crucial action, decision, or realization occurs, marking a turning point or reversal of (usually) the **protagonist's** outlook or fortune. While the **climax** of a plot tends to be executed through the action, the crisis is sometimes an internal struggle in a main character. In Mark Twain's *Huckleberry Finn* (1884), Huck reaches a crisis moment when, after facing down the pro-slavery values of his society and his conscience, he decides to help the slave Jim escape, thus accepting, "All right, then, I'll *go* to hell." In *Hamlet* (1601), the protagonist faces a crisis when he spots the usurper Claudius praying but decides not to slay him as he is speaking to God, a crisis that leads directly to the accidental killing of Polonius and points forward to the horrors of Act V. Typically the crisis inaugurates the **falling action** (after Hamlet's killing of Polonius, Claudius controls the events) until the catastrophe or conclusion arrives (in *Hamlet* the death of the Prince, King Claudius, Queen Gertrude, and Laertes). (*See also* **Climax, Conflict, Plot.**)

Cultural studies   An interdisciplinary field of academic study that focuses on the social relations and power structures encoded in texts. Influenced by Marxist theory, which denies the independence of art from concrete political and economic circumstances, cultural studies expands the domain of criticism to all manifestations of culture, defining a text as any signifying phenomenon, be it a classic novel, an advertising image, a modern museum, a sitcom, or an actor's face. An editorial statement in the journal *Cultural Studies* exemplifies the heterogeneous objects of the practice: it "seeks work that explores the relation between everyday life, cultural practices, and material, economic, political, geographical and historical contexts"—a description broad enough to include just about any humanistic inquiry, though it goes on to highlight work on postcolonial relations, nationality and globalization, "gendered, sexual, and queer identities," and race, class and ethnicity. As such, cultural studies crosses disciplinary boundaries, broaches high art and **mass culture** equally, and casts itself as both academic scholarship and political intervention.

The practice was first developed as a distinct method of analysis at the Centre for Contemporary Cultural Studies at Birmingham University in England. Founded in 1964, the program expanded the range of literary study beyond traditional aesthetic and philological approaches to canonical literature in order to explore a broader spectrum of historical, cultural, and political issues. Raymond Williams, a leading figure in the movement, argued that scholars should study literature as an evolutionary process involving an entire society. "We cannot separate literature and art," he insisted, "from other kinds of social practice." Indeed, all the fixtures of art and art criticism—beauty, taste, form, genius, etc.—are themselves a type of social practice, each one bearing an ideological content with broad political implications.

If the object of analysis were a short story by Saul Bellow, the cultural studies adherent would begin by unearthing the social and political assumptions buried in the work, at the same time making sure not to implement any critical tools that might lead him or her to reinscribe those assumptions in the interpretation. Specifically, the interpreter would trace the meanings and values embedded in the plots and characters that hold those assumptions in place and give them the appearance of objective representation. These include the racial, gender, and class dynamics of the action. How do African Americans appear in the work? What economic relations are represented in the ordinary descriptions of setting? How do the representations match up with the real Chicago of Bellow's life? These are standard questions of literary analysis, but cultural studies doesn't stop there. Next, the critic steps outside the work and determines what social practices match Bellow's representations. That is, Bellow's characters, landscapes, and incidents form a more or less coherent **ideology** in dramatic form. The cultural studies critic converts it into political form, determining which individuals, classes, and gender and ethnic identities benefit or suffer from it.

The latter step is what makes cultural studies a political critique as well as a literary criticism. It is a hybrid activity that borrows from many schools of literary analysis to forge Left wing interpretations of widespread social conditions.

From Marxism it takes a theory of history as a process of class struggle, with art cast as an expression of class interest and ideological support structures. Marx's belief that artists and intellectuals constitute a subclass serving in one way or another the needs and vanities of the powers that be is one of the root postulates of cultural studies thought. From **deconstruction** it adopts an intricate formal analysis of deep conflicts and contradictions in the text, particularly certain fundamental oppositions (nature/culture, reason/madness) and the values that go with them. Because ideological content is often veiled by innocent-seeming images and natural-seeming events, an interpretation must be sensitive to the unsaid and unseen, the implicit and subtly tendentious. This is what deconstruction provides—a window onto buried and repressed realities, an awareness of the political work a metaphor and an image can do. From **feminist criticism** and race-oriented criticism, cultural studies imports a protest against racial and gender inequality. In its naked uses, racism and sexism can be resisted with straightforward action; but in cultural products such as television shows, racism and sexism can work in subtextual ways, and race and gender theory helps expose them. Each borrowing is mobilized into what stands as the ultimate purpose of cultural studies—to advance the cause of social justice.

Because of its political slant and its open agenda, and despite its moral claims, cultural studies has been criticized for abandoning norms of academic inquiry and disciplinary coherence. Without a set critical method (it is the political thrust and the textual focus that identify individual interpretations as cultural studies, not the methodology), cultural studies appears to draw haphazardly from whatever interpretative tools are appropriate to the text at hand and the politics in mind. It presumes to speak about real-world conditions, yet its language is riddled with jargon and its arguments fraught with indignation. It focuses on apparently trivial phenomena, such as advertisements for cigarettes, then drafts broad indictments of capitalism, globalization, and imperialism, a judgment uninitiated readers consider overdone and remote from their experience. Forsaking the traditional scholarly trait of objectivity—theorists treat objectivity as a spurious trait masking a reactionary outlook—cultural studies reaches political conclusions that appear ordained from the start. As a result, in the United States cultural studies has occupied an embattled position in the university, scorned by traditionalists in the humanities and social sciences, and ridiculed in the public sphere as mere political correctness.

Despite these criticisms, however, cultural studies has come to dominate certain areas of inquiry in the humanities. Critics who believe in expanding the curriculum beyond purely literary subjects praise its copious interdisciplinarity, and egalitarian minds favor its tendency to level all culture productions and break down the high art versus mass culture divide. Moreover, those professors who wish to become more engaged with public life and bring literary methods to real-world phenomena find in cultural studies a sanctioned method for doing so.

Dactyl   [DAK–tul] A metrical foot of verse in which one stressed syllable is followed by two unstressed syllables (*bat*-ter-y or *par*-a-mour). The dactylic meter is less common in English verse than it was in classical Greek and Latin verse, where it served as the basis for narrative poetry. Henry Wadsworth Longfellow's *Evangeline* (1847) is the most famous American poem written in dactylic meter, with lines such as:

> *Faint* was the *air* with the *odorous breath* of magnolia *blossoms.*

Because of its sing-song rhythm, dactylic verse is rarely found in serious English poetry, but appears often in children's songs and nursery rhymes:

> *Hick*ory *dick*ory dock . . .

> Merrily, merrily, merrily, merrily, life is but a dream . . .

(*See also* **Meter**, **Prosody**.)

Dead metaphor   A **metaphor** that has lost its figurative aspect. Metaphors "die" when repeated use makes their metaphorical side come to seem literal, as in the common phrases "Time is running out" and "Keep your shirt on!" "Live" metaphors entail a relation between two meanings, but dead metaphors have fused those two into one. When one hears them, one doesn't register the literal meaning (time running, a shirt coming off), only the figurative one ("there's little time left," "don't get upset").

Deconstructionist criticism   A school of interpretation conceived by French philosopher Jacques Derrida and enjoying a wide vogue in the humanities in the United States in the 1970s and 80s. In landmark essays from the 1960s, such as *"Différance"* and "Structure, Sign, and Play in the Discourse of the Human Sciences," Derrida combined aspects of philosophy, linguistics, and psychoanalysis into an innovative far-reaching strategy of textual analysis. Although a complex and difficult enterprise, deconstruction stands on a few basic principles regarding language and truth. First, deconstruction posits that language is an unstable medium, with the meaning of statements ambiguous and wavering because of the workings of context and **metaphor**. The same word in one text means one thing, in another yet another thing. Literal meanings are always being twisted into figurative meanings and alternate connotations. Second, language is a system of differences, not identities. The meaning and value of words are not due to an inherent quality they bear, but to their differences from other words. The word *brown* signifies a color, but we understand it not simply by relating the term directly to the color itself, but through the mediation of other terms and colors (Derrida extends this dialectical principle to things as well, to all existences). Finally, all texts have a structure, and what gives that structure coherence is a centering mechanism that orients each element of the text toward a governing meaning. The "center" of the Bible is God;

the center of a poet's corpus, to a psychologist, is the poet's psyche. As Derrida describes it, "The function of this center was not only to orient, balance, and organize the structure . . . but above all to make sure that the organizing principle of the structure would limit what we might call the *play* of the structure." The center acts to contain the variations of language, to circumscribe the play of meaning (in the sense of the play in a steering wheel as well as the play in a game).

Without a center, too much of the text would be indeterminate and unaccounted for. We would not be able to anchor the ambiguous meanings and figurative language in a coherent pattern. The Bible is a heterogeneous complex of stories, ideas, parables, laws, authors, etc., and what gives them unity is, precisely, God. But, Derrida observes, the center occupies a contradictory position: it rules the pieces of the text, but is itself separate from the text—God is manifest in the Bible, yet transcends it. Here lies a logical problem that forces a rethinking of textuality, specifically, an implication of the center in the textual play that it heretofore regulated. God is to be understood textually just as are different books in the Bible, or rather, God is an object of interpretation just as much as is the Bible. Interpretation is endless, and any center that purports to close off interpretation is to be understood as a false closure.

In practice, assuming the fugitive nature of meaning and the spuriousness of the old centers, deconstructionists drop the goal of determining the truth or ultimate significance of the text. The text becomes a field of verbal play, with words acting more like tokens in a strategic game than representations of reality. In literary criticism, the strategy sometimes becomes a type of formalism in which critics detail fuzzy distinctions, oblique metaphors, and contradictory motifs in the work. But whereas other formalists try to demonstrate how the diverse elements of the work cohere into an overall import, deconstructionists explore how the text deconstructs—that is, how it contains irreconcilable, indeterminate elements, how it won't dovetail on a stable meaning, how it problematizes the very centers that purport to explain it. One early subject of deconstructive criticism was the poetry of William Carlos Williams, in which beginnings and origins are repeatedly invoked as if Williams were searching for a basic springboard for creation. Traditional critics might take this search at face value, and interpret Williams's poetry as succeeding or failing to realize an original poetry. Deconstructionist critics proceed differently. Citing the many instances in Williams's corpus in which the pursuit of origins is frustrated, they view the whole question of originality as a misleading one, for no pure origin is possible. To achieve it would be to step out of language and time, to achieve unmediated contact with reality. But though Williams's search is futile, this does not lead deconstructionists to dismiss his work. Instead, they concentrate on the way in which the pursuit of origins functions in the poetry and prose, how it generates fruitful dilemmas and interesting themes leading Williams into serious meditations on history and tradition. Criticism in this case is not the answer to questions—what does the poem mean?—but the elaboration of why such questions cannot be answered.

Such approaches show that the value of deconstruction lies not in its specific readings of literature, but in its theory of interpretation. According to Derrida, standard interpretations rely upon fundamental principles or beliefs to determine the meanings of different elements of a text. Biographical readers use the author's life and intentions, Marxist critics invoke class struggle. The radical thrust of deconstruction is to claim that these extra-textual entities are themselves just as much subject to interpretation as the texts they supposedly structure. Interpretation is generalized into an inescapable condition of life, however much uncertainty and anxiety it produces. Truth, God, reality, and intention are fluid concepts themselves in need of interpretation. This is the point at which some deconstructionists extend beyond formalism and engage in political criticism (armed with deconstructionist skepticisms). They step outside the text and explore how truth, God, etc., function as tools of social organization and rationales for social conditions. Critiquing the nature of God then becomes, they claim, an active intervention in the putatively transcendent grounds of social and political structures.

Clearly, deconstruction calls for intellectual subtlety and skill, plus extensive training in the history of philosophy. Though it has nihilistic tendencies, its practitioners often expose some of the assumptions and simplifications of conventional criticism. Nevertheless, several thinkers have criticized deconstruction for what they feel are its predictability and rigidity. It is predictable in its insistence on fissures and disharmonies in the text, sometimes enlarging minor ambiguities into major uncertainties and problems. It is rigid in its knack of ruling out of hand various empirical materials such as historical events (because they are too "mediated" to serve as adequate explanations of the text), even when the text seems to point directly and unproblematically to them. When leading deconstructionist critic Paul de Man maintains "the impossibility of making the actual expression coincide with what has to be expressed, of making the actual signs coincide with what is signified," one senses a skeptical temperament at odds with ordinary experience. After reading many deconstructionist works of criticism, one observes a routine pattern at work, with individual texts run through a deconstructive wringer to yield the same conclusions again and again. (*See also* **Formalist criticism, Hermeneutics, Literary theory.**)

Decorum   [duh–KOR–um] Propriety or appropriateness in language. In poetry, decorum usually refers to form and **diction** that are matched to an occasion or subject matter. Formal events, such as funeral orations and epic invocations require an elevated language and a weighty structure. Certain verse patterns complement one topic and not another. For instance, with their curt, bounding rhythm, tetrameter couplets clash with the scope and heroism proper to serious **epic**. Decorum can also apply to characters, setting, and the harmony that exists between the elements in a poem. A scene showing rural folk speaking inner-city slang violates decorum, as does a moment of somber feeling in the midst of a farce. Each classical genre (tragedy, comedy, lyric, etc.) had its decorum, and one of the things that marks modern genres such as the novel is its loosening of the standards of diction and treatment. Still, errors in decorum indicate a writer who hasn't mastered the conventions of a genre—unless, that is, a writer deliberately breaks decorum for ironic or ideological purposes—for instance, having a king-character speak in stilted, hyperbolic language in order to mock the pretenses of royalty. (*See also* **Diction, Genre, Irony.**)

Denotation The dictionary meaning of a word, as opposed to its figurative uses and the associations it may attract in one context or another. Denotation is fixed (except over long periods of time), and it stands as a baseline from which writers "bend" words to other meanings and implications. Routinely contrasted with **connotation**, denotation may be divided into the thing the word refers to (its "extension") and the abstract contents that make up the word itself (its "intension"). The denotation of *zebra*, for instance, includes both the real animal and the general attributes of it (four-legged, white coat with black stripes, etc.). (*See also* **Connotation.**)

Dénouement [DAY–new–mawn] French for "unknotting" or "untying," *dénouement* signifies the resolution or conclusion of a literary work. More than just an end, the *dénouement* entails the untangling of complications and a sense of completion to the action, although an **open *dènouement*** allows for a measure of ambiguity. (*See also* **Closed *dénouement*, Conclusion.**)

Deus ex machina [DAY–us ex MAH–key–nah] Latin for "a god from a machine," the phrase originally referred to the Greek playwrights' frequent use of a god, mechanically lowered to the stage from the roof (*see* **Skene**), to resolve the human conflict represented in the drama. Uttering judgments and commands, the god settles issues in the play that the action had left hanging. To Aristotle, such arbitrary resolutions failed to address the conflicts in the play artistically or realistically. Letting the gods decide the outcome was an artificial contrivance: "It is therefore evident that the unraveling of the plot . . . must arise out of the plot itself, it must not be brought about by the *deus ex machina*" (*Poetics*). The issue is a dead one today, as no literal *deus ex machina* appears on modern stages, but the term survives in naming any forced or improbable device used to terminate a plot. (*See also* **Dènouement, Plot.**)

Dialect A variety of language spoken by an identifiable regional group or social class. Distinguished from other varieties of the language by differences in vocabulary, pronunciation, and grammar, a dialect is distinct from the standard language but has rules and usages consistent enough to mark the dialect as an established practice. In English and American literary history, dialects have characterized some of the most important works of literature. In Middle English, there was no clear standard for the language, and the two major works of the fourteenth century, *The Canterbury Tales* (1386–1400) and *Sir Gawain and the Green Knight* (ca. 1375–1400), are written in different dialects. In the United States, ever since the nineteenth century, regional and ethnic literatures have invoked dialects to represent the diversity of multicultural American experience. Mark Twain's writings made the Mississippi River vernacular a national entertainment, Langston Hughes explored urban Black English at length in modernist verse, and translations of Isaac Bashevis Singer's stories preserved the resources and feel of Yiddish (Singer personally supervised the translations). Although such dialects entail errors of Standard English, literary critics should approach them as local modes of expression, as the idiom of a region, a culture, a racial or ethnic identity. (See also **Regionalism.**)

Dialogue   The direct representation of conversation between two or more characters. Apart from conventions such as utterances by the **chorus** and the **aside**, **drama** is built mainly on dialogue. Scenes may begin or end with a **soliloquy**, but it must be used sparingly; and the revelation of motive and the creation of tension generally grow out of exchanges between characters. Having two voices on stage allows for multiple conflicts—declarations rejected, lies told, messages misconstrued—and the audience's greater or lesser knowledge of the characters adds yet another level of irony and interest.

In fiction, dialogue is framed by descriptions of **setting** and **character**, and so it bears a lesser burden of exposition than it does in drama. Statements are less elaborate and theatrical, and the rhythms of speech sound more conversational. While certain novelists occasionally use dialogue in near-dramatic ways (for example, Ernest Hemingway often turns an episode on a verbal exchange having little supporting description), most of the time novelists treat dialogue as but one element of fiction. In the late fiction of Henry James, ordinary dialogue is eclipsed by subtle and convoluted musings upon the dramatic situation, while in the **stream-of-consciousness** novels of James Joyce and William Faulkner, external dialogue becomes less important than the words and images passing through the narrators' heads.

When dialogue appears in poetry—in a lengthy **ballad**, for example—it functions the same way that it does in fiction, with the important exception of poems that are themselves structured as dialogues. Alexander Pope's "Epistle to Dr. Arbuthnot" (1735) is an imagined conversation between the poet and his physician/friend, their words marked, respectively, "P." and "A," while William Wordsworth's "Expostulation and Reply" (1798) contains three stanzas spoken by "Matthew" and four in response by Wordsworth. Andrew Marvell's "A Dialogue between the Soul and Body" (1681) has four stanzas, two spoken by "SOUL" and two by "BODY," while William Butler Yeats echoes the pattern in "A Dialogue of Self and Soul" (1929). In such cases, when words are placed explicitly in the mouths of identifiable figures, the lyric directness is blunted, and the statements become mediated by the subjectivity of the speaker of them. (*See also* **Dramatic irony, Monologue.**)

Diction   Word choice or vocabulary. Most works have an identifiable diction, some using one kind consistently, others mixing **dialects** and styles. Diction can be literal or figurative, **colloquial** or idiomatic (as in a professional jargon), concrete or abstract, high, middle, or low. That is, diction may be evaluated by its meaning, reference, occasion, rhetorical purpose, and social status. A scientific report requires a diction that imparts a professional seriousness and is free of metaphor and irony. A **lyric** poem, on the other hand, may be one extended simile in ornate, concrete diction. Although the measurement of diction is somewhat fuzzy, one can distinguish concrete diction (referring to what we can immediately perceive with our senses) from abstract diction (words that express general ideas or concepts), and separate high diction (Latinate, multisyllabic words), middle diction (the language one hears in casual, but polite conversation), and low diction (the language of the street). Concrete diction would offer *bouncing puppy* rather than *youthful canine*, and *harsh yell* rather than *angry utterance*. Slang is low diction (Walt Whitman's "the blab of the pave"), whereas the language of John Milton's *Paradise Lost* (1667) is high. In a line from James Thomson's *The Seasons* (1744), the diction is literal and concrete:

> The Black-bird whistles from the thorny Brake . . .
> ("Spring," l. 601)

But when Thomson refers to a female bird as a "patient dam" and a male as "Her sympathizing Lover," the diction shifts higher, more formal and stylized. The latter is a case of **poetic diction**, a flowery vocabulary that substitutes fanciful epithets and inverted syntax for simple names and direct word order. Such changes signify broader issues of style and audience, and show that diction has social, regional, and ethnic dimensions. The Romantic poet William Wordsworth considered poetic diction an artificial style remote from the "language of men," and so he composed his *Lyrical Ballads* (1798) in diction nearer to that of rustic laborers. Wordsworth's argument was decisive, and forms one of many cases in which literary history turns on a prevailing diction being challenged, upheld, or reinvented. (*See also* **Levels of diction, Poetic diction.**)

Didactic literature   [die–DAK–tik] Fiction and poetry intended to teach a specific moral lesson, exemplify a doctrine, or provide a model for proper behavior. It sets education above entertainment, and in the best examples preserves aesthetic quality while remaining true to the pedagogical goal. Samuel Johnson's "The Vanity of Human Wishes" (1749) is filled with moral precepts, yet skillful in its verse; and Thomas Gray's "Ode on a Distant Prospect of Eton College" (1742) ends with a didactic ruling—"where ignorance is bliss, / 'Tis folly to be wise"—that has become commonplace in English. While most works of serious literature have didactic elements, didactic literature is distinguished by a clear instructional purpose underlying the plot and characters. For instance, Dante's early fourteenth-century epic *The Divine Comedy* (1314–21) contains a multitude of fascinating personages and affecting stories, but its overriding function is to chart the way through sin to Christian salvation. Lesser forms of didactic literature lack imagination, but are equally prescriptive. In the mid-nineteenth-century, for example, a popular genre of fiction was the "temperance novel," a narrative that typically chronicled an upright, hardworking husband and father who is lured into a barroom by a friend. He slips into alcoholism, loses his job, abandons his family, and ends in suicide, the entire sequence a warning of the dangers of drink.

The heavy-handedness of such didactic fiction has made the term a pejorative one, applied to stories in which the events seem manipulated in order to press a moral opinion. Art declines into propaganda, and the moral and aesthetic complexity of serious literature is sacrificed to a single teaching. This is a modern interpretation, however, for throughout the Medieval and Renaissance Periods didactic aims were fundamental to great literature. As Sir Philip Sidney put it in "An Apology for Poetry" (1595):

> Poetry therefore is an art of imitation . . . a representing, counterfeiting, or figuring forth—to speak metaphorically, a speaking picture; with this end, to teach and delight.

The dual purpose of art is what led Samuel Johnson in "Preface to *Shakespeare*" (1765) to criticize the Bard: "He sacrifices virtue to convenience, and is so much more careful to please than to instruct, that he seems to write without any moral purpose." Not until the nineteenth century, with the advent of **aestheticism, realism, naturalism,** and other nonmoral artistic movements, did instruction in literature become a suspect motive. (*See also* **Theme.**)

Dimeter   [DIM–it–er] An uncommon verse meter consisting of two feet per line:

> Your ugly token
> My mind hath broken
> From worldly lust;
> For I have discussed,
> We are but dust
> And die we must.
>   (John Skelton, "Upon a Dead Man's Head"; 1498)

Doggerel   [DOG–er–ul] Crude verse that brims with cliché, predictable rhyme, and inept rhythm. Some doggerel strives for sentiment and sincerity, such as greeting card verse, but fails because of the hackneyed versification and conventional thoughts. Another kind of doggerel aims only for low comedy, such as vulgar limericks, and revels in crudity and irreverence. A third kind mixes the two, parodying the language of "serious" doggerel to produce the silliness of "comic" doggerel. In *Huckleberry Finn* (1884), Mark Twain includes an elegy by a young deceased poetess for a young man who died falling down a well:

No whooping-cough did wrack his frame,
    Nor measles drear, with spots;
Not these impaired the sacred name
    Of Stephen Dowling Bots.

Despised love struck not with woe
    That head of curly knots,
No stomach troubles laid him low,
    Young Stephen Dowling Bots.

O no. Then list with tearful eye,
    While I his fate do tell.
His soul did from this cold world fly,
    By falling down a well.

The target of the parody is the lugubrious drama of mid-century American **sentimentality**. The means is the rough mixing of high and low ("sacred name" and "stomach troubles") and the simplistic rhymes (*eye-fly, tell-well*). (*See also* **Parody.**)

Double plot   A double plot, or subplot, is a second story or plotline that is complete and interesting in its own right, often mimicking or inverting the main plot. By analogy or counterpoint, a skillful subplot broadens understanding of the main plot to enhance rather than dilute its effect. It may provide **comic relief** or a different version of the primary conflict—for instance, when a romantic plot involving aristocratic figures edging toward marriage is paralleled by a romantic double plot involving servant figures edging toward sexual dalliance. English Renaissance dramatists often insert double plots into their works, as in Shakespeare's *Othello* (1604), when Iago's duping of Roderigo reflects the main plot of Iago's treachery to Othello. John Dryden terms them "underplots or by-concernments, of less considerable persons and intrigues, which are carried on with the motion of the main plot" ("An Essay of Dramatic Poesy," 1668). Such minor plotlines risk violating the so-called "unity of action," which demands that all the plot elements in a play coalesce in a single, complete course of events. But when integrated as a reflection upon or contrast with a main plot, a double plot serves to develop a theme and complicate the audience's perspective. (*See also* **Plot, Unities.**)

Drama   Derived from the Greek *dran*, "to do," drama originally named actions or deeds immediately represented, not narrated. As opposed to fiction and poetry, dramatic compositions are designed for performance on a stage, in which actors assume the roles of characters, execute the indicated movements, and speak the written dialogue. In the *Poetics*, Aristotle defines **epic** poetry, **lyric** poetry, and drama as "in their general conception modes of imitation," but he distinguishes epic from drama on formal grounds: "the poet may imitate by narration . . . or he may present all his characters as living and moving before us." The purported realism of drama has remained a controversial subject ever since, and has posed numerous critical problems. Critics have wondered why people enjoy bloody deeds, lamentations, and horrifying outcomes on stage, when the same scenes in real life appall them. In *The Decay of Lying* (1889), Oscar Wilde maintained that in carrying realism too far ("The characters in these plays talk on the stage exactly as they would off it . . . they would pass unnoticed in a third-class railway carriage"), the modern English drama had become wearisome and pointless—why attend a drama if the drama aims to reproduce what may be heard in the street? Another problem arose when, given the burden of verisimilitude, Renaissance and seventeenth-century dramatists pondered how best to represent time and place on stage. The French tragedian Pierre Corneille believed that one should "compress the action of the poem into the shortest possible period, so that the performance may more closely resemble reality" (*Of the Three Unities of Action, Time, and Place*, 1660). He also advised that the action transpire as much as possible in the same place, and thus produce in the audience an illusion of real happenings. In the "Preface to *Shakespeare*" (1765), however, Samuel Johnson dispeled the entire question: "The truth is, that the spectators are always in their senses, and know . . . that the stage is only a stage, and that the players are only players." To leap from place to place and time to time doesn't hinder the audience's involvement, so long as the changes are warranted by the plot. The twentieth-century philosopher Ernst Cassirer echoes the point by affirming, "At a Shakespeare play we are not infected with the ambition of Macbeth, with the cruelty of Richard III, or with the jealousy of Othello" (*Essay on Man*, 1944). Nonetheless, he added, "Dramatic art discloses a new breadth and depth of life. It conveys an awareness of human things and human destinies, of human greatness and misery, in comparison to which our ordinary existence appears poor and trivial." The ambivalence Cassirer highlights rests upon the simultaneous engagement/distance of the audience's experience, a situation more intense than that of reading a play in a book at home. (*See also* **Closet drama, Realism, Unities**.)

Dramatic irony   A special kind of suspenseful expectation, when the audience understands the meaning or implication of a situation onstage but the character does not. Characters speak, unaware of the full import of their words; they take action, intending one result but (as the audience realizes instantly) producing another. The irony lies in the contrasting degrees of knowledge, in the discrepancy between the information the audience brings to the play and the awareness the characters have of themselves. In ancient Greek and Roman drama, theatergoers knew in advance the outcome of the action, whose plot was based upon popular myths and stories, and so they could judge the characters' conduct against their eventual fate. Dramatic irony is pervasive throughout Sophocles' *Oedipus*, because everyone knows from the beginning what Oedipus does not. We watch with dread and fascination the spectacle of a morally good man, committed to the salvation of his city, unwittingly pursuing his own catastrophe. On a simpler level, it may operate through brief verbal clues. In the first scene of Shakespeare's *Macbeth* (1605), the three witches chant "Fair is foul, and foul is fair." Two scenes later Macbeth appears for the first time with the words "So fair and foul a day I have not seen." The audience hears the echo and suspects a connection between the two, but Macbeth has no inkling of it. Later in the play it will be borne out. (*See also* **Character development**, **Drama**, **Irony**.)

Dramatic monologue A poem written as a speech made by a character. Typically, in the course of the monologue, the character acquires a delineated personality and reveals private desires, weaknesses, crimes, and sins, sometimes inadvertently. A life situation unfolds, and elements of confession and justification fuel the self-display. As a further complication, the speaker usually addresses a silent listener, for instance, the "you" in T. S. Eliot's "The Love Song of J. Alfred Prufrock" (1915) and the Count's emissary in Robert Browning's "My Last Duchess" (1842), which begins:

> That's my last Duchess painted on the wall,
> Looking as if she were alive. I call
> That piece a wonder, now; Frà Pandolf's hands
> Worked busily a day, and there she stands.
> Will't please you sit and look at her?

Browning is the acknowledged master of the dramatic monologue, which flourished in England in the mid-nineteenth century, and his portraits of historical and imagined personages achieve arresting depths of temperament and motive. (*See also* **Monologue**.)

Dramatic poetry Although dramatic poetry loosely names any poetry involving a dramatic situation (for example, the **dramatic monologue**), strictly speaking it signifies verse written for the stage—a generic definition wide enough to include the plays of classical Greece and Rome, the Renaissance, and the Neoclassical period, as well as scattered contemporary efforts. Indeed, the works of Euripides and Seneca, all of Shakespeare's plays except *The Merry Wives of Windsor*, and the Neoclassical works of Racine, Corneille, and Molière count as dramatic poetry. Not until the late-seventeenth century did prose begin to dominate the language of drama, and into our own day dramatic poetry has had its defenders. In "A Defense of Poetry" (1821), Percy Bysshe Shelley judged drama "that form under which a greater number of modes of expression of poetry are susceptible of being combined than any other," and in the twentieth century T. S. Eliot championed dramatic poetry as a popular art. Poets Wallace Stevens, William Carlos Williams, Robert Lowell, and James Merrill essayed plays in verse, and Bertholt Brecht and Samuel Beckett inserted metrical passages into their otherwise prosaic dramas. For the most part, though, dramatic poetry in recent times is rarely performed, functioning as an experimental genre in which writers test the limits of verse dialogue.

Dramatic point of view   A point of view in which the narrator merely reports dialogue and action with minimal interpretation and little access to the characters' minds. Authors implementing the dramatic point of view write prose fiction but approximate the situation of theater, in which readers are provided only with set descriptions, stage directions, and dialogue, and thus must infer motivations based solely on external evidence. The narrator has no personality, no discernible angle of vision, but instead stands neutral to the characters and events. (*See also* **Point of view.**)

Dramatic situation   The basic conflict that initiates a work or establishes a scene. It usually entails both a protagonist's **motivation** and the forces that oppose its realization. In *Hamlet* (1601), the dramatic situation is a simple one, established quickly by Hamlet's father's ghost. He was murdered by his brother, he tells Hamlet, and Hamlet must wreak revenge. This is the dramatic situation from which all ensuing actions follow, and the **plot** doesn't end until it is resolved. (*See also* **Antagonist, Character, Complication, Plot, Rising action.**)

Dumb show   In Renaissance theater, a mimed dramatic performance whose purpose is to prepare the audience for the main action of the play to follow. Jacobean playwrights such as John Webster used it to show violent events that occur some distance from the play's locale. The most famous Renaissance example is the dumb show preceding the presentation of "The Murder of Gonzago" in *Hamlet* (1601).

Dynamic character   A character who, during the course of the narrative, grows or changes in some significant way. This means that a dynamic character must not only be complex and three-dimensional, but also must develop as the **plot** develops. In the *Bildungsroman*, for instance, the growth of the **protagonist** is, in fact, coincident with the course of the plot. (*See also* **Character development.**)

Echo verse   A poetic technique dating back to classical Greek poetry in which the final syllables of verse lines (or their near equivalent) are repeated back as a reply or commentary:

Of now done darkness I wretch lay wrestling with (my God!)
  my god.
                (Gerard Manley Hopkins, "Carrion Comfort"; 1918)

Editorial omniscience   [awm–NISH–ints] Narration becomes editorial when
an **omniscient narrator** goes beyond reporting the thoughts of his or her characters to make a critical judgment or commentary. The narrator of Lord Byron's
Don Juan (1819–24), for instance, repeatedly inserts his own opinions into the
exposition. A description of Juan's parents leads him to reflect upon mismatched marriages; Juan's education, his first crush, etc., evoke similar editorial
remarks. As the innocent Haidée brims with love for Juan, the narrator waxes:

> Alas! The love of women! It is known
>   To be a lovely and a fearful thing;
> For all of theirs upon that die is thrown,
>   And if 'tis lost, life hath no more to bring
> To them but mockeries of the past alone . . .
>   (Canto II, ll. 1585–89)

If such digressions occur frequently, they become a functional part of the narrative and the narrator achieves an independent identity. He or she, too, is a character and raises critical questions—Is the narrator to be trusted? Is the narrator a
moral authority? An object of irony?—forcing readers to interpret the editorial-
izing as they would the statements of other figures. (*See also* **Point of view.**)

Editorial point of view   Also called "authorial intrusion," the editorial point
of view assumes the perspective of a **third-person narrator** who inserts his or
her own comments into the narrative. Usually representing the ideas and
opinions of the author—unless the author wishes to criticize precisely that attitude and makes the narrator a target of ridicule—the editorial point of view
presumes a copious knowledge of the events and characters. The narrator
looks down upon the fictional materials with an authoritative judgment,
adding an initial layer of interpretation to the exposition. Sherwood Anderson's *Winesburg, Ohio* (1919) is a sequence of portraits of small-town
denizens articulated through the editorial point of view. In unveiling different
midwestern "types," Anderson has his narrator look deep into the characters'
hearts and minds, then step out and regard them with coldness. In introducing
an aged writer, the narrator observes:

> He had once been quite handsome and a number of women had been
> in love with him. And then, of course, he had known people, many
> people, known them in a peculiarly intimate way that was different
> from the way in which you and I know people. At least that is what
> the writer thought and the thought pleased him. Why quarrel with
> an old man concerning his thoughts?

The first few sentences one believes on faith, until the "At least" puts them into the writer's head, not the narrator's, and insinuates a note of vanity ("pleased him"). The final question completes the "editorialization," setting the old man up as an object scrutinized by reader and narrator. (*See also* **Editorial omniscience, Point of view.**)

Elegy [EL–uh–jee] A lament or a meditative poem, often written on the occasion of a death or other solemn event or theme. Although an elegy may appear as a discrete section in a larger work (as in the oration at the funeral of Beowulf), it is usually a complete poem in a formal style. A famous example is Thomas Gray's "Elegy Written in a Country Churchyard" (1751), whose thirty-two stanzas ruminate upon the passing of time and souls:

> Can storied urn or animated bust
>   Back to its mansion call the fleeting breath?
> Can Honor's voice provoke the silent dust,
>   Or Flattery soothe the dull cold ear of Death?
>
> Perhaps in this neglected spot is laid
>   Some heart once pregnant with celestial fire;
> Hands that the rod of empire might have swayed,
>   Or waked to ecstasy the living lyre.

One kind of elegy that is especially important in English literary history is the pastoral elegy, whose highlights include John Milton's "Lycidas" (1637) and Percy Bysshe Shelley's "Adonais" (an elegy for the dead John Keats, 1821). Pastoral elegies combine pastoral themes and images—nature deities, seasonal vegetation—with a memorialization of a deceased friend or comrade. (*See also* **Pastoral.**)

Elizabethan Era The period in English literary history named for Queen Elizabeth, who reigned from 1558–1603, roughly coincident with the English Renaissance. The period is said to begin with mid-century poets Sir Thomas Wyatt, who incorporated Italian models into English poetry, and Henry Howard, Earl of Surrey, who introduced **blank verse**. What followed was an outpouring of poetry and drama virtually unmatched over the centuries: sonnet cycles by Sir Philip Sidney, Edmund Spenser, Michael Drayton, Samuel Daniel, and Shakespeare; lyrics by Sir Walter Raleigh, Spenser's epic *The Faerie Queene* (1590), and Sidney's pastoral fiction *Arcadia* (1590); and the dramas of Christopher Marlowe, Shakespeare, and Ben Jonson.

Endnote A citation or piece of information that the author includes in a note at the end of a paper or book. Endnotes usually contain material that the author has borrowed from, or believes is significant to, the main body of the text, but not sufficiently so to be included there. (*See also* **Footnote.**)

End rhyme Rhyme that occurs at the ends of lines, rather than within them (as **internal rhyme** does).

> For never was a story of more woe
> Than of this Juliet and her Romeo.
> (Shakespeare, *Romeo and Juliet*, V.iii; 1596)

(*See also* **Rhyme.**)

End-stopped line A line of verse that ends in a full pause, usually indicated by a mark of punctuation. **Heroic couplets**, for instance, tend to be end-stopped at the second line, while **ballad stanzas** have an end-stop at the second and fourth lines. (*See also* **Enjambment.**)

English sonnet Also called **Shakespearean sonnet**, the English sonnet is written in **iambic pentameter** with a rhyme scheme organized into three quatrains with a final couplet, usually *abab cdcd efef gg*. While the **Italian sonnet** turns—that is, shifts in mood or argument—at the eighth line, the English sonnet postpones the turn until the final couplet. In Spenser's Sonnet 67 from *Amoretti* (1595), for instance, the first twelve lines tell a story, while the final two reflect upon it. (Note also Spenser's variation on the typical rhyme scheme.)

Lyke as a huntsman after weary chace,	*a*
Seeing the game from him escapt away,	*b*
Sits downe to rest him in some shady place,	*a*
With panting hounds beguiléd of their pray:	*b*
So after long pursuit and vaine assay,	*b*
When I all weary had the chace forsook,	*c*
The gentle deare returnd the selfe-same way,	*b*
Thinking to quench her thirst at the next brooke.	*c*
There she beholding me with mylder looke,	*c*
Sought not to fly, but fearless still did bide:	*d*
Till I in hand her yet halfe trembling tooke,	*c*
And with her owne goodwill hir fyrmely tyde.	*d*
Strange thing me seemd to see a beast so wyld,	*e*
So goodly wonne with her owne will beguyld.	*e*

(*See also* **Italian sonnet, Sonnet.**)

Enjambment [en–JAM–ment] When one verse flows into another without grammatical pause—that is, the opposite of end-stopped. In these lines from Wallace Stevens's "Sunday Morning" (1915), the first two are enjambed, the last three are end-stopped:

Supple and turbulent, a ring of men
Shall chant an orgy on a summer morn
Their boisterous devotion to the sun,
Not as a god, but as a god might be,
Naked among them, like a savage source.

(*See also* **End-stopped lines.**)

Envoy (or *Envoi*)   [AWN–voy] A short, summary stanza that appears at the end of certain poetic forms (most notably the **sestina**, *chant royal*, and the French *ballade*) and contains the poet's parting words. The word comes from the French *envoi*, meaning "sending forth," and many envoys begin with the words go or *forth*, as if the poet were sending the poem out into the world. The first line of the "Envoi (1919)" section of Ezra Pound's *Hugh Selwyn Mauberley* (1920) announces, "Go, dumb-born book"; and the final stanza of Algernon Swinburne's "A Ballade of Life" (1866) begins, "Forth, ballad, and take roses in both arms." Swinburne's "A Ballad of Burdens" (1866) ends with a "*L'Envoy*" of four didactic lines:

> Princes, and ye whom pleasure quickeneth,
>   Heed well this rime before your pleasure tire;
> For life is sweet, and but after life is death.
>   This is the end of every man's desire.

Epic   A long narrative poem composed in an elevated style recounting the trials and adventures of a **hero**, superhuman achievements in battle and migration, and fateful exchanges with the gods or God. The most prominent epics in Western literature—Homer's *Iliad* and *Odyssey*, Virgil's *Aeneid*, John Milton's *Paradise Lost* (1667)—because of their historical influence, aren't just literary compositions. They are cultural expressions, embodying political and moral codes essential to their respective societies. The epic poet selects familiar materials from myth, legend, religion, and oral tradition and turns them into a grand portrayal of the origin of a nation, the nature of the cosmos, the ultimate workings of fate, the meaning of heroism. The events they narrate have long-term consequences, the characters are larger than life, and the settings have panoramic scope. As philosopher Thomas Hobbes observed long ago, "The delight of an epic poem consisteth not in mirth, but admiration. Mirth and laughter are proper to comedy and satire. Great persons that have their minds employed on great designs have not leisure enough to laugh." In *The Iliad*, the raging skirmishes outside the walls of Troy are bloody and pitiless, and on their outcome rest the honor and future of Greece. *Paradise Lost* is a Christian epic focused on the Fall, but the thematic significance lies in its dramatic exploration of tenets of Puritan theology, specifically, the motives of sin and the path of salvation.

In terms of their form and meter, epics generally share set conventions, including:

1. an **episodic plot**—the action jumps from one adventure or scene to another, without a strong determinate sequence;
2. an invocation to the Muses—the poet begs the Muse to inspire him with the story he must sing, in part because the Muses are the daughters of memory (Mnemosyne) and must help him remember the long poem he must recite without notes (Homeric tales came out of an oral tradition);
3. a copious verse form—the elevation of the subject matter requires a line length of comparable breadth and flexibility, for instance, the **hexameter** of Roman epic and **blank verse** in English epic;
4. epic similes and lengthy catalogues—figurative descriptions and comparisons of heroes, armies, armor, and physical objects that run for several lines and become a minor set piece of their own;
5. *in medias res* (Latin for "in the middle of things")—epic poems begin in the middle of the action. For example, Milton's defeated angels wake up in Hell after the battle in Heaven is over, and only in later sections is the background filled in.

Epigram A short poem, often comic, that ends with a sharp turn of wit or meaning. For instance, Ben Jonson's "To Fool or Knave," printed in his book of *Epigrammes* (1616):

> Thy praise or dispraise is to me alike:
> One doth not stroke me, nor the other strike.

Epigrams have the advantage of brevity and concentration, making them easy to remember. One reason Alexander Pope is so often quoted is that many of his heroic couplets stand independently as epigrams:

> A little learning is a dangerous thing;
> Drink deep or taste not the Pierian spring.
> (*Essay on Criticism*, 215–16; 1711)

A parallel saying in prose is an aphorism, such as Oscar Wilde's "A little sincerity is a dangerous thing, and a great deal of it absolutely fatal" ("The Critic as Artist," 1888).

Epigraph A brief quotation preceding a story or other literary work. An epigraph usually suggests the subject, theme, or atmosphere the story will explore. Ralph Waldo Emerson's essay "Self-Reliance" (1841) begins with three epigraphs, one from Persius's Satire ("Do not search outside yourself"), one from a Jacobean play (first two lines: "Man is his own star, and the soul that can / Render an honest and perfect man"), and one a poem of Emerson's own making:

Cast the bantling on the rocks,
Suckle him with the she-wolf's teat:
Wintered with the hawk and fox,
Power and speed be hands and feet.

Each one bears upon the essay's central theme—that conformity is taking over social life in the United States, and only a vigilant individualism can counteract it.

Episode   An incident in a large narrative that has a measure of unity in itself. An episode may bear close relation to the central narrative, or it may be a digression. Mark Twain's *Huckleberry Finn* (1884) is structured as a series of episodes loosely connected by a journey down river. Several times Huck and Jim land near a Mississippi River village and Huck sallies forth to investigate. The events he witnesses—a lynch mob, a blood feud, etc.—are more or less complete and independent, and when they are finished Huck returns to the raft and the novel continues. (*See also* **Episodic plot, Plot.**)

Episodic plot, episodic structure   A form of plotting in which the individual scenes and events are presented chronologically without any deep cause-and-effect relationship. In an episodic narrative the placement of many scenes could be changed without greatly altering the overall effect of the work. Instead of the plot moving forward with each scene following logically upon the previous one and leading logically to the succeeding, episodic plots jump casually from one scene to another. The transition could be due simply to a change of time or place. For example, the episodes in Homer's *Odyssey* are the result of the hero's effort to return home to Ithaca. They don't build upon themselves; they stand independently as stories and could be rearranged without the epic losing its integrity. Because of the episodes' casual, not causal, relation to one another, Aristotle asserted that "Of all plots and actions the episodic are the worst" (*Poetics*). Episodic writers may compose entertaining vignettes, he argued, but they lack the artistry required to weave the vignettes into a plot having the "air of design," in which each episode becomes part of a necessary course of events. (*See also* **Episode, Plot, Unities.**)

Epistle   A poem addressed to a friend, lover, or patron. Although some ironical examples exist (Alexander Pope's "Epistle II: To a Lady," 1743), most epistles honor the addressee, singling out personal traits and reflecting upon them. Pope's "Epistle to Dr. Arbuthnot" (1735) is a supreme example in English literary history, a tribute to Pope's friend and physician composed just a few weeks before Arbuthnot's death. Taking Arbuthnot's ministrations as a pretext for ruminating upon his famed, tempestuous career, Pope slashes at his enemies and detractors with surgical wit, then balances it with short testimonials to the doctor ("O friend! may each domestic bliss be thine!").

Epistolary novel   A novel in which the story is told by way of letters written by one or more of the characters. The epistolary form often lends an authenticity to the story, leading readers directly into the characters' lives and thoughts. Narration takes the form of a series of partial perspectives, with the characters commenting privately upon one another, providing different versions of a single event, and representing different styles of expression. One of the earliest and longest novels in English (the first to be published in the American colonies), enormously popular in its day, Samuel Richardson's *Clarissa* (1747–48) is an epistolary novel. (*See also* **Novel.**)

Epistrophe   [eh–PIS–tro–fee] The opposite of **anaphora**, epistrophe is the repetition of the same word or words at the end of lines, sentences, or clauses:

> There was never any more inception *than there is now,*
> Nor any more youth or age *than there is now,*
> And will never be any more protection *than there is now,*
> Nor any more heaven or hell *than there is now.*
> (Walt Whitman, "Song of Myself," ll.40–43; 1855–92)

Etymology   [ET–uh–MAW–low–jee] The study of word origins, etymology follows words from one language to another, analyzes their parts (prefixes, roots, suffixes), and discovers cognates in different languages. An etymological study of the word *euphony* breaks it into semantic pieces (*eu-* "good" + *phon-* "sound, voice") and traces them back to ancient Greek. Etymology is useful for literary study in that the etymological meanings carry associations not always evident in the current definition. For instance, the word *supercilious* today means "coolly and patronizingly haughty," but its etymological background is *super-* "above" + *-cilious* "eyelid, lash," that is, the raising of an eyelid or eyebrow.

Euphony   [YOU–fo–nee] Language that has both melodious sound and harmonious relation to meaning, so that the words please and comfort the ear and mind. A sensuous example is Walt Whitman's address to the ocean, "Cushion me soft, rock me in billowy drowse, / Dash me with amorous wet" ("Song of Myself," ll.452–53; 1855); and Lord Tennyson's "The Lotus-Eaters" (1832) is filled with euphonious lines rendering the easeful calm of lotus-induced rest:

> There is sweet music here that softer falls
> Than petals from blown roses on the grass,
> Or night-dews on still waters between walls
> Of shadowy granite, in a gleaming pass;
> Music that gentlier on the spirit lies,
> Than tired eyelids upon tired eyes . . .
>   (46–51)

Although euphony is difficult to quantify and is susceptible to impressionistic descriptions, clearly certain sounds in English are smoother than others, and some arrangements of them more sonorous. Phonological analysis shows that vowels have greater resonance than consonants, and that consonants without a vocal stop (l, m, n, r) are more pliant than consonants with a stop ($b, d, k \ldots$). The presence of the latter often produces the opposite of euphony, **cacophony**, as in Edmund's complaint in Shakespeare's *King Lear* (1605) over his illegitimacy:

> Why brand they us
> With base? With baseness? bastardy? base, base?
> (I.ii. 9–10)

Exact rhyme   A full rhyme in which the sounds following the initial letters of the words are identical in sound, as in *follow* and *hollow*, *go* and *slow*, *disband* and *this hand*. (*See also* **Eye rhyme, Rhyme, Slant rhyme.**)

Experimental theater space   *See* **Flexible theater.**

Explication   Literally, an "unfolding," explication is one of the central modes of literary analysis. In an explication, the lexical features of an entire work (usually a poem) are explained in detail, every verbal element analyzed and each stylistic pattern expounded. Broad thematic and conceptual elements in the work are placed in the background while explication delineates the implications of a **metaphor**, the **connotations** of the diction, the nature of the syntax, and so on. Poetic language is often obscure, ambiguous, and multilayered, and before the full meaning of the work can be grasped, the nuances and complexities of each part must be elucidated. That requires a close attention to semantic features (for instance, the way in which words are turned to figurative or ironic meanings) and a cogent use of textual evidence (knowing what is valid and sufficient evidence for interpreting an image one way or another).

An explication of the opening lines from John Keats's "Ode on a Grecian Urn" (1819) would fall into two parts.

> Thou still unravish'd bride of quietness,
> Thou foster-child of silence and slow time, . . .

First, it would note prosodic features, such as the pentameter verse length, and rhetorical features, such as the **apostrophe** ("Thou") and the impassioned epithets ("unravish'd bride," "foster-child"). Next, it would determine the indirect references of the epithets—that is, the urn and the figures on it—and the ambiguities of the word "still" (both "motionless" and "enduring"). Then, it would proceed to more complex semantic questions, tracking the course of Keats's descriptions and analyzing the ornate metaphors: what is a "bride of quietness," a "foster-child of silence"? What is "slow time"? These questions would not be answered in the abstract, but with later lines in the poem that bear precisely upon quietness and time, with pertinent materials from Keats's life and writings, and with the literary history of the ode and other poems ruminating on beauty, truth, and temporality. (*See also* **Formalist criticism, Hermeneutics.**)

Exposition The opening portion of a narrative or drama. In the exposition, the scene is set, the **protagonist** is introduced, and the author discloses any background information necessary to allow readers to understand and relate to the events that are to follow. Writers use different techniques to present their materials. James Baldwin's short story "Sonny's Blues" (1957) begins with a man reading a story in the paper about his younger brother Sonny being arrested for peddling heroin. The shock leads him to reflect upon Sonny's adolescence, his commitment to jazz, and the dissolution of their family. The brother then bumps into a friend of Sonny's who confesses that he may have led Sonny into drug abuse. The exposition establishes the main characters and initiates the dramatic **conflict** between the siblings. (*See also* **Plot**.)

Expressionism A powerful movement in literature, painting, film, and other arts developed between 1910 and 1924 in Germany. Against **realism**'s focus on surface details and external reality, expressionism emphasizes a dreamlike (or nightmarish) subjective realm, often in intense and extreme states. Expressionistic artistic styles involve **episodic plots**, ecstatic characters, distorted lines, exaggerated shapes, abnormal coloring, mechanical physical movement, and telegraphic speech (for instance, the broken syntax of a disordered psyche). In its subject matter, expressionist works range from utopian visions of a fallen, materialistic world redeemed by the spirituality of "new men" to dark pessimistic visions of universal catastrophe. From the philosophical poetry of Friedrich Nietzsche's *Thus Spake Zarathustra* (1883–85), it draws its dominant attitudes: alienation from bourgeois society, disbelief in secular progress and enlightenment, and premonitions of apocalypse, all registered not objectively in the world but subjectively through an innervated temperament.

Eye rhyme A "false" rhyme in which the spelling of the words implies an ordinary rhyme, but the pronunciations differ, as in *laughter* and *daughter*, *idea* and *flea*. (*See also* **Rhyme**.)

Fable A brief, often humorous narrative told to illustrate a moral. The characters in fables are animals or objects whose behavior manifests human traits. In the tradition of fables, particular animals have come to represent specific human qualities or values—the ant represents industry, the fox craftiness, the lion nobility, etc. As a genre of **didactic literature**, fables employ different narrative means to impart their lesson. One way is to place a summary statement at the end of the story, separated from the text proper. Aesop's fables follow this pattern, as when "The North Wind and the Sun" concludes with the moral "Persuasion is better than force." Other fables, such as those by seventeenth-century French writer Jean de La Fontaine, are more sophisticated in their instruction, incorporating ambiguities and ironies that work against the simple equation of story and message. (*See also* **Allegory.**)

Fairy tale A traditional genre of short narrative **folklore**, originally transmitted orally, which features witches, giants, fairies, lost and endangered children, and animals with human traits. In fairy tales, the ordinary laws of nature and society are suspended and fantasy takes over, sometimes happily as when an unlikely hero or heroine achieves a desirable fate such as marrying a prince or princess, becoming wealthy, or destroying a renowned enemy; sometimes unhappily, as when siblings are chopped up and cooked in a pie by an evil stepmother. The fantastical, child-like content of fairy tales has led psychological and anthropological critics to broach them as serious expressions of human nature. Cataloguing motifs and character types in hundreds of fairy tales, and marking significant changes in different versions of the same tale, scholars relate actions and figures to primal fears and desires. What appears to be an accidental element in one fairy tale—for example, a substitute parent (a guardian, a stepfather, etc.) who despises the children—turns out to be a fundamental condition or anxiety when it is repeated in others. (*See also* **Stock character.**)

Falling action The events in a narrative that follow the **climax** and bring the story to its **conclusion.** As with other plot elements, falling action is a "deep structure," not just a sequence of actions but their underlying pattern. What distinguishes the pattern of falling action is that the actions have a "downward" momentum, that is, a progress toward a *dènouement*. In general, in the falling action no new conflicts are introduced, nor are characters further developed. Rather, the falling action involves the working out of established conflicts, and it often begins once a crucial development of character has taken place. In F. Scott Fitzgerald's *The Great Gatsby* (1925), for instance, the falling action begins after the confrontation between Gatsby and Tom Buchanon as they compete for Daisy's love. The subsequent events—Daisy and Gatsby drive home, Myrtle is run over, Myrtle's husband kills Gatsby, Nick encounters Tom and Daisy on the street, Nick returns to Gatsby's abandoned mansion—bring the novel to its end. (*See also* **Plot.**)

Falling meter A meter whose feet are accented on the first syllable. Trochaic and dactylic meters "fall" in their level of stress, as in the words *aw*-ful and *com*edy, and in the lines:

> Margaret, are you grieving
> Over Goldengrove unleaving?
> (Gerard Manley Hopkins, "Spring and Fall"; 1880)

(*See also* **Dactyl, Meter, Rhythm, Trochee.**)

Fantasy (or Fantastic) literature A narrative that depicts events, characters, or places that defy the physical and/or psychological laws of the ordinary world.

Fantasy literature freely pursues the dreamy and nightmarish possibilities of the imagination, keeping open the question of whether the events have a natural, supernatural, or psychic source. In the case of **fairy tales**, fantasy populates the scene with supernatural figures of uncertain moral bearing, and the story often climaxes with magical transformations (for instance, a frog becoming a prince). In more psychological versions of fantasy fiction, such as the old television show *The Twilight Zone*, strange situations take on a pathological cast. In one episode, a man wakes up one day to find everything has changed—he doesn't recognize his wife, his friends, his co-workers, but they all recognize him and treat him casually. The contrast between the outer normalcy and the man's inner estrangement marks an uneasy space of fantasy. Has the world really changed, or is it all in his head? Such complications prompt critics to relate fantasy literature to real world conditions and the psyches that inhabit them. Fantastic situations may be read as renditions of profound doubts about the nature of reality, or of the dissatisfactions of an alien world. That is, underlying the surface play, magic, grotesqueries, and dreamscapes are existential cruxes that can only be addressed in fantastical form. (*See also* **Fiction**.)

Farce   A type of **comedy** featuring exaggerated character types in ludicrous and improbable situations, provoking belly laughs with social mix-ups, crude verbal jokes, pratfalls, and knockabout horseplay. Whereas higher forms of comedy such as **satire** have critical and moral purposes (say, to mock pretense), farce lays no direct claim to criticism. It merely entertains, providing an outlet for ribald and ludic impulses. It may have critical implications, as when Groucho Marx plays a college president and addresses a faculty meeting with the song "Whatever It Is, I'm Against It" (thus taunting academic contrariness), but what makes the Marx Brothers movie a farce isn't the message, but the zaniness. (*See also* **Burlesque, Slapstick comedy**.)

Feminine rhyme   A rhyme of two or more syllables with a stress on a syllable other than the last, as in *tur*-tle and *fer*-tile. Sometimes an entire poem, stanza, or sequence of lines contains feminine rhyme, as in the narrator's reminiscences in Canto IV of Lord Byron's *Don Juan* (1819–24):

> As a boy, I thought myself a clever fellow,
>   And wished that others held the same opinion;
> They took it up when my days grew more mellow,
>   And other minds acknowledged my dominion:
> Now my sere fancy "falls into the yellow
>   Leaf," and Imagination droops her pinion . . .

(*See also* **Masculine rhyme, Rhyme**.)

Feminist criticism   *See* **Gender criticism**.

Fiction From the Latin *ficio*, "act of fashioning, shaping, making," fiction covers any literary work that, although it might contain information true to reality, is not bound by existing facts and events. Rather, it imparts a world spun out of the author's imagination. **Drama** and poetry (especially narrative poetry) can be considered modes of fiction, and when the term became popular in the seventeenth century it named all forms of fanciful invention. But today it usually refers to prose stories and novels. Historical and other factual writing also require shaping and making, but they are distinct from fiction because they are not free to invent people, places, and events; forays from documented fact must identify themselves as conjecture or hypothesis.

Nonfiction, as the name suggests, is a category separate from fiction, and only appeared in the twentieth century after the novel became the dominant literary genre. Certainly an essay or work of literary journalism is a "made thing," and writers of nonfiction routinely employ the techniques used by fiction writers (moving forward and backward in time, reporting the inner thoughts of characters, etc.). But the materials handled in this way originate in the world of fact and opinion, not that of imagination. Nonfiction writers may recount actual events with all the tools of narrative, but they must be guided by the fact. Truth in nonfiction is fidelity to an actual state of affairs. Truth in fiction, if we may apply the term at all, rests on how plausibly and convincingly the writer has drawn the fictional world. (*See also* **Verisimilitude**.)

Figure of speech An expression or comparison (sometimes termed *trope*—"to turn") whose meaning is metaphorical, ironic, or rhetorical, not literal. Although the boundary between figurative and literal is often fuzzy, as in the case of **dead metaphors**, a figure of speech is distinguished as a semantic composite: at least two meanings are in play. On one side is the ordinary usage, on the other the divergence from it. The dualism of meaning may be due to the immediate sense of the figure, as in the opening line from William Carlos Williams's "Spring and All" (1923):

> By the road to the contagious hospital . . .

Hospitals aren't literally contagious, but contagions do reside there. Thus, we recognize the line as a **metonymy**, and the inventiveness of the figure rests in the application of a disease-based term to the institution in which diseases are treated. In other cases, however, a larger contextual awareness is necessary for the figurative meaning to emerge. In Jonathan Swift's "A Modest Proposal" (1729), a kindly narrator outlines a plan to relieve the poverty and hunger of Ireland: to take one-year-old infants from indigent parents and sell them as meat for consumption at dinner tables of the middle and upper classes. The scheme is outrageous, but the sentences issue so consistently from the earnest, deadpan perspective of the narrator that they sound straightforward and literal. Only by stepping outside the essay and learning something about the early-eighteenth-century economies of Ireland and England do readers apprehend the irony.

Ever since Plato, and up through contemporary theories of literature, figures of speech have been considered essential constituents of literary language. Plato considered literature a mode of falsehood and singled out the "turns" of figurative language away from proper meaning as literature's fundamental wrongdoing. Renaissance rhetoricians compiled exhaustive taxonomies of tropes and ironies for use in the training of orators and writers, while twentieth-century critics, such as I. A. Richards, detailed the workings of **metaphor** as central to poetic meaning. Interpretation of literature is always, at least in part, the delineation of figures of speech, and the first technique students must master is discerning where and how language becomes figurative. (*See also* **Denotation, Irony, Simile, Synecdoche.**)

First-person narrator   A **narrator** that has a distinct personality and speaks from a consistent subjective position. First person narrators refer to themselves as "I" and may be major or minor figures in the story or human-like observers of it. Their attitude and perspective shape the reader's perception of the incidents and characters, and must be accounted for as an independent element in the storytelling. In F. Scott Fitzgerald's *The Great Gatsby* (1925), narrator Nick Carraway is instrumental to the action, and his judgments of Gatsby, Daisy, Tom, and Jordan Baker color everything we learn about them. (*See also* **Point of view.**)

Fixed form   A traditional verse form requiring certain predetermined elements of structure—for example, a stanza pattern, set **meter,** or predetermined line length. A fixed form such as the **sonnet,** for instance, must have fourteen lines, follow an iambic pentameter verse length, and rhyme according to conventional patterns. Those sonnets that diverge from the norm are accepted as sonnets, precisely because they can be understood in terms of the norm from which they diverge. (*See also* **Closed form.**)

Flashback   A scene in drama or narrative that recounts a prior event. A flashback may be represented as a function of a character's memory, or it may involve a character or a narrator describing the past to another character or directly to readers, as when Aeneas describes the fall of Troy to Dido in Book II of *The Aeneid.* But, as the term suggests, flashbacks usually require a strong dramatic rendition, as if the past were still affecting the present. They allow authors to include events that occurred before the opening of the story, which may reveal something significant that happened in a character's past and indicate how the character and situation have changed. (*See also* **Plot.**)

Flat character   A term coined by English novelist E. M. Forster to describe a character with only one prominent trait. Remaining the same throughout the story, flat characters are rarely the central characters in a narrative and are often based on **stock characters**. This doesn't mean that flat characters are unimportant. Indeed, they are often crucial to the drama—witness the role of Dr. Watson in the Sherlock Holmes stories—reflecting the more complex traits of the protagonist or providing a frame within which the **protagonist** develops. (*See also* **Dynamic character, Round character.**)

Flexible theater   Also called **black box** or **experimental theater space**, flexible theater is a modern, nontraditional performance space in which actor-audience relationships can be flexibly configured, with moveable seating platforms. Usually seating anywhere from 100 to 250 spectators, flexible theaters can accommodate staging in the round, thrust staging, tennis court staging, and even temporary **proscenium arch** (fourth wall) staging. (*See also* **Box set.**)

Folk ballads   Anonymous popular narrative songs, often composed in **ballad stanza**, that were transmitted orally and bear the customary traits of folk verse—flexible text, colloquial diction, frequent refrains, formulaic settings and characters. In folk ballads, the story is the central issue. **Character development** is slight, **point of view** simple, and the narration moves swiftly toward climactic episodes. The stories are presented as if intended for public viewing, rendered for a collective audience and joining other ballads, tales, **myths**, and **legends** in the repository of a community culture. Characters have a token identity, such as the outlaw in "Sam Bass," the cowboy in "The Streets of Laredo," and the lovers in "Frankie and Johnny"; and what happens to them stands as a kind of folk wisdom. (*See also* **Ballad.**)

Folk epic   A long narrative poem composed in a regular, nonstanzaic verse form that traces the adventures of a tribe or nation's popular heroes. Whereas literary epics, such as *Paradise Lost* (1667), are composed by an individual author consciously emulating earlier epic poetry, folk epics are anonymous creations whose words vary with every performance. Grounded in a folk culture and transmitted through **oral tradition**, folk epics have the same literary traits as **folk ballads**—flexible text, colloquial diction, frequent refrains and epithets, formulaic settings and characters—but they strive for greater scope and heroism. Although by virtue of its length, the folk epic has more variety of character and setting than other folk genres, **character development** and narrative commentary remain subordinate to the action. The stories belong to the community, so to speak, the characters have a typological value (the hero, the lovers, the enemy), and the outcomes offer a sort of folk wisdom in dramatic form. (*See also* **Epic.**)

Folklore   The body of traditional wisdom and customs of a people as collected and continued through **oral tradition**. Broken down into its pieces, *folk-lore*, the term combines the sense of "knowledge" with that of "a people," and bears connotations of preindustrial, preliterate, prescientific cultures. It includes songs, stories, **myths**, **proverbs**, and any rituals, customs, medicines, etc., that have a putative origin in the mythic past of the "folk." For some, this means that folklore signifies a world of ignorance and pseudoscience, captive to bias and prejudice; for others, it signifies an authentic expression of agrarian or village life. In either case, folklore offers rich materials for cultural and anthropological analysis, and literary specimens of folklore such as **folk ballad** and **folk epic** have had a profound influence upon genres of high art.

Folktale   A short anonymous narrative that forms part of the **folklore** of a people and a region and is passed down through **oral tradition**. While the contents of folktales may appear simple and conventional, they amount to more than just single stories having entertainment value. They are *folk*tales—that is, expressions of a people's world view, the narratives and images through which a folk renders its values and beliefs. (*See also* **Fairy tale, Legend.**)

Foot   The basic unit of measurement in metrical poetry. Whereas **accentual verse** counts only the number of stresses per line, **fixed forms,** such as **blank verse, sonnets, heroic couplets,** and so on, count all the syllables and categorize them as feet. That is, different meters are identified partly by the pattern and order of stressed and unstressed syllables, the pattern arranged in two- and three-syllable units. Thus lines of verse may be subdivided:

> my fa / ther moved / through dooms / of love
> (E.E. Cummings, "my father moved through dooms of love"; 1940)

> All hon / or and praise / to the right- / hearted bard
> Who was true / to The Voice / when such ser / vice was hard, . . .
> (James Russell Lowell, "A Fable for Critics"; 1848)

The Cummings line follows the most common foot in English, the **iamb,** which has two syllables, an unstressed followed by a stressed, while the Lowell poem follows anapestic meter, unstressed-unstressed-stressed (except for the iamb of "All hon-"). (*See also* **Anapest, Dactyl, Meter, Prosody, Spondee,** and **Trochee.**)

Footnote   An additional piece of information that the author includes at the bottom of a page, usually signaled by a small reference number in the main text. A footnote might supply brief facts about a historical figure or event related to the argument, the definition of a foreign word or phrase, or any other relevant information that may help in understanding the text or from which the author has derived ideas and conclusions. Most importantly, footnotes document sources and attribute credit to prior discussions. Without them, authors risk committing plagiarism. (*See also* **Endnote.**)

Foreshadowing   In plot construction, the technique of arranging events and information in such a way that subsequent doings are prepared for, or "shadowed," beforehand. An author may introduce specific words, images, or actions in order to suggest significant later events, or "plant" a character or minor occurrence that will later play a critical role in the story. The effective use of foreshadowing by an author may prevent a story's outcome from seeming haphazard or contrived. For instance, near the beginning of Stephen Crane's Civil War novel *The Red Badge of Courage* (1894), two fresh soldiers have a quiet talk about running away once the fighting starts, thereby foreshadowing the protagonist's flight in the upcoming battle. The foreshadowing inserts a tension into the narrative, encouraging readers and spectators to form expectations as the action progresses. (*See also* **Plot.**)

Form   The means by which a literary work renders its content. A capacious and malleable term, *form* designates elements as specific and concrete as the verse length of a poem, and as broad and categorical as the generic course of the story. Whatever appears as the material side of meaning (the sound of a word, not its denotation; the arrangement of incidents in a plot, not the incidents themselves) may be considered a feature of form. Although formal elements may be distinguished from **theme**, action, and other contents, critics agree that form and content are inextricably connected, though their relation is notoriously difficult to pin down. The former is more than the external framework or envelope of content; and certain forms are predisposed to certain contents, as the **novel** is better suited to panoramic representations of social life than is the **lyric**. Determining the functionality of form in the meaning of a literary work, then, is a crucial task. Indeed, analyses that overlook form and address only the content don't qualify as complete interpretations of the work *as* literature or art. Instead, they take the work as a statement of ideas, attitudes, politics, values, etc., broaching the work not as an aesthetic object but as a proposition ("In the novel, author so-and-so is saying that . . ."). When, for example, an aristocrat objects to Walt Whitman's poetry because of its egalitarian assertions, the judgment treats the poetry as social doctrine, not as poetry. This isn't to say that *Leaves of Grass* (1855–92) may not function as social doctrine—it surely can, and was recognized as such in its time—but only that a complete, literary interpretation of it accounts for the free verse, the slang, the sequence of individual poems, and other formal elements.

Formal English   The heightened language of civilized discourse, suitable for dignified occasions such as funeral orations and serious literary genres such as the **ode**. Formal language is characterized by Latinate diction, ceremonial rhetoric, and solemn tone. The speeches of the fallen angels in John Milton's *Paradise Lost* (1667) are examples, as when Beelzebub answers Satan's first utterance:

> "Oh prince, O chief of many thronéd powers
> That led th'embattled seraphim to war
> Under thy conduct, and, in dreadful deeds

Fearless, endangered Heaven's perpetual King,
And put to proof his high supremacy,
Whether upheld by strength, or chance or fate!
Too well I see and rue the dire event
That with sad overthrow and foul defeat
Hath lost us Heaven . . ."
(I. 128–36)

(*See also* **Levels of diction.**)

Formalist criticism A school of criticism that focuses on the **form** of the literary work, downplaying outside influences and information such as events in the writer's life. The foundational principle of formalism is that literature is a discrete form of expression whose significance lies in its form as much as in its content. Literary language, formalists argue, is such because the material and structural aspects of it (sound, rhythm, irony, etc.) are prominent enough to claim explicit attention. As one early-twentieth-century theorist put it, in a literary work the "linguistic patterns acquire *independent value.*" To appreciate them properly, formalist critics treat the work not primarily as a social, historical, or biographical document, but as a literary artifact, one understood mainly by reference to its intrinsic literary features—**style, imagery, genre, figures of speech,** etc.

Because form is such a varied concept, there are many different methods of formalist criticism. Some formalisms focus upon narrative, analyzing the structure of the **plot.** Others concentrate on the poetic surface, searching for patterns and motifs in the concrete language of the verse. The New Critic Cleanth Brooks believed that the task of formalism is to explicate a poem's "structure of meanings," the general form "balancing and harmonizing connotations, attitudes, and meanings." Hence, he analyzed the ways in which words, metaphors, and images were contextualized by the individual poem in which they appear— for instance, how the word "adoration" in a William Wordsworth sonnet accumulates multiple resonances when placed in juxtaposition to other words in the poem. What makes the Brooks's analysis formal is that the meanings he uncovers arise from the relation *between* the words as written, not simply from the dictionary meaning of each one.

Although different approaches disagree about the grounds of literary value—for instance, some maintain that superior literary forms are organically unified, with all the parts cohering into a whole—formalists all agree that the meaning of a literary work is inextricable from (although not entirely reducible to) its form. Too often, they say, critics and students approach literature by trying to extract its content, thinking that an abstract paraphrase is the goal of interpretation. This is to convert the literature into history, philosophy, commentary, or some other nonliterary mode, and to consider the literary aspects of the work as mere ornament. In the best examples of formalist criticism, the meaning of a poem is shown to be grounded in a dynamic connection of form and content. Too much form leads to a mechanical enumeration of figures of speech, metrical feet, etc., and too much content leads to a colorless summation of themes and concepts—both of them worthwhile but incomplete exercises.

Found poetry   Poetry that purports to be constructed out of bits of found verbiage. The "recovered" fragments may form all or part of the final text, but the convention rests on their ability to suggest a missing context, the place from which the verbiage was "lost." Antecedents of found poems date back to the Renaissance; but the subgenre is essentially a twentieth-century development, practiced extensively by surrealist poets in France and by Americans Ezra Pound and William Carlos Williams, who includes (among other items) personal letters and a geological survey document in his long poem *Paterson* (1949).

Franglais   [FRAWN–glay] An idiom of French characterized by the incorporation of English words, most of them taken from mass and commercial culture: for example, *weekend, burn-out, shopping, parking, hamburger, Walkman, bonus, jogging.* Franglais is considered an ominous phenomenon in French-speaking regions whose inhabitants worry about the integrity of their culture and the survival of their heritage.

Free verse   From the French *vers libre*, free verse is poetry whose lines fall into no consistent meter. It may have internal and external **rhyme**, and it may contain intricate rhetorical patterns, but none of them are regular enough to mark it as a **fixed form**. Precursors of free verse poetry may be found in the works of Jean de La Fontaine (seventeenth-century France), Johann Wolfgang von Goëthe (eighteenth-century Germany), and Alexander Pushkin (nineteenth-century Russia), each of whom developed verse forms different from the conventional forms popular in their respective countries. But free verse didn't become a distinct verse form until the advent of Walt Whitman, who in *Leaves of Grass* (first edition 1855) conceived a revolutionary poetic medium. Whitman's verse lines are wholly inconsistent, his verse paragraphs without pattern. **Internal rhyme, anaphora, assonance, consonance**, and other rhetorical, poetic features abound in the poems:

> I fly the flights of a fluid and swallowing soul,
> My course runs below the soundings of plummets.
>> (*Song of Myself*, 11.800–01)

> O you singer solitary, singing by yourself, projecting me,
> O solitary me listening, never more shall I cease perpetuating
>> you,
> Never more shall I escape, never more the reverberations,
> Never more the cries of unsatisfied love be absent from me.
>> ("Out of the Cradle Endlessly Rocking")

But the patterns seem to emerge at random, as if the only order to the verse is the rhythm of Whitman's own fluctuating impulse. It isn't that Whitman breaks the verse protocols of different fixed forms such as the **sonnet**. Rather, his compositions dispense with *any* relationship with fixed form, imitative or transgressive. Herein lies the "freedom" of free verse, not that it has no organization at all, but that the organization is due to something other than systematic metrics. In *Song of Myself*, lines 756–70 all begin with "Where," lines 771–773 with "Through," and lines 774–78 with "Pleas'd with the," but although the anaphora marks a pattern, the lines still count as free verse, because Whitman never repeats the pattern and he might just as well have altered it without breaking any metrical rule.

Whitman's work has deeply influenced twentieth-century poetry, and free verse has become a customary practice. While some Modernist poets (Robert Frost, T. S. Eliot, Wallace Stevens) opted for regular metrics, others such as William Carlos Williams (in *Paterson*, 1949) and Ezra Pound (in *Cantos*, 1954) experimented with free verse in their most ambitious works. The **Beat Generation** poets employed free verse as a habit, and today free verse has no claims to unconventional expression. Indeed, it is the most standard convention in contemporary verse. (*See also* **Open form**.)

Gender criticism   A school of criticism that examines how sexual identity influences the creation, interpretation, and evaluation of literary works. As an organized academic study, gender criticism sprang from the feminist movement in the Sixties, borrowing its premises from foundational texts such as Simone de Beauvoir's *The Second Sex* (English trans. 1953) and Kate Millett's *Sexual Politics* (1970), and from woman-centered studies in sociology, psychology, and anthropology. As a first principle, it states that Western culture, including the tradition of literary study, is a patriarchal one based upon unexamined male-oriented assumptions, habits, and values. Gender critics see their work as correcting this imbalance by recasting gender as a socially-constructed norm, not a biological grounding, then analyzing the patriarchal mindset and combating its practices. Many previous interpretations of literature, they claim, pass off a patriarchal outlook as a general truth. For example, a half-century ago formalist critic Allen Tate emphasized the universality of Emily Dickinson's poetry, affirming how powerfully the language, imagery, and mythmaking of her poems combine to affect a generalized reader. But Sandra Gilbert, a leading feminist scholar, identifies attitudes and assumptions in Dickinson's poetry that are characteristically female, greatly attributable to the difficult position of an intellectual woman in nineteenth-century Massachusetts. Tate's hypothetical reader is (putatively) sexless; Gilbert's reader is sexually-determined. To feminists, Tate's approach is a repressive sexism.

Gilbert's approach (and gender criticism's in general) aims to lift the repression and recover women's experience as it was and is apart from the filter of the masculine outlook. First, it insists that "sexless" interpretation—that is, a gender-neutral approach—is impossible; second, it articulates the sexual meanings and identities embedded, distorted, and submerged in the history of literature and literary study.

In recent years, gender criticism has expanded beyond traditional feminist concerns to include sexual orientation in its conceptual arsenal. Whereas feminism focused upon male/female identity, current gender studies turns to heterosexual/homosexual identity as well. Critical practice explores the "compulsory heterosexuality" of Western culture, the course of gay and lesbian identities in the Western world from the ancients to the moderns, and similar historical and social themes. Gender theorists ponder the existence of liminal figures such as cross-dressers and "butch" women, figures who blur the boundaries of sexual identity and show its ultimate fluidity.

The pitfall of gender criticism is the pitfall of all theories with a strong social commitment: it tends to predestine interpretation to a general conclusion. In unskilled hands, the literary work turns into an illustration of feminist beliefs, another case of sexism and repressed identity. Because it is a social agenda as much as it is a critical practice, gender criticism sometimes handles literary works crudely, translating them into customary feminist themes. But despite its biases, few challenge the fact that gender criticism has opened literary studies to new areas of research and enriched the meanings and values to be ascertained through critical interpretation. As a scholarly endeavor paralleling the Women's Movement of the 1960s and 1970s, the recovery and reassessment of women's literature and history has placed traditional literatures and histories in a new light and yielded a more balanced understanding of the past.

General English   The ordinary speech of educated native speakers. Most literate speech and writing is general English, the discourse one finds in *The New York Times* and *The New Republic* magazine. Its diction is more sophisticated than that of **colloquial English**, yet not as elevated as that of **formal English**. (*See also* **Levels of diction.**)

Genre   [JAWN ruh]   A term for the different kinds of literary work—**epic**, **novel**, **tragedy**, etc. Classifications of literary genres are based upon their combination of literary form and subject matter. An epic is a genre whose literary form includes an **episodic plot** and a consistent, expansive verse form such as **blank verse** or **heroic couplets**, and whose subject matter includes a **hero** and grand martial adventures. Make the hero a comical character and the adventures a set of petty incidents and you have the subgenre of **mock-epic**. In social terms, a genre implies a preexisting understanding between the artist and the reader about the purpose and rules of the work. A horror story, for example, combines the form of the **short story** with certain conventional subjects, styles, and themes—a monster, a vulnerable heroine, etc.—with the expectation of frightening the reader.

The concept of genre is as old as the extant theories of literature, that is, those of Plato and Aristotle, and up until the eighteenth century generic distinctions were essential to the practice of writing and criticism. In *Republic*, Book III, Plato distinguished between "poetry and mythology [that] are wholly imitative," and works "in which the poet is the only speaker"—in other words, the genre of **drama** and the genre of narration. In *Poetics*, Aristotle accepted the division of genres by medium and added a division of genres by character types: "comedy aims at representing men as worse, tragedy as better than in actual life." Renaissance and Neoclassical critics added further categories and ranked them accordingly—tragedy stood higher than comedy, epic higher than **lyric**—insisting that the divisions be respected. To mix genres, such as in **tragicomedy**, was to produce inferior artworks. During the eighteenth century, however, new genres appeared (for instance, the **novel, sentimental comedy**, the literary essay, "graveyard poetry") that captured a wide readership and upset the long-standing hierarchy of forms. Genre now has little prescriptive force, and instead serves as a comparative tool helping critics describe a work as an echo or irony of another, say, the way William Wordsworth's *Lyrical Ballads* (1798) relate to the genre of the **folk ballad**. (*See also* **Convention**.)

Gothic fiction   A genre whose dominant mood is terror and suspense, whose setting is an isolated castle, mansion, or monastery, and whose characters include an ingenuous hero or heroine surrounded by mysterious or threatening individuals. Plots often involve young women thrown into scary situations in which they uncover dark motives and long lost secrets. Beneath the surface of rural landscapes, aged churches, and country estates lie bloody deeds from the past, illicit passions, and ghostly presences, as if beneath the order of civil society and rational thought lay evil forces and insane motives. Inaugurated by Horace Walpole in *The Castle of Otranto* (1764), Gothic fiction almost coincides with the rise of the novel and has survived in one form or another ever since. The term *gothic* originally applied to medieval church architecture, and Gothic fiction often exploits mysterious architectural spaces in its plotting, featuring dungeons, crypts, torture chambers, locked rooms, and secret passageways. During the eighteenth century in England, Gothic fiction became wildly popular; and in the nineteenth century, American writers such as Nathaniel Hawthorne, Edgar Allan Poe, and Charlotte Perkins Gilman brought the genre into the mainstream of American fiction.

Grotesque   An image or characterization that exaggerates its subject to the point of unnatural, bizarre distortion. Wavering between the humorous and the off-putting, a grotesque representation might picture a corrupt rural politician as enormously fat, sweaty, leering, and grasping, each trait serving as a physical counterpart of his moral deformity. Political cartoonists often sketch grotesque portraits of famous figures, and fiction writers employ the same tactic to distinguish minor characters and their ruling passions, as in the numerous menacing and thwarted characters in Dickens's novels.

Haiku [high–KOO] A Japanese verse form that has three unrhymed lines of five, seven, and five syllables. Traditional haiku is often serious and spiritual in tone and minimizes figures of speech, relying mostly on imagery and having one of the four seasons as its setting:

> Temple bells die out.
> The fragrant blossoms remain.
> A perfect evening!
> (Matsuo Basho)

Hamartia [huh–MAR–tee–uh] Greek for "error," *hamartia* denotes either an offense committed in ignorance of some material fact (without deliberate criminal intent) and therefore free of blameworthiness; or a mistake unintentionally made as a result of an intellectual error by a morally good person, usually involving the identity of a blood relation. Although a *hamartia* does not make the person who commits it entirely guilty, in **tragedy** it is accompanied by punishment, and to many critics the necessity of suffering for unintentional error is essential to the tragic effect. Aristotle singled out the importance of *hamartia* to the tragic hero: "a man who is not eminently good and just, yet whose misfortune is brought about not by vice or depravity, but by some error or frailty" (*Poetics*). The *hamartia* of Oedipus stems from his ignorance of his actual parentage; inadvertently and unwittingly he commits the *hamartia* of patricide and incest.

Because of its role in causing a tragic situation (and because of its importance to Aristotle), *hamartia* has been a central concept in theories of tragedy and character. To Aristotle, it is not a defect in the hero's personal makeup, but a lack of knowledge. If the hero were vicious, Aristotle argued, then his downfall would not be tragic—it would be deserved. But later theorists such as the French neoclassicist Dacier interpreted *hamartia* as, precisely, a grave flaw in the character's moral nature. That notion became popular among German Romantic dramatists due to the influence of Shakespeare, and they cited cases such as Othello and his inordinate capacity for love (loving "not wisely but too well"), which leads him into irrational jealousy and murder. (*See also* **Recognition**.)

Heptameter [hep–TAM–uh–ter] A verse meter consisting of seven metrical feet, or seven primary stresses, per line:

Beneath them sit the aged men, wise guardians of the poor;
Then cherish pity, lest you drive an angel from your door.
(William Blake, "Holy Thursday"; 1790)

Hermeneutics [HER–muh–NEW–tiks] The study of interpretation. Hermeneutics arose as a discrete field of inquiry in the late-eighteenth century, when a new sense of historical change led scholars to recognize a distance between past texts and present readers. How could a reader in France in 1790 understand a text such as the Gospels, they asked, which were composed seventeen hundred years earlier by writers of wholly different cultures and understandings? Hermeneutics attempted to solve the problem through methods of historical reconstruction—specifically, restoring the conditions under which the text was created. Protestant scholars breaking from the Catholic Church sought to interpret the Bible outside the tradition of Church commentary (which emphasized allegorical meanings of the text) and rely solely on the historical beginnings of Scripture. Renaissance scholars discovering ancient texts employed philology as a hermeneutical science, believing that careful analysis of the original languages of Pindaric odes, Horatian epistles, etc. would render the ancients' world view.

Nineteenth-century scholars expanded hermeneutics to the interpretation of all texts, indeed to all acts of cognition. To figures such as Friedrich Schleiermacher and Wilhelm Dilthey, texts were the embodiment of a subjectivity determined both by personal experiences and dispositions and by cultural conditioning (the beliefs, values, and attitudes that prevail at the time, many of which are held unconsciously by people within the culture). Interpretation, then, strives to reimagine a mental outlook, what was termed a "horizon of understanding," something equivalent to the emotional/cognitive framework of the author's creations. To twentieth-century thinkers, however, this proposal begged the initial hermeneutical question of the *critic's* horizon: if an author's labors issue from a historically- and personally-determined mindset, then do an interpreter's labors also? Philosopher Hans-George Gadamer addressed the problem by making the critic's prejudices a functional part of interpretation. Interpretation is really a dialogue, he asserted, an exchange between an author's and a critic's understandings. The critic's point of view is just as much in question as is the text's meaning, but this is taken as a fruitful crux, as a chance for the critic to examine his or her historical condition.

From the 1960s to the 1980s, such questions were important topics in literary studies, but in recent years they have been largely cast aside. Having raised issues of objectivity and historical bias, hermeneutics has failed to answer them satisfactorily. The problems remain and critics make practical adjustments to them (for instance, remaining mindful of their own historical moment), but they are no longer live issues among academic scholars. Other questions of identity, politics, and cultural history have displaced them.

Hero The central character in a narrative whose virtues and vices, choices and experiences, are raised to meaningful levels. The term is derived from the Greek epic tradition, in which heroes were the leading warriors among the princes—men who own armor and chariots and are trained in the arts and labor of war. Fifth-century Athenian tragedians, such as Aeschylus and Sophocles, created idealized stage-figures out of Homer's Achilles, Agamemnon, and Ajax—men whose lives are lived at the level of action, in the public eye, and whose moral choices have weight because their communities depend upon them.

In discussing tragedy in the *Poetics*, Aristotle treated the hero in less glorious terms, describing him (always a male) as a man "who is not eminently good and just, yet whose misfortune is brought about not by vice or depravity, but by some error or frailty." Assigning heroes to high genres such as **epic** and **tragedy**, writers and theorists continued to reflect upon heroes and produced as many versions as there are conceptions of heroism. Dante's confused spiritual pilgrim guided by Virgil and Beatrice was one kind of hero; Shakespeare's dithering, reflective Hamlet another; Samuel Butler's bungling, pedantic knight Hudibras still another. Milton's *Paradise Lost* (1667) posed a moral crux: is Satan a hero? He possesses the great martial powers of Achilles, the canny eloquence of Odysseus, and the psychological depths of Shakespeare's protagonists, yet he commits unfathomable sin. By the time of Lord Byron's *Don Juan* (1819–24), the hero had undergone so many forays into satire, sentimentality, and psychologizing that Byron could begin:

> I want a hero: an uncommon want,
>> When every year and month sends forth a new one,
> Till, after cloying the gazettes with cant,
>> The age discovers he is not the true one . . .

Today, the term signifies merely the principal male or female figure in a narrative or dramatic literary work. When a critic terms the protagonist a *hero*, however, the choice of words implies a positive assessment of the character, or at least a sympathetic understanding of the figure's flaws. (*See also* **Antihero, Hamartia, Protagonist**.)

Heroic couplet *See* **Closed couplet**.

Hexameter [heck–SAM–uh–ter] A verse meter consisting of six metrical feet, or six primary stresses, per line:

> Loving in truth, and fain in verse my love to show,
> That the dear she might take some pleasure of my pain,
> Pleasure might cause her read, reading might make her know,
> Knowledge might pity win, and pity grace obtain . . .
> (Sir Philip Sidney, *Astrophel and Stella*, Sonnet 1; 1591)

High comedy   A comic genre directed to the intelligence and cultivation of spectators and readers. Whereas **low comedy** relies on **slapstick, farce,** and the like for its humor, high comedy relies on verbal sparring and urbane irony. Smart characters speak in clever repartee and express sophisticated sentiments. Wit prevails over clownishness. A man slipping on a banana peel is low comedy; a woman fending off the advances of a clever rake with subtle skepticisms that puncture his overtures is high comedy. The audience observes the action from a distance, appreciating the refined humor of the situation without becoming too engrossed in the characters' fates. The French playwright Molière and the English dramatists of the Restoration Period developed a special form of high comedy in the **comedy of manners,** focused on the social relations and amorous intrigues of sophisticated upper-class men and women conducted through pointed and ironic dialogue. In *Love for Love* (1695) by William Congreve, the opening conversation between a witty, but profligate, lover and his servant marks the play as refined social comedy:

> *Valentine:* Well, and now I am poor, I have an opportunity to be revenged on 'em all. I'll pursue Angelica with more love than ever, and appear more notoriously her admirer in this restraint than when I openly rivaled the rich fops that made court to her. . . . And for the wits, I'm sure I'm in a condition to be even with them.
>
> *Jeremy:* Nay, your condition is pretty even with theirs, that's the truth on't.
>
> *Valentine:* I'll take some of their trade out of their hands.
>
> *Jeremy:* Now Heav'n of mercy continue the tax upon paper! You don't mean to write!
>
> *Valentine:* Yes, I do; I'll write a play.

(*See also* **Comedy.**)

Historical criticism   The practice of analyzing a literary work by investigating the social, cultural, and intellectual context that produced it, a context that includes the artist's biography and milieu. Historical critics are less concerned with explaining a work's literary significance for today's readers than with recreating the historical moment in which it arose. Every literary work issues from a particular time and place, they insist, and until we can reconstruct that setting our knowledge of the work is incomplete. There have been so many social, cultural, and linguistic changes over time that some older texts are incomprehensible without scholarly assistance.

A historical analysis, then, requires extensive study beyond the text itself. A full interpretation ties all the materials of the text to relevant conditions of the time. Words must be aligned with their meanings back then, not with those of today. Basic events in the plot must be situated within contemporary social practices. For example, Daniel Defoe's *Robinson Crusoe* (1719) portrays a merchant captain stranded on a remote island, and the situation has provided materials for everything from children's stories to Marxist economics. But a historical critic hesitates to lift the story out of its early-eighteenth-century setting. Such scholars would address the novel with information about late seventeenth- and early eighteenth-century global politics, the slave trade, and European voyages of discovery and colonization. In the process, images and events in the novel that mean little to us emerge as significant elements.

Obviously, historical criticism enriches the significance of literary works. Without it, readers overlook casual allusions and meaningful references and misconstrue the polemical or satirical aspects. It also has an educational benefit in that it forces scholars and students to widen their studies, to incorporate historical, sociological, legal, religious, and economic material into their research. Finally, because of its empirical nature, historical criticism also serves to curb speculative interpretations of literature. If a speculative reading of a poem begins by noting a double-meaning in a particular word in the title, but historical analysis shows that the second meaning did not develop for another two hundred years, the speculative reading is discredited. While historical criticism may skirt the stylistic details that are highlighted by **formalist criticism,** its recovery of context is essential to the full understanding of literature.

Historical fiction   A type of fiction in which the narrative is set in another time or place, with marked attention to historical accuracy. In historical fiction, the author usually attempts to recreate a faithful picture of daily life during the period, letting it serve as the backdrop for the local action. Hence, historical fiction writers bear a double burden of telling a good story and getting the past right. For example, Robert Graves's *I, Claudius* (1934) depicts the lives of the ancient Roman ruling class in the early Imperial age, choosing famed personages from the past as its characters. On the other hand, the Romantic writer Sir Walter Scott invented in his Waverley novels imaginary heroes, but placed them amidst the action of real historical events, such as the mid-eighteenth-century Jacobite uprisings against Hanoverian rule. The effect of such portrayals is to lend authenticity to the fiction, adding a layer of historical fact and imagery to the imaginary action; and readers are often compelled as much by the historical detail as they are by the invented plot and characters. Indeed, historians sometimes complain that people in the United States learn more about history by watching movies and reading narratives, such as Nathaniel Hawthorne's stories of Puritan New England, than by reading straightforward historical scholarship.

Hubris   [HOO–bris] Overweening pride, the insolence that leads to ruin, *hubris* was in the Greek moral vocabulary the antithesis of moderation or rectitude. Creon, in Sophocles' *Antigone*, is a good example of a character brought down by his *hubris*. Creon's decision to deny Antigone's brother Polyneices burial is a violation of the ancient unwritten law requiring kin to inter their dead.

Though he initially acts to restore order to a city destabilized by war, his inability to change his mind in the face of mounting evidence against his course targets him for suffering. When he does change his mind, it's too late. Antigone has already hanged herself, Haemon destroys himself, and Eurydice the Queen curses him as she, too, commits suicide.

Hyperbole [high–PER–bo–lee] *See* **Overstatement**.

Iamb [I–am] A metrical foot in verse in which an unaccented syllable is followed by an accented one, as in "a-*rouse*" and "a *cat*." The iamb is the most common metrical foot in English poetry, the rhythm of stressed-unstressed matching the rhythms of ordinary speech. **Fixed forms** such as the **ballad stanza** and the **sonnet** naturally fall into iambic patterns, and, indeed, the regular verse forms that resist iambic structure are rare (trochaic tetrameter, for instance). Unrhymed iambic pentameter (five iambs per line) is **blank verse**, the meter of *Paradise Lost* (1667) and *The Prelude* (1850)—a form so flexible and natural that even among the verse experiments of the Modernist period it remains a favored structure (especially in the poetry of Wallace Stevens and Robert Frost). Another advantage of iambic meter is that it easily accommodates metrical variations, allowing an extra syllable, a **trochee**, a **dactyl** while maintaining the general pace of the verse. Hence, although Keats begins "Ode to a Nightingale" (1819) with syllables unstressed-stressed-stressed-unstressed, the lines smoothly settle into flowing iambs after "and":

My heart aches, and a drowsy numbness pains
My sense, as though of hemlock I had drunk . . .

Ideology A term associated with Marxist thought, *ideology* has a range of meanings and connotations. In its basic sense, ideology is a set of ideas that are arranged by an overarching theory. Although this is a neutral definition in widespread usage today, ideology has pejorative connotations. It signifies doctrinaire beliefs and rigid attitudes, and to call an opinion ideological is to condemn it as a partisan one that places ideas ahead of facts. For example, we might say that the concept of capitalism rests on notions of human decisionmaking, free markets, the power of money, etc., all of which go to support a particular economic vision. To go further and call capitalism an ideology is to question the truth of those notions, to insinuate that capitalism is, in fact, more driven by the vision than by the observable results of markets, money, etc. In other words, suspicions arise once thinkers ponder the role of ideology in social and political settings. Because of this close tie to theory plus its claim to set social agendas, *ideology* has acquired connotations of unreality and blind self-interest. Napoleon Bonaparte applied the term to any social outlook that appeared abstract or impracticable, and Karl Marx and Friedrich Engels considered ideology a falsification of reality, specifically, a denial of the material conditions of life through the elevation of ideas to independent status. To them and their Marxist followers, ideology is a case of "false consciousness," of minds living by putatively natural and self-evident ideas without realizing their basis in class differences.

The latter definition has been the most influential one in literary criticism. Critics of a Leftist bent cite "bourgeois ideology," "the ideology of modernism," and so on, designating a system of ideas and representations that correlates with political-economic conditions. Their conversion of ideas into ideology, they maintain, keeps criticism from being too idealistic, too caught up in matters of Beauty, Taste, and Truth (which they regard as ideological constructs). Criticism in this sense is a strategy of "unmasking," of laying bare the ideology that produces a social network, a political system, and artworks.

Image   A series of words that refers to a sensory object, usually an object of sight. In effect, an image is a direct or literal recreation of perceptual experience, correlating literary language with what is immediately seen, felt, heard, touched, and tasted. In critical practice, simple references—for example, the mention of a star—are insufficient to stand as images, and **metaphors**, **symbols**, and other figurative creations are only imagistic if they contain a measure of sensuous content. John Keats writes in "Ode on Melancholy" (1820):

> But when the melancholy fit shall fall
>   Sudden from heaven like a weeping cloud . . .
>   (11-12)

The statement is a simile, but not quite an image. An image must involve a more detailed description, a fuller complex of sights, sounds, etc. In Langston Hughes's "The Weary Blues" (1927), the first line quoted names a place, but the reference doesn't count as an image until the concrete particulars of the subsequent line:

> Down on Lenox Avenue the other night
> By the pale dull pallor of an old gas light . . .
>   (4–5)

Impartial omniscience   A **third-person narrator** who knows all, but does not judge or comment. Impartial omniscience sees into the minds of characters, remembers past events, jumps easily from one setting, time, and character to another, and recounts secret motives and distant actions, yet withholds opinion. (*See also* **Editorial omniscience.**)

Implied metaphor   A metaphor that uses neither connectives nor the verb *to be*. If we say "John crowed over his victory," we imply metaphorically that John acted like a rooster but do not say so explicitly. (*See also* **Metaphor.**)

Impressionism   An artistic movement originating with French painters of the late-nineteenth century, such as Edouard Manet, Claude Monet, and Pièrre

Auguste Renoir. On the premise that reality is a matter of perception and mood, impressionists sought images of a momentary impression, a concrete perspective, rather than the objectively realistic or conventional representation of objects. Although initially scorned by the academic and museum worlds, within two decades impressionism became the dominant expression in the visual arts, and its influence extended into the language arts. Poets in Europe and England adopted the habit and wrote poetry that cultivated reflective emotion and refined **rhythm** and **diction**. Novelists composed stories that explored the inner lives of characters rather than the reality they inhabited. The historian and critic Walter Pater spoke for many of them when he emphasized a world "not of objects in the solidity with which language invests them, but of impressions, unstable, flickering, inconsistent." The latter are the root of cognition, he argued, and they mark a wall of personality: "Every one of those impressions is the impression of the individual in his isolation, each mind keeping as a solitary prisoner its own dream of a world." In "Arques—Afternoon" (1897), Arthur Symons follows impressionist practice in his rendition of a dreamy landscape colored by a brooding personality:

> Gently a little breeze begins to creep
> Into the valley, and the sleeping trees
> Are stirred, and breathe a little in their sleep,
> And nod, half-wakened, to the breeze.
>
> Cool little quiet shadows wander out
> Across the fields, and dapple with dark trails
> The snake-gray road coiled stealthily about
> The green hill climbing from the vales.
>
> And faintlier, in this cooler peace of things,
> My brooding thoughts, a scattered flock grown few,
> Withdrawn upon their melancholy wings,
> Float farther off against the blue.

While adopting some impressionist ideas about self and reality, Modernist poets such as Ezra Pound and T. S. Eliot, however, considered impressionism a watery art, fuzzy and narcissistic, and called instead for a poetry of sharp description and impersonality. In his programmatic essay "Tradition and the Individual Talent" (1919), Eliot explicitly disclaimed the focus on individuality:

> . . . the poet has, not a "personality" to express, but a particular medium, which is only a medium and not a personality, in which impressions and experiences combine in peculiar and unexpected ways. Impressions and experiences which are important for the man may take no place in the poetry, and those which become important in the poetry may play quite a negligible part in the man, the personality.

(*See also* **Modernism**.)

Incremental refrain A refrain whose words change slightly with each recurrence. For example, in Thomas Traherne's "On Christmas-Day" (ca. 1665), the following lines recur throughout: "While Angels sing," "With Angel sing," "His Praises sing," "The Praises sing," "His Prais to sing," "Thy Prais to sing," "To whom I sing," "The whole Assembly sings." They don't appear in precisely the same place in each stance, but they echo sufficiently to create an oracular effect and underscore the celebratory devotion evoked by Christ's birthday. (*See also* **Refrain**.)

Initiation story Also called **Coming-of-age story**, an initiation story is a narrative in which the main character, usually a child or adolescent, undergoes an important experience or rite of passage—often a difficult or disillusioning one—that prepares him or her for adulthood. James Joyce's "Araby" (1914) is an initiation story in its portrayal of a young boy who is infatuated with an older girl and promises to buy her a gift at an upcoming bazaar. He anticipates the moment with passion and impatience, his schoolwork lags, his mind wanders. But when the evening comes, his uncle returns late and dinner is delayed. When he finally is able to leave the home, he reaches the bazaar just as it is shutting down. The episode becomes a lesson in hopes dashed and plans waylaid, and the boy concludes with an adult dramatization: "Gazing up into the darkness I saw myself as a creature driven and derided by vanity; and my eyes burned with anguish and anger."

In medias res [in MAY–dee–us race] A Latin phrase meaning "in the midst of things," taken from Horace's *Ars Poetica* (circa 20 B.C.E.): the poet "always hastens to the climax, and plunges the listener *into the middle of things* as though they were already known." The term refers to the narrative tactic of beginning a story midway in the events it depicts (usually at an exciting or significant moment) before explaining the context and preceding actions. *In medias res* is a basic convention of epic poetry, so that Virgil's *Aeneid* (19 B.C.E.) begins after the sacking of Troy, and John Milton's *Paradise Lost* (1667) begins after the battle in Heaven and the fallen angels have been cast into Hell. Earlier events are recounted later, for instance, in an expository sequence in which the narrator introduces characters, or in a dramatic scene in which a hero describes to a beloved what happened to him long before they met.

Innocent narrator Also called "naïve narrator," an innocent narrator is one who fails to comprehend the implications of the story he or she tells. Of course, many narrators possess some degree of innocence or naïveté, but the innocence of the innocent narrator—often a child or childlike adult—is a consistent and functional part of the story. His or her point of view generates **irony**, sympathy, or pity by creating a gap between what the narrator understands and what the reader understands. The first narrator of William Faulkner's four-part novel *The*

Sound and the Fury (1929) is mentally handicapped, so his **stream-of-consciousness** impressions and memories mean little to him, but resound with readers. Not all cases are so extreme: Mark Twain's Huckleberry Finn has a mischievous nature and recognizes villainy all around him, but his responses to it betray an innocence that heightens the cruelty and corruption. (See also **Point of view**.)

Interior monologue An extended presentation of a character's thoughts in a narrative. Usually written in the present tense and printed without quotation marks, an interior monologue reads as if the character were speaking aloud to himself or herself. Charlotte Perkins Gilman's story "The Yellow Wallpaper" (1892) is an interior monologue in short paragraphs, the narrator an unbalanced woman growing ever more absorbed in her delusions:

> We have been here two weeks, and I haven't felt like writing
>   before, since that first day.
> I am sitting by the window now, up in this atrocious nursery,
>   and there is nothing to hinder my writing as much as I please,
>   save lack of strength.
> John is away all day, and even some nights when his cases are
>   serious.
> I am glad my case is not serious!

(*See also* **Stream of consciousness**.)

Internal refrain A refrain that appears within a stanza, generally in a position that stays fixed throughout a poem. In Robert Burns's "For A' That and A' That" (1795), the title phrase appears in the fifth line of each of its five stanzas. (*See also* **Refrain**.)

Internal rhyme Rhyme that occurs within a line of poetry, as opposed to **end rhyme**. For example:

> The fair breeze *blew*, the white foam *flew*,
> The furrow followed free;
> We were the *first* that ever *burst*
> Into that silent sea.
>   (Samuel Taylor Coleridge, *Rime of the Ancient Mariner*,
>   11:103–06; 1798)

> And the wild re*grets*, and the bloody *sweats*,
>   None knew so well as I.
>   (Oscar Wilde, *The Ballad of Reading Gaol*, Pt. 3, Stanza 37;
>   1898)

Ironic point of view The perspective of a character or narrator whose voice or position is rich in ironic meanings. Sometimes the irony lies in the disinterested superiority of the narrator, who describes the actions and feelings of the characters with a knowing detachment. In Alexander Pushkin's *Eugene Onegin* (1834), for example, the narrator recounts his hero's passions, the high society of St. Petersburg, life in the country, a fateful duel, and loneliness and death with a partly-sympathetic, partly-mocking voice. One isn't always sure where the irony ends and the sincerity begins. In other ironic points of view, the irony turns upon the narrator himself. In Vladimir Nabokov's *Pale Fire* (1962), the narrator is a scholarly critic who has taken the unfinished work of an acquaintance, a famous poet who lived next door and was murdered, and set about explicating it. We soon discover that the critic has one aim in mind: to read the poem as a reflection of the critic's own colorful life. The self-absorption of the narrator (or, perhaps, his hallucinatory vision) leads him into a series of hilarious misinterpretations of the work. (*See also* **Irony**.)

Irony　As a feature of language, irony is a statement whose intended meaning is the opposite of its literal meaning. As a quality of life, irony is a discrepancy between an expected outcome and a real outcome. In both cases, we need a context in which (or a distance from which) to recognize the meaning as ironic, not straightforward. Simplicity and sincerity provide earnest, literal expressions; irony requires duplicity and play. As the early-eighteenth-century theorist Giambattista Vico put it, "Irony certainly could not have begun until the period of reflection."

Irony of a linguistic sort can be as simple as **sarcasm** (for example, the word *sure* pronounced with an exaggerated *u* so that it really means, "No way!") or as complex as **satire**, in which characters are drawn with exact, but ludicrous detail so as to attack a specific person or group for its vices (for instance, the manners of mid-eighteenth-century rural gentility in Henry Fielding's *Tom Jones*, 1749). Along with them range a host of ironic genres—**burlesque, mock epic, parody**, etc.—that operate through a discordance of style and subject matter—for instance, a low, trivial subject treated in elevated, heroic language. Their fundamental tactic is to employ **verbal irony**, whereby literal and intended meanings are opposed and the opposition implies criticism, a jab at someone's pretense, stupidity, vanity, willfulness, and so on. To diminish someone, an ironist might praise him to the sky. Soon the audience recognizes a gross disparity between the praise and the person, and the irony does its work more effectively than would a straightforward attack. In Shakespeare's *Julius Caesar* (1599), when Antony addresses the multitude after Caesar's assassination, he doesn't directly accuse Brutus and the conspirators of murder. He acknowledges Caesar's sins and calls the conspirators "honorable men" over and over, overdoing the point until the crowd believes the opposite and demands revenge.

Another form of irony in literature takes place when a work offers a statement that appears straightforward at first, but becomes ironic in light of other statements. In one of William Wordsworth's Lucy Poems (1800), the word "thing" wavers between literal and playful:

A slumber did my spirit seal;
    I had no human fears:
She seemed a thing that could not feel
    The touch of earthly years.

No motion has she now, no force;
    She neither hears nor sees;
Rolled round in earth's diurnal course,
    With rocks and stones and trees.

In the first stanza, "thing" sounds like a playful term for a beloved; but in the second stanza, when we learn she has died, "thing" comes to signify an inert object, like the "rocks and stones and trees" of the final line. She *seemed* a thing before; now she *is* a thing.

A form of irony in literature that is not founded on verbal irony is **dramatic irony**, in which the audience recognizes something about a character's actions or statements that the character himself or herself does not.

Irony of a "life" sort is called **situational irony**. For example, in Jean-Paul Sartre's story "The Wall" (1939), a Spanish Civil War fighter is held captive by opposition soldiers. They want the prisoner to betray a comrade, but the man doesn't know where his friend is hiding. Faced with torture, he pretends to divulge a hiding place, believing that when the guards search it and find it empty, they will return and kill him. But when they return, they let the prisoner go. Amazingly, he directed them to precisely the right place. He never intended to do so, even though it means his life was saved. Something about the outcome seems more than random, as if the universe were playing a bitter joke upon us mortals. Our strivings are mocked, our pretenses teased. (*See also* **Cosmic irony, Irony of fate.**)

Irony of fate   A type of **situational irony** that can be used for either tragic or comic purposes. Irony of fate marks the discrepancy between actions and their results, between what characters deserve and what they get, between expectation and reality. In Sophocles's tragedy *Oedipus Rex*, for instance, Oedipus unknowingly acts for his own ruin, even as he takes the actions a wise leader should. The irony lies in the course of the plot: with each step toward uncovering the mystery of the plague of Thebes, Oedipus edges closer to his shocking discovery of past crimes. Underneath the incidents, a fateful design seems to be operating, and Oedipus is its unwitting instrument. This sense of design, of a pattern underlying human experience that only becomes evident after the fact, is central to irony of fate. (*See also* **Cosmic irony.**)

Italian sonnet   Also called **Petrarchan sonnet**, an Italian sonnet falls into two parts—the first eight lines (the **octave**) and the final six lines (the **sestet**). The octave follows the rhyme scheme *abba abba*, while the sestet rhymes in a variety of ways—for instance, *cdecde*—though it tends not to end in a couplet. The poem traditionally turns or shifts in mood or tone after the octave:

Milton! thou shouldst be living at this hour:	*a*
England hath need of thee: she is a fen	*b*
Of stagnant waters: altar, sword, and pen,	*b*
Fireside, the heroic wealth of hall and bower,	*a*
Have forfeited their ancient English dower	*a*
Of inward happiness. We are selfish men;	*b*
Oh! raise us up, return to us again;	*b*
And give us manners, virtue, freedom, power.	*a*
Thy soul was like a Star, and dwelt apart;	*c*
Thou hadst a voice whose sound was like the sea:	*d*
Pure as the naked heavens, majestic, free,	*d*
So didst thou travel on life's common way,	*e*
In cheerful godliness; and yet thy heart	*c*
The lowliest duties on herself did lay.	*e*

(William Wordsworth, "London, 1802"; 1807)

Wordsworth's sonnet doesn't share the devotion-of-the-lover theme of most traditional sonnets, but structurally it meets the Italian criteria. The rhyme scheme is consistent; and after line eight, Wordsworth turns the poem from criticizing England to eulogizing Milton. (*See also* **Sonnet**.)

Katharsis, catharsis [ka–THAR–sus] Translated as "purgation" or "purification," the term is drawn from the last element of Aristotle's definition of **tragedy**, relating to the final purpose of tragic art. Catharsis is, he writes, "carrying to completion, through a course of events involving pity and fear, the purification of those painful or fatal acts which have that quality." This is the feeling of emotional release and subsequent calm the spectator feels at the end of tragedy, despite having watched scenes of intense and shocking suffering. To Aristotle, *katharsis* is the final effect of the playwright's skillful use of plotting, character, and poetry, whereby the dismay and outrage the audience feels is converted to rational acceptance of the action portrayed. The conflicts have been resolved and the outcome has been justified, even though the audience has identified with characters such as Oedipus who do not deserve their horrible end.

Plato believed that drama was dangerous because it "feeds and waters the passions." Spectators observe the action and become carried away, thus threatening the stability of society. (If one thinks this is an alarmist fear, remember how frequently in history a work of literature has provoked social upheaval.)

Aristotle agrees that drama excites the audience with scenes of bloodshed, wickedness, heated emotion, and injustice—but only temporarily. If the plot is well-constructed, he argues, these excitations are expelled in a controlled fashion. Ultimately, a social benefit follows: the audience learns compassion for the vulnerabilities of others, and absorbs lessons in justice and other civic virtues.

Kitsch [kitch] Popular, commercial art and literature produced for mass consumption, *kitsch* is an important constituent of **mass culture**. What distinguishes *kitsch* is that it contains trace materials of the very high culture that it disregards. As art critic Clement Greenberg observed, "The precondition for *kitsch* . . . is the availability close at hand of a fully matured cultural tradition, whose discoveries, acquisitions, and perfected self-consciousness *kitsch* can take advantage of for its own ends" ("Avant-Garde and *Kitsch*," 1946). *Kitsch* borrows characters, plots, and themes from cultural traditions and adapts them to mass tastes. Thus Disney and Hollywood can mine the corpus of American literature for stories and icons (such as Huck Finn), water down the content (remove the killings, the savage portraits of Midwestern society, etc.), package it in familiar terms (a boy's adventure story), and market it for maximum profits. This is why Greenberg calls *kitsch* "ersatz culture."

Language poetry A school of poetry that emphasizes the medium of poetry itself—that is, the grammar and syntax of language. Emerging in the 1970s and led by Ron Silliman, Charles Bernstein, Bob Perelmen, and others, language poetry was in part a reaction to the personal modes of poetry common in the 1950s and 1960s. **Confessional poetry** and similar styles that highlighted the private self and treated language as an expressive vehicle of subjective experience (the language poets believed) fail to recognize the shaping power of the language that imparts the self. The understanding of language as a mere instrument for expression is naïve, and however familiar and unconscious are the workings of idiom, grammar, etc., they are functional to our mental and social lives. Hence language poets compose works in verse and prose that "problematize" expression. Poet Bernadette Mayer advises language poets to "systematically derange the language," "eliminate all connotation from a piece of writing," "consider word & letter as forms," and "design words." Perelman's poem "Chronic Meanings" (1999) begins:

> The single fact is matter.
> Five words can say only.
> Black sky at night, reasonably.
> I am, the irrational residue . . .

Perelman describes this poem as "an attempt on my part to see what happened to meaning as it was interrupted." While they have limited appeal to most readers, such language experiments attract a dedicated following in the university and among a small coterie of poets (many of whom teach in Creative Writing Programs).

Legend   Originally, the story of a life, often that of a saint. Today, the term signifies a traditional narrative handed down through **oral tradition** to illustrate and memorialize a remarkable character or an important event, or, in its more mythical forms, to explain the unexplainable (although myths usually involve superhuman figures, while legends tend to portray human characters). Unlike **folk tales**, legends claim to have some basis in historical truth and take place in recognizable locations, often populated by genuine historical personages. (*See also* **Myth**.)

Levels of diction   In English, there are conventionally three basic levels of formality in word choice, or three levels of diction. From the least formal to the most elevated, words fall into low, middle, and high registers, or, in more precise terms **colloquial English** (low-middle), **general English** (middle-high), and **formal English** (high). Low English includes slang, street idioms, and the like; high English includes Latinate diction, professional jargons, and the language of formal occasions such as acceptance speeches. No doubt, the distinctions are fuzzy, but rough assignments may be given and the language of literary works tabulated along a normative scale:

low	middle	high
catty	spiteful	acrimonious
wasted	drunk	inebriated
slip-up	blunder	miscalculation
pushy	assertive	pugnacious

(*See also* **Diction**.)

Limerick   A short, usually comic verse form of five iambic/anapestic lines rhyming *aabba*. The first, second, and fifth lines have three stressed syllables each; the third and fourth lines have two stresses:

> There was an old man of Calcutta,
> Who coated his tonsils with butta,
> Thus converting his snore
> From a thunderous roar
> To a soft, oleaginous mutta.
>   (Ogden Nash, "Arthur"; 1935)

Limited omniscience   Also called third-person limited point of view, limited omniscience is a **point of view** in which the narrator sees into the minds of some but not all of the characters. Typically, limited omniscience narrates through the eyes of one major or minor character, but extends somewhat beyond that character, mediating between the immediacy of first-person narration and the mobility of third person. The omniscience allows the narrator to enter the mind of a central or peripheral figure, recording thoughts and feelings and building an identification of reader and character. The limitedness, however, constrains knowledge to that character's perspective, adding a level of suspense or irony as readers encounter other characters and actions through that perspective.

Literary ballad   As opposed to **folk ballads**—which are meant for singing, orig-inate in **oral tradition**, and are circulated in folk communities—literary ballads are composed for literate readers by individual poets. The literary ballad adopts ballad conventions (**ballad stanza**, fast-paced narrative) and contents (**stock characters**, melodramatic events), but with the sophistication and conscious-ness of a trained writer. In a professional literary world, the poet emulates the folk ballad as a more primitive, natural expression closer to the actual beliefs and values of ordinary people. The most famous literary ballads are the poems in William Wordsworth's *Lyrical Ballads* (1798), which include stories of old huntsmen, simple-minded children, and deceased loves. (*See also* **Ballad**.)

Literary epic   Whereas ancient epics were originally the product of oral cultures whose myths were passed down through dramatic performances by storytelling bards, literary epics are written by authors living in advanced societies that have developed writing technologies and historiographical inquiries. Poets are not inspired bards performing mythical dramas before a village audience; they are learned writers composing sophisticated narratives for enlightened readers. Although the past they speak of retains distant mythical meanings, it is not ex-perienced by poets and readers as a mysterious time of supernatural heroism and cosmic creation. In sum, the materials of literary epic are, precisely, literary, not historical. Homeric epics emerge out of folk epic stories, but works such as Virgil's *Aeneid* (19 B.C.E.) and Dante's *Divine Comedy* (1314–21) are entirely literary epics, even though they spring out of deeply-held political and religious beliefs. (*See also* **Folk epic**.)

Literary theory   Literary theory is the search for explanations, laws, and princi-ples of different literary phenomena in the world. It poses general questions about literature such as: What distinguishes literature from other kinds of com-munication? What is the nature of poetic language? What are the standards by which we should judge literary works? How do we discriminate one kind of lit-erature from another? It may derive theoretical notions through interpretations of specific works, or construct taxonomies of literature by gathering and classi-fying specimens of each; but generally it favors abstract argument over practical criticism. Most readers rest content with enjoying literature, but faced with its power and popularity, theorists are compelled to explain it. Since the ancient Greeks, inquirers have sought to clarify the forms, ethics, and appeals of litera-ture, and outpourings of theory have transpired among Renaissance humanists, eighteenth-century rhetoricians, twentieth-century modernist poets, and aca-demic critics in the 1970s and 1980s.

Today we witness diverse literary theories running in political, psychological, historical, and aesthetic directions. To distinguish them, the Romantic scholar M. H. Abrams has usefully distinguished four orientations of literary theory. First is the mimetic orientation. In mimetic theories, literature is measured by how well it represents the real world (whatever those theorists conceive the real world to be). Plato censured poetry because he believed it distorts reality, for instance, showing the gods as petty tyrants and presenting the mere appearances of things as their truth. In the twentieth century, Marxist critics praised works of social realism because they depicted what they considered the heart of social life and human history: class relations. By holding up a mimetic standard, theorists provide a yardstick by which to distinguish true representations from false ones, and hence to discriminate good literature from bad.

Second is the pragmatic orientation. In these theories, literature is judged by the effects it produces. Didactic theories of literature fit this category because they approach literature in terms of what it teaches. As the eighteenth-century man of letters Samuel Johnson put it, "The end of writing is to instruct; the end of poetry is to instruct by pleasing." Under didactic criteria, literature that shows evil triumphing, makes sin appear attractive, and has no moral compass is suspect, and graded accordingly. If theorists have other pragmatic aims in mind, not didactic ones but social or political ones, they may prefer literature that dramatizes a historical condition—for instance, slave society in Harriet Beecher Stowe's *Uncle Tom's Cabin* (1851–52) and totalitarian thinking in George Orwell's *Nineteen Eighty-Four* (1949). The assumption behind these pragmatic theories is that literature has a direct influence upon the individuals who read it. Some pragmatic theorists disagree with that premise, however, stating that the reading experience is a more complex affair. A psychologist, for example, might claim that the representations have an opposite effect, so that violence in art actually curbs violent behavior in that it provides a safe outlet for such urges. Aristotle's theory of **katharis** endows drama with precisely the capacity to elicit, then drain, chaotic feelings. Current debates on the prevalence of sex and violence in movies and on television turn on this pragmatic question: whether watching behaviors in art will inspire people to enact them in their lives.

Third is the expressive orientation. In these theories, literature is understood as an expression of the author. The creative process is an externalization of what the author feels, perceives, or thinks inside. As Romantic poet William Wordsworth put it, "Poetry is the spontaneous overflow of powerful feeling." Literature is the conversion of private memories, experiences, traumas, and opinions into artistic form, and criticism works backward, disclosing the subjectivity "behind" the words. Although literature represents real things (mimetic) and influences readers (pragmatic), the important thing is how the writer intervenes, reshaping the world in his or her own vision and drawing readers into it. As might be expected, expressive theories are tied to Romantic conceptions of art and artists, which place the individual mind—not the medium, the tradition, or the society—at the center of the work. In extreme cases, as in some forms of **Symbolism** and **Surrealism**, the poet disregards the outside world altogether, heeding only his or her inner life in the creation of art.

Fourth is the objective orientation. In these theories, literature is measured as a discrete object, more or less independent of the world, the reader, and the author. Although they admit these latter elements into the creative and reading processes, objective critics concentrate on the work itself. It is the objective qualities of the language, **plot**, images, and so on that count, not the externals of the world outside, the reader's impressions, or the author's mind. Objective theories pose the question of what kind of object the work of literature is, what concrete elements go into it, and how words and meanings come together to form a *literary* thing. Objective theorists often begin with empirical analyses detailing the verbal ingredients of the work, then draw large conclusions about literature from them. **Formalist criticism** fits this category by focusing on the work's formal properties—**diction, prosody**, etc.—without trying to explain their existence by recourse to something outside the work. For Cleanth Brooks, William Empson, and other mid-century formalists, poetic language lay in **paradox, irony**, and **ambiguity**—that is, turns of language that complicate the semantic and instrumental functions of language. They claimed that what made literary language stand out as an object was, precisely, those elements that made it not a transparent representation of something else, or a simple communication that is forgotten once it has been read or heard. The work is an object because its language draws attention to itself *as* language, as a memorable phrase, a striking metaphor, an evocative statement.

These categories are not exhaustive, and in practice they frequently overlap. Plato mixes mimetic and didactic criticisms of literature, while Aristotle blends formalism and didacticism into a defense of literature. Eighteenth-century England was dominated by pragmatic theories, nineteenth-century England by expressive theories. The common element to them all is that they address literature as a discrete mode of communication. Herein lies the disciplinary difference between literature in the hands of literary scholars and literature in the hands of historians, philosophers, political scientists, and other inquirers. The latter often include literature in their studies, but when, say, the historian does so, he or she considers literature a piece of historical evidence in the same way that sculpture, battles, elections, and so on are pieces of historical evidence. The work illustrates a historical moment, and its literary idiosyncrasies tend to be downplayed as mere ornament. The literary critic, on the other hand, accepts that a work is a historical artifact, but believes that it is a work of art as well, and qualifies for an aesthetic analysis—as an imitation of reality, an expression of subjectivity, a literary object. The putatively ornamental aspects of literature are in fact fundamental constituents of aesthetic experience, which in turn is irreducible to historical, scientific, or political categories. Indeed, unless literary theorists establish the distinctiveness of literature and aesthetic experience, then there is no warrant for literary studies to exist as a discrete field of inquiry.

Local color   The inclusion of specific regional material—customs, dress, habits, and speech patterns of ordinary people identified with a social and geographical locale—to create a regional environment in a literary work. Washington Irving's famous short story "The Legend of Sleepy Hollow" (1820) begins with several long paragraphs on the geography of Tarry Town and Sleepy Hollow, on the legends that hung about the community, and on the schoolhouse world of Ichabod Crane. Irving singles out the "spacious coves which indent the eastern shore of the Hudson," summarizes the tale of the Headless Horseman, and calls forth the "populations, manners, and customs" of the region. The meandering descriptions indicate that local color is just as important to the **plot** as are the characters, and that one of Irving's goals is to evoke a unique time and place.

Low comedy   A comic style arousing laughter through jokes, **slapstick**, sight gags, and boisterous clowning. Unlike **high comedy**, it has meager intellectual content, opting for the belly laugh that comes from pratfalls rather than the knowing smile that comes from witty turns of phrase and sharp-edged commentary on social mores. (*See also* **Comedy**.)

Lyric   Originally distinguished from narrative and dramatic poetry, lyric poetry emphasized a speaker's emotional and intellectual state and was meant to be sung (hence the connection to the Greek lyre). Today, the musical element has disappeared, and the term now applies to any poem that focuses upon a speaker's feelings, as long as it doesn't veer into narrative. It may be wildly emotional or quietly meditative, and may assume any poetic form, although lyrics usually bear a more or less musical rhythm and have a short length (because of the difficulty in sustaining a consistent emotional expression). If the lyrical style extends into longer sequences, as in Rainer Maria Rilke's *Duino Elegies* (1923), the work is considered just that, a lyric sequence. Although the lyric may contain characters (for example, the love object of Renaissance sonnet sequences), the most important figure in the lyric is the lyric voice. The attitude, the outlook, and the prevailing mood of the speaker—all shape the objects described and establish the dramatic situation of the poem. The voice may address the reader directly or an auditor imagined in the work; it may recall the past or envision a future; it may speak from spite, jealousy, love, or joy. In other words, the variations of voice are infinite, but a lyrical voice of some identifiable characteristics is central to the lyric poem.

Madrigal   [MAD–rih–gul] A short secular song for three or more voices arranged in counterpoint. Originating in Italy in the fourteenth century and enjoying a popular vogue in England during the **Elizabethan Age**, the madrigal often speaks of love or **pastoral** themes.

Magic (or Magical) Realism   A type of contemporary narrative in which the magical and the mundane are mixed in an overall context of realistic storytelling. The term was coined by Cuban novelist Alejo Carpentier in 1949 to describe the matter-of-fact combination of the fantastic and the everyday in Latin American fiction. Magic Realism has become the standard name for an international trend in works of fiction, such as Gabriel Garcia Marquez's *One Hundred Years of Solitude* (1967).

Masculine rhyme   A rhyme of stressed syllables, either one-syllable words (as in *fox* and *socks*) or polysyllabic words whose final syllables are stressed (as in con-*trive* and sur-*vive*). (*See also* **Feminine rhyme**.)

Masks   In Latin, *personae*. In classical Greek theater, full facial masks made of leather, linen, or light wood, with accompanying headdress, allowed male actors to embody the conventionalized characters (or *dramatis personae*) of the tragic and comic stage. Later, in the seventeenth and eighteenth centuries, **stock characters** of the *commedia dell'arte* wore characteristic half-masks made of leather. (*See also* **Persona**.)

Mass culture   The sum of artifacts produced in a mass society and intended for widespread consumption. Mass culture began in the eighteenth century, when a growing reading public and improved technologies of printing and circulation enabled producers (writers, artists, journalists, cartoonists, etc.) and distributors (newspaper editors, publishers, advertisers, manufacturers, etc.) of cultural objects to reach an entire population quickly and uniformly. Fostered by democratic political systems and universal education, mass culture reaches across social classes and ethnic, racial, and religious groups. Critic Dwight Macdonald sums up the political effects of mass culture in apocalyptic terms: "Mass Culture is a dynamic, revolutionary force, breaking down the old barriers of class, tradition, taste, and dissolving all cultural distinctions. It mixes and scrambles everything together, producing what might be called homogenized culture . . . It thus destroys all values, since value judgments imply discrimination. Mass culture is very, very democratic: it absolutely refuses to discriminate against, or between, anything or anybody. All is grist to the mill, and all comes out finely ground indeed" ("A Theory of Mass Culture"; 1953).

In contrast to high culture, mass culture cares little for aesthetic virtues, traditional forms and genres, and coterie audiences. Its primary impulse is the profit motive. Although it resembles older forms of folk culture, it differs in that mass culture doesn't emerge out of a distinct community. Rather, it is the creation of business enterprises, such as Hollywood studios and media conglomerates.

Macdonald's example of mass culture is *Life Magazine*. There, he examines one issue and notes an exposition of atomic theory followed by reports on the love life of a celebrity; a photo of a mother arguing a call with a Little League umpire balanced by a series of Impressionist paintings; pieces on starving Korean children competing with advertisements for tv sets and brassieres. All content is evened out, leveled as material for leisurely consumption.

What worried critics in the 1930s and 1940s, and continues to trouble intellectuals who believe in cultural discriminations, is that mass culture swallows up everything else. Urban subcultures, regional identities, elite and popular traditions, artisanship and handicrafts—all are incorporated in mass production and standardized to the lowest common denominator. Irving Howe, a critic and colleague of Macdonald's, compares mass culture to industrial labor in that each depersonalizes individuals and makes them passive and bored. "The movie house," he says, "is a psychological cloakroom where one checks one's personality" ("Notes on Mass Culture," 1948). There, we may sit back in soothing mindlessness and "escape from our frayed selves."

Today's critics apply the critique of mass culture to globalization processes. Whereas globalization is hailed by economists and politicians as the opening of national borders to free trade and improved standards of living, cultural critics see globalization as the disappearance of indigenous cultures in a flood of brand names, restaurant franchises, and Hollywood images. Youths in far-flung regions abandon local heritages for clothes from The Gap and food from McDonald's. They prefer Western movies to village **folk tales**. Commentators in the West wonder about what is gained and lost in the spread of U.S.-based mass culture. Fundamentally, the debate turns upon the cultural status of capitalist society; for mass culture is certainly the most profitable kind of artistic production, yet also the most unimaginative and undifferentiated.

Melodrama   Originally tied to the advent of opera, melodramas were stage plays featuring background music and songs to underscore the emotional mood of each scene. Melodramas were weak in **characterization** and **plot** but strong in action, **suspense**, and passion. Characters were stereotyped villains, heroes, and young lovers, and plots followed formulae of good vs. evil, love triumphant, and daring rescues. Today, the term has less generic specificity. It now signifies any work that contains extravagantly emotional content rendered in conventionalized, sentimental action. In 1940s Hollywood movies, for example, filmmakers strove for high drama and intense situations, employing lugubrious music, closeups of tearful faces, extreme situations (a wife plotting to kill her husband, a man struggling with alcoholism), and moralistic outcomes to produce a melodramatic experience for moviegoers. The emotionalism may be entertaining, especially when one senses a tongue-in-cheek attitude toward the materials, but it also shows the pitfall of melodrama. That is, the urgency of it all indicates a lack of psychological depth and credibility of action, as if emotional excitement and adventurous happenings were making up for weaknesses of plot and character. (*See also* **Sentimentality**.)

Metafiction   Fiction that consciously explores its own nature as a literary creation. The Greek prefix *meta* means "upon" or "beyond," and is often attached to preexisting words to denote a reflective activity. Metaphysics is the physics "beyond" physics, metacriticism is criticism about criticism. Metafiction is a mode of narrative that eschews the illusion of **verisimilitude** and delights in its own fictional nature, often by speculating on the story it is telling. The term is usually associated with twentieth-century writers, such as John Barth, Italo Calvino, and Jorge Luis Borges, authors who experiment with **plot** and representation. For example, in Barth's story "Lost in the Funhouse" (1968), the narrator frequently interrupts the narrative to remark upon how the characters are drawn and where the plot is going. The story opens with a trivial question:

> For whom is the funhouse fun? Perhaps for lovers. For Ambrose it is *a place of fear and confusion.*

The italics emphasize what the funhouse represents to the central character, Ambrose, a sensitive boy in the midst of puberty. But Barth doesn't just italicize the words; he explains the italicization one sentence later:

> A single straight underline is the manuscript mark for italic type, *which in turn* is the printed equivalent to oral emphasis of words and phrases as well as the customary type for titles of complete works, not to mention. Italics are also employed, in fiction stories especially, for "outside," intrusive, or artificial voices, such as radio announcements, the texts of telegrams and newspaper articles, et cetera. They should be used *sparingly.*

The ironies accumulate in this metafictional commentary. Barth the narrator of Ambrose's world turns into Barth the author recounting his own compositional choices. He refers to himself indirectly—the "intrusive" voice—and mocks his own italics—"They should be used *sparingly.*" The tactic creates a double-layered narrative—on one level a story of a boy at the beach, on another level a writer telling a story of a boy at the beach. (*See also* **Postmodernism**.)

Metaphor   A figurative statement asserting that one thing is something else, which, in a literal sense, it is not. A metaphor may attribute a property to an entity that does not strictly possess it, as when Wallace Stevens writes, "One must have a mind of winter" ("The Snow-Man," 1921), giving "wintry" qualities to a mental substance. Or, it may equate one thing with another, as when Percy Bysshe Shelley calls the pines at the base of Mont Blanc "Children of elder time" ("Mont Blanc," 1817). By asserting one thing's figurative connection to another, a metaphor establishes an association that may be compelling, funny, illuminating, or strained. Shelley's metaphor lies in the attribution of childhood to tall trees, and gains strength from the jarring connection of *children* and *elder*.

Critic I. A. Richards breaks metaphors into the vehicle and the tenor—that is, the literal meaning of the words themselves and the object to which the words are figuratively applied. In Emily Dickinson's line, "I felt a Funeral, in my Brain" (ca. 1861), the vehicle is a funeral and the tenor (we discover) is her sense of falling into madness. The tenor comes largely from the literal meaning of the words, while the vehicle rests upon the context of their usage. When a metaphor gets used so often that its figurative nature dissipates—that is, its vehicle fades in meaning—it becomes a **dead metaphor**. For example, in current usage the literal meaning of *grasp* in "grasp an idea" has been lost. *Grasp* signifies only its tenor "comprehend," not "grab hold of." Dead metaphors indicate that one of the processes of language change is the advent and disappearance of metaphorical meanings, and that one important site of language change is literature, where figurative language sometimes establishes new usages of words in ordinary discourse. (*See also* **Conceit, Mixed metaphor.**)

Meter   A systematic rhythmic pattern of stresses in verse. When stresses fall at regular intervals, the result is meter, and the many existing meters are classified by differences in those intervals. In metrical compositions, the organization of stresses may vary from line to line, but not so much as to break the general pattern. For example, a work in **blank verse**—unrhymed iambic pentameter—may include lines with more trochees than iambs, as long as the iambic rhythm is the most common.

The following verses each have a distinct meter that colors their entire nature:

> A milk-white Hind, immortal and unchang'd,
> Fed on the lawns, and in the forest rang'd;
> Without unspotted, innocent within,
> She feared no danger, for she knew no sin.
> (John Dryden, "The Hind and the Panther," ll. 1–4; 1687)

> The time is not remote, when I
> Must by the course of nature die;
> When, I foresee, my special friends
> Will try to find their private ends:
> Though it is hardly understood
> Which way my death can do them good.
> (Jonathan Swift, "Verses on the Death of Dr. Swift," ll. 73–78; 1739)

> O thou by Nature taught
> To breathe her genuine thought,
> In numbers warmly pure and sweetly strong;

Who first on mountains wild,
In Fancy, loveliest child,
Thy babe or Pleasure's, nursed the powers of song!
(William Collins, "Ode to Simplicity"; 1746)

Each meter speeds up the reading or slows it down, sets rhythmic patterns that structure the content and establish a **tone**. There is an intimate connection between subject matter and meter, and serious treatments call for certain meters, comic treatments for others.

Obviously, meter is a phonological measurement. All depends upon how the words are pronounced, which means different languages tend to fall naturally into different meters. In Roman epic poetry, the **hexameter** line is the most common, while the French neoclassicists Corneille, Racine, and Molière (influenced by the Romans) prefer **alexandrines** in their dramas. In English poetry during the **Restoration** and **Augustan Eras, tetrameter** and **heroic couplets** prevail in ambitious poetic works by Dryden, Pope, Swift, and Butler, and most sonnets in English stick to the pentameter line.

We define meter in quantitative terms, but we must realize that meter is essential to the poetic experience. Critic Paul Fussell says that "meter is a prime physical and emotional constituent of poetic meaning" ("Poetic Meter and Poetic Forms," 1965), and many of the epochal careers of English literary history involved a liberating exploration of one metrical form or another: Milton and blank verse, Dryden and the heroic couplet, Byron and *ottava rima*. Their example shows that what may appear to be merely a pattern of stresses and syllables can, in fact, release powerful creative energies and yield new and influential expressions. Readers take them in as they do the tempo of music, and theorists relate their incorporations of meter to bodily functions such as heartbeats and breathing. Meter is, to be sure, a mechanical construct, but it issues from and sinks deep into human instincts for rhythm, song, time, and expression. (*See also* **Free verse**.)

Metonymy [muh–TAWN–uh–mee] A **figure of speech** in which one thing stands for another on the basis of prior association in reality. The association may involve a cause/effect relationship—for example, citing the symptoms of a disease for the disease itself—or an object/characteristic relationship—calling a nation suffering from famine a "hungry nation"—or almost any other actual relationship that preexists the metonymic figure. In the phrase, "The State ordered his release from jail," "State" is a metonymy for some person representing State power. In "Did you study Jefferson for the poli sci test?" "Jefferson" is a metonymy for materials associated with him and assigned for the exam. Metonymy is distinguished from **metaphor** in that metaphor involves a comparison of things with no prior association in reality. It is distinguished from **synecdoche** in that synecdoche involves a substitution of actual part for whole (or whole for part), as in "All hands on deck." As the examples above show, the effects of metonymy range from simple economy (it's easier to say "Jefferson" than to say "the works by Jefferson assigned in the course") to multilayered association (to say "The State" is to conjure up not only a single functionary, but all the powers, the history, and the responsibilities of a governing body).

Middle English   The English language as it was spoken from the twelfth to the sixteenth centuries. The transition from **Old English** to Middle English began with the Norman invasion in 1066. With the conquest, Middle English developed as an evolving combination of Old English and Norman French. Because of the social and political flux of the times, Middle English remained in constant change, with various forms scattered throughout England. Geoffrey Chaucer's *The Canterbury Tales* (1386–1400) and the anonymous poem *Sir Gawain and the Green Knight* (ca. 1375–1400) are written in different dialects, and William Langland's *Piers Plowman* (ca. 1372–89) has elements of several dialects. Not until geographical advantages and the influence of Chaucer made the Midland speech prevail in the late-fourteenth century did Middle English evolve into **Modern English**. To modern readers, the biggest problems with Middle English lie in vocabulary and spelling (and the pronunciation implied by it). Silent consonants in Modern English are pronounced in Middle English (*g-nat*, *k-nave*), the final *e* often gets a long sound, and many basic lexical features have disappeared (*thou*, *ye*, *hir* for *their*, *hem* for *them*, verb forms ending-*est* and -*eth*). But in its more influential dialects, the grammar of Middle English is largely familiar, as is the syntax. The opening to *The Canterbury Tales* indicates the similarities and differences:

> Whan [When] that April with his showres [showers] soote [sweet]
> The droughte of March hath perced [pierced] to the roote [root],
> And bathed every veine in swich [such] licour [liquid],
> Of which vertu [power] engendred is the flowr . . .

Mime   A play or sketch without words, narrated only through gesture and movement, though sometimes accompanied by music. The genre dates back to ancient Greece and Rome (Greek *mimesis*, "imitation") and ranges in content from the bawdy episodes of **farce** to the high seriousness of **drama**, the Dumb Show in *Hamlet* (1601) being an example of the latter. (*See also* **Pantomime**.)

Minimalism   Contemporary art and literature that adopts the principles of spareness, simplicity, abstract form, and minimal content. The term first applied to sculptors and painters in the 1960s (Donald Judd, Carl Andre, Sol LeWitt, and others) who fabricated artworks out of basic materials such as concrete blocks and fluorescent lighting, or canvases of "color-fields" rather than representations, thus reducing the distinction between material and meaning. The term drifted into poetry and fiction soon after, with poems pared back to near-pure description and fiction written in a deliberately flat, unemotional tone and an appropriately unadorned style. Take, for example, the following poem by Karl Kempton (1991):

ANTIQUE QUESTION

anti question

a we

awe

Because of its looser form and narrative requirements, minimalist fiction cannot attain the blankness of minimalist poetry and art. It often becomes "minimal" by relying more on dramatic action, scene, and dialogue than on narration or authorial summary.

Mixed metaphor A metaphor that trips over another metaphor already in the statement, usually without the speaker's awareness. The two or more metaphors are combined, resulting in ridiculousness or nonsense. For example: "The smoke-screen worked, and worked like a charm"; "Mary was such a tower of strength that she breezed her way through her work" (a tower of strength does not breeze).

Modern English The English language spoken from the sixteenth century to our own time. Philologists date Modern English from around 1550, because at that time the language had settled roughly into its current lexical and grammatical form. In the previous four hundred years—the **Middle English** period—different dialects of English had been evolving, each with a distinct vocabulary and pronunciation. By the **Elizabethan Period**, though, English had acquired a relative uniformity. From then on, in part because of the influence of Shakespeare and other Elizabethan writers, along with the King James Bible (1611), the major changes were of vocabulary and rhetoric. The invention of printing in the fifteenth century gave the language a new stability, and changes such as the loss of the final -e sound and the Great Vowel Shift (a change in *a*, *e*, and *i* sounds) were completed by 1650. Although orthography wasn't regularized for another one hundred years, when students today read Ben Jonson they have the sense of reading the same language as their own, whereas with Chaucer they require a significant amount of translation.

Modernism A movement in literature and the arts concentrated in the first third of the twentieth century. Because of the complexity of modernism, any generalization about it is inevitably inadequate, but in leading literary practitioners one can isolate some fundamental strands.

First, modernism is characterized by experimentation in form. British and American poets such as T. S. Eliot and William Carlos Williams compose works that cross a range of styles and genres. Eliot's *The Waste Land* (1922) jumps from one verse form to another, gathers allusions in a collage-like manner, and incorporates a host of narrative voices. Williams's volume *Spring and All* (1923) mingles prose effusions—complete with errant typography—and brief poems bearing little ostensible relation to one another. Each is an artistic experiment working against the norms of poetic convention. It is not that modernists are incapable of composing traditional works—Ezra Pound's "A Virginal" (1912) is a closely-observed Elizabethan love sonnet—but that they wish to expand the forms of poetry to test its powers of expression.

Second, modernism is an outlook upon modern life. In the rise of technology, consumerism, and mass entertainment, modernists see culture in a crisis moment. The advent of automobiles, warfare on a world scale—many thought that World War I was nothing but a pointless bloodbath—massive factories, commercial phenomena such as advertising, and vulgar attitudes in general made life in the West a sordid and confusing experience. Many writers and intellectuals considered its worst symptom the loss of tradition and high art. Some set out to revive a sense of beauty and history, while others tried to discover in the new materials of life new material for art. For example, in *Hugh Selwyn Mauberley* (1920), Pound creates a protagonist who "strove to resuscitate the dead art / Of poetry; to maintain 'the sublime' / In the old sense," while in "Of Modern Poetry" (1940) Wallace Stevens asserts that poetry "has to be living, to learn the speech of the place. / It has to face the men of the time and to meet / The women of the time."

Third, modernism is an aesthetic. Against the emphasis on self in **Romanticism** and upon the fluid sensuousness of **Impressionism**, modernists preferred a language of sharp outlines and concentrated diction. The critic T. E. Hulme advocated a poetry of concrete images ("The great aim is accurate, precise and definite description"—"Romanticism and Classicism," 1924); and T. S. Eliot advised writers to curb their egotism and adopt an impersonal pose ("Poetry is not a turning loose of emotion, but an escape from emotion; it is not the expression of personality, but an escape from personality"—"Tradition and the Individual Talent," 1919). To break out of individualism, Hulme maintained, we need a revival of the classical spirit, which claims that human beings are "intrinsically limited, but disciplined by order and tradition to something fairly decent." Eliot thought that writers must acquire a "historical sense"—that is, an abiding awareness of the tradition of art from classical times to the present.

The resulting literature, then, contained rigorous images and crisp word play:

> Call the roller of big cigars,
> The muscular one, and bid him whip
> In kitchen cups concupiscent curds . . .
>> (Wallace Stevens, "The Emperor of Ice-Cream"; 1922)

learned allusions and sophisticated variations on classic forms:

> In Breughel's great picture, The Kermess,
> the dancers go round, they go round and

around, the squeal and the blare and the
tweedle of bagpipes . . .
> (William Carlos Williams, "The Dance"; 1944)

crisis portraits of contemporary life:

This is the way the world ends
Not with a bang but a whimper.
> (Eliot, "The Hollow Men"; 1925)

and ruminations upon the plights of selfhood:

They cannot scare me with their empty spaces
Between stars—on stars where no human race is.
I have it in me so much nearer home
To scare myself with my own desert places.
> (Robert Frost, "Desert Places"; 1934)

These strands came together to constitute one of the major episodes in English and American literary history. Its influence lingers today in the conception of art as a challenge to conventional modes of seeing, in the alienation of the artist from middle-class society, and in presentations of contemporary life as a crisis moment (though the nature of that crisis has changed).

Monologue   An extended speech by a single character. The term originated in drama, where it describes a solo speech that has listeners (as opposed to a **soliloquy**, in which a character speaks only to himself or herself). A short story or even a novel can be written in monologue form if it is an unbroken speech by one character to another silent character or characters, or to the reader. (*See also* **Dramatic monologue.**)

Monometer   A verse meter consisting of one metrical foot, or one primary stress, per line.

Monosyllabic foot   [MAW–no–sil–LAB–ik] A foot, or unit of **meter**, that contains only one syllable.

Moral   A message or lesson implied or directly stated in a literary work. Commonly, a moral is placed at the end of the work. At the end of Aesop's fable "The Lioness and the Vixen," for instance, we have a message set off from the text: "Do not judge merit by quantity, but by worth." (*See also* **Didactic literature.**)

Motif   An element that recurs significantly throughout a narrative. A motif can be an image, idea, theme, situation, or action, and was first commonly used as a musical term for a recurring melody or melodic fragment. A motif can also refer to an element that appears in diverse literary works, such as a beautiful lady in medieval romances who turns out to be an evil fairy, or three questions that are asked a protagonist to test his or her wisdom. Usually, motifs serve to underscore a thematic point, but they can also operate on a structural level, as with the journey motif that structures the plot of *The Odyssey*, *The Aeneid*, Mark Twain's *Huckleberry Finn* (1884), and Joseph Conrad's *Heart of Darkness* (1899).

Motivation   What a character in a story or drama wants; the reasons an author provides for a character's actions. Motivation can be either *explicit* (in which reasons are specifically stated in a story) or *implicit* (in which the reasons are only hinted at or partially revealed). For some characters, motivation is simple. In Shakespeare's *Julius Caesar* (1599), Brutus's motivation is to end the imperial ambitions of Caesar and preserve republican freedoms. In Fitzgerald's *The Great Gatsby* (1925), Gatsby's motivation is to regain the love of Daisy Buchanon. For others motivation is complex. In *Hamlet* (1601), Hamlet's initial motivation is to revenge his father's murder; but that is complicated by his feelings for his mother and for Ophelia, as well as his need to verify the murder and question the morality of his plans. (*See also* **Character development**.)

Multiculturalism   A social and educational movement in the United States that maintains the multicultural basis of past history and contemporary society. Our world, multiculturalists say, is comprised of cultural materials derived from different racial, ethnic, religious, and national backgrounds. Up until the 1960s, white, male, and Eurocentric traditions and values dominated the classrooms and mainstream venues such as television. This was more a reflection of power than of reality or goodness, they argue, for "other" creators and traditions have been operative all along and bear their own aesthetic and moral criteria. Hence multiculturalism begins with an assertion of cultural relativism, which states that cultures should be judged by their own standards, not by another's. Assuming that, multiculturalists set about trying to restore the heritages that were formerly excluded—for example, bringing women writers into the canon and supporting ethnic studies programs on college campuses. While some commentators believe multiculturalism has introduced into education and the arts a pernicious identity politics—that is, the distribution of resources and value on the basis of group identity—few deny that in its alteration of curricular content, multiculturalism has yielded a richer, more diverse sense of the past and present. Although many dispute the educational value of diversity and believe that multiculturalist attitudes thrive on resentment and guilt, today multiculturalism is the prevailing outlook in schools and universities.

Myth   A traditional narrative of anonymous authorship that arises out of a culture's oral tradition and that portrays gods and heroes engaged in epochal actions and decisions. Myths characteristically dramatize fundamental beliefs about existence, time, and morality, explaining the origin of creation, the nature of human psyche, the beginnings of nations and natural objects. The story of the Fall in Genesis explains the presence of human frailty and corruption; the myth of Zeus and the other Greek gods rebelling against the Titans renders the endless battle of one generation against another. Through them a culture's values and cosmic outlooks are consolidated and passed from generation to generation, and in ritual enactments of myths community members experience their most profound understanding of life and existence. Scholars of myth take a more objective approach, regarding myth in social terms as a means of tribal unity, or in mental terms as a conversion of natural processes into human form. That is, they substitute for the truth or falsity of myth the instrumental or psychological value of it.

Mythological criticism   The practice of analyzing literature by looking for recurring patterns of plot and character and relating them to the universal experiences of humanity. An interdisciplinary approach that combines anthropology, psychology, history, and comparative religion, mythological criticism assumes that human creativity has certain traits and impulses common to all cultures and epochs. These show up in **motifs, heroes,** villains, situations, and outcomes that appear in works of literature spanning vast times and places. How else to explain the presence of, say, quest motifs and creation stories in so many cultures? The Swiss psychologist Carl Jung named these fundamental elements **archetypes,** claiming that they evoked deep psychic realities. Jung believed that all individuals share a "collective unconscious," a set of primal memories common to the human race, existing "beneath" each person's conscious awareness. In his writings, Jung connected the collective unconscious with archetypal images (which often involve primordial phenomena such as the sun, moon, fire, night, and blood). Later literary critics adopted archetypal thinking while downplaying Jung's metaphysical speculations. Critic Northrop Frye defined the archetype in less occult terms as "a symbol, usually an image, which recurs often enough in literature to be recognizable as an element of one's literary experience as a whole." Because of its comparatist nature, mythological criticism links the individual text under discussion to a broader context of works that share an underlying pattern. In discussing Shakespeare's *Hamlet* (1601), for instance, a critic might relate the Danish prince to other mythic sons avenging the deaths of their fathers, such as Orestes from Greek tragedy and Sigmund of Norse legend. Joseph Campbell took such comparisons even further; his compendious study *The Hero with a Thousand Faces* (1949) demonstrates how certain mythic characters arise in virtually every culture on every continent.

Although mythological criticism enjoyed a vogue in the mid-twentieth century, few literary critics practice it today. But researchers working in other fields, especially anthropology, often engage in mythological criticism when they include literature in their scholarship.

Naive narrator   *See* **Innocent narrator.**

Narrative poem   A poem that tells a story. Narrative is one of the four traditional modes of poetry, along with **lyric, drama,** and **didactic. Ballads** and **epics** are two common forms of narrative poetry.

Narrator   A voice or character that tells a story, providing readers with information and insight about characters and incidents in the narrative. A narrator's perspective and personality greatly affect how a story is told, and thus shape the meaning of the work. Speaking in the first or third person, a narrator may be reliable or unreliable, opinionated or nonjudgmental, a participant in the action or a storyteller outside the action. In either case, readers must determine the narrator's role in the presentation. For instance, in Jonathan Swift's *Gulliver's Travels* (1726), the narrator, Captain Gulliver, has undergone experiences that render him insane, and yet the entire story comes through his eyes. Such complications force readers not only to judge the materials of the narrative, but to examine the motives and limitations of the narrator himself. Added to the actions and figures is an all-too-human outlook. In other words, the distance between narrator and narrative is where ironies set in, where identifications of reader with storyteller are problematized, and where the significance of the events undergoes an initial interpretation. In narratives such as Edgar Allan Poe's tales (for example, "The Tell-Tale Heart," 1843), the real drama lies in the narrator's own head, not in the ostensible events taking place before him. In Mark Twain's *Huckleberry Finn* (1884), we see a fundamental narrative distinction: Huck is a voluble, observant first-person narrator, but as a character interacting with other characters he is quiet and unassuming. (*See also* **Innocent narrator, Nonparticipant narrator, Omniscient narrator, Participant narrator, Point of view, Unreliable narrator.**)

Naturalism   A school of fiction and drama in which the characters are presented as products or victims of environment and heredity. Influenced by evolutionary theory, naturalism portrays human beings as natural creatures set apart from other animals only by virtue of their intelligence. Society is a veneer of civility under which simmer ruling urges of fear, lust, and acquisitiveness. No supernatural entities appear, and the world runs on an unforgiving natural law of cause and effect, the strong preying upon the weak. Plots move forward through the conflict of inner motive and outward circumstance, with characters thrown into social and economic milieus that more or less fail to meet their primitive needs.

   Naturalism was first formally developed by French novelist Émile Zola in the 1870s. In promoting naturalism as a theory of human behavior, Zola urged the modeling of naturalist literature and drama on the scientific case study. The writer, like the scientist, was to record objective reality in all its amoral abundance with detachment; events should be reproduced with sufficient exactness to demonstrate the strict laws of material causality. Important American Naturalists writing in fiction include Jack London, Stephen Crane, Frank Norris, and Theodore Dreiser. Crane's *Maggie: A Girl of the Streets* (1893) opens with an exemplary naturalistic scene:

> A very little boy stood upon a heap of gravel for the honor of Rum Alley. He was throwing stones at howling urchins from Devil's Row

who were circling madly about the heap and pelting him. . . . In the yells of the whirling mob of Devil's Row children there were notes of joy like songs of triumphant savagery.

Here, the setting is a New York slum, the ideal of honor is a false pretense, joy stems from violence, and children behave like wild pack animals. Important examples in drama are Henrik Ibsen's *Ghosts* (1881), dealing in adultery, incest, and syphilis; Maxim Gorky's *Lower Depths* (1924), set in a Moscow flophouse; and Eugene O'Neill's *The Iceman Cometh* (1946), featuring washed-up drunks in a New York City bar. (*See also* **Realism**.)

Neoclassical Period   *See* **Augustan Age.**

New Formalism   A recent literary movement (begun around 1980), in which young poets employed traditional genres, rhyme, meter, and narrative. The dominant strain of poetry from the Fifties to the Eighties favored dense, difficult lyric expression in a more or less free verse form, and it was especially popular among academics and poets working in an academic milieu. Form was considered an artificial restraint or an elitist holdover alien to the poetic impulse. New Formalists tried to revive traditional form as both an enabling structure of expression (that is, forms such as the **terza rima** provided poets an inspiring medium and tradition of expression) and as an entertaining feature of verse (readers like **rhyme**, etc.). They observed that unstructured poetry had become a cliquish endeavor, appealing only to other poets, and proposed to compose works for a broader audience and to make poetry a popular form as it was in the eighteenth and nineteenth centuries before the advent of **Modernism**. Timothy Steele, Gertrude Schnackenberg, R. S. Gwynn, David Mason, and Marilyn Nelson are poets commonly associated with the movement.

New Naturalism   A term describing some American plays of the 1970s and 1980s, frankly showing the internal and external forces that shape the lives of unhappy, alienated, and/or impoverished characters. Examples include the plays of Sam Shepard, August Wilson, and David Mamet. (*See also* **Naturalism.**)

Nonfiction novel   A literary genre in which actual events are presented as a novel-length story, using the techniques of fiction (flashback, interior monologues, etc.). Truman Capote's *In Cold Blood* (1966), which depicts a multiple murder and subsequent trial that took place in Kansas, is a classic example of the method. Basic facts are respected and characters are profiled accurately, but they are represented within a frankly literary narrative and style.

Nonparticipant narrator   A narrator who does not appear in the story as a character but is capable of revealing the thoughts and motives of one or more characters. A nonparticipant narrator is also capable of moving from place to place in order to describe action and report dialogue. (*See also* **Omniscient narrator**.)

Nouvelle   The French term for a short prose tale (called *novella* by Italian Renaissance writers) that usually depicts in realistic terms illicit love, ingenious trickery, and sensational adventure, often with an underlying moral. Gaining popularity in the late-Middle Ages, the *nouvelle* often appears in collections, as in Marguerite de Navarre's *Heptameron* (ca. 1550) and Giovanni Boccacio's *Decameron* (ca. 1350). Today, the *nouvelle* is defined solely in terms of length, running longer than a short story but shorter than a novel (approximately 30,000 to 50,000 words), long enough to be published independently as a brief book. In this middle ground, the *nouvelle* strives for the focus of a short story but cannot be read in a single sitting. Some of the most influential works of the twentieth century include examples of the subgenre: Thomas Mann's *Death in Venice* (1913), Joseph Conrad's *Typhoon* (1903), and James Joyce's *A Portrait of the Artist as a Young Man* (1916). (See also **Novel**, **Short story**.)

Novel   An extended work of fictional prose narrative. The term *novel* implies a book-length composition (as compared to more compact forms of prose fiction such as the ***nouvelle***) with abundant characters, varied scenes, and a broader coverage of time than a shorter work provides. Given the looseness of the form, however, a novel may have the sweep of an era (as in Sir Walter Scott's historical fictions) or the narrowness of an episode in the life of a poor rural family (as in William Faulkner's *As I Lay Dying*, 1930).

As the most popular literary genre from the late-eighteenth century to our own time, the novel has evoked from scholars and critics lengthy commentary. Literary historians have traced its origins back to the medieval prose **romance**, the Italian *novella* of the fourteenth century, the **picaresque**, and medieval **legends** (especially those chronicling the lives of Christian saints). The German philosopher G. W. F. Hegel judged the novel the modern version of epic, and hence the most thorough representation of the spirit of the age. In English literary history, it reached its current shape in the eighteenth century, in the prose fictions of Daniel Defoe, Henry Fielding, and Samuel Richardson. Sociohistorical critics tie the novel to social changes such as the rise of the bourgeois class, the advent of a reading public not schooled in the classics, and the withdrawal of religion from daily life. Critics interested in questions of narrative favor the novel because of its narrative complexities—that is, its potential to contrast different points of view, to shift from person to person and from objective to subjective, and to experiment with alternative perceptions of reality (as in **stream-of-consciousness** narrative).

In other words, the novel is the most pliant and indefinable of contemporary literary genres. The tone ranges from comic to tragic, the scope from individual consciousness to thirty years in the life of a nation, the number of characters from one to hundreds, the narrative form from a sequence of letters (**epistolary novel**) to an omniscient panorama of society. There are detective novels, the ***Bildungsroman*, historical novels, romances,** and more, and examples of virtually every aesthetic school are to be found among them (**realism, naturalism, fantasy,** etc.) Novels have provided escapism for readers and they have produced social reforms, as when Upton Sinclair's *The Jungle* (1906) dramatized conditions in the meatpacking industry and sparked Federal investigations. Whereas it started out as a popular literary genre with little pretensions to high art, by the twentieth century the novel had come to equal all other genres; and many of the landmark works of world literature since the mid-nineteenth century are novels, such as Herman Melville's *Moby-Dick* (1851), Leo Tolstoy's *War and Peace* (1869), Fyodor Dostoyevsky's *The Brothers Karamazov* (1879–80), Marcel Proust's *Remembrance of Things Past* (1913–27), and James Joyce's *Ulysses* (1922).

Objective point of view   *See* **Dramatic point of view.**

Observer   A type of **first-person narrator** who is relatively detached from or plays only a minor role in the events described. (*See also* **Narrator.**)

Octameter   [awk–TAM–uh–ter] A verse meter consisting of eight metrical feet, or eight primary stresses, per line.

Octave   A **stanza** or grouping of eight lines. *Octave* often refers to the first eight-line of the **Italian sonnet,** as distinct from the **sestet** (the final six lines), but any organized eight-line unit qualifies. A **triolet** is an octave, as are the stanzas in *ottava rima* ("eighth rhyme"—*abababcc*), the verse form of Lord Byron's *Don Juan* (1819–24). Irish poet William Butler Yeats wrote several of his best-known later poems in octaves of various line lengths and rhyme schemes, including "A Prayer for My Daughter" (1927), "A Dialogue of Self and Soul" (1929), "The Circus Animals Desertion" (1939), "Sailing to Byzantium" (1927), "Among Schoolchildren" (1928), and "Byzantium" (1932):

> The unpurged images of day recede;
> The Emperor's drunken soldiery are abed;
> Night resonance recedes, night-walkers' song
> After great cathedral gong;
> A starlit or a moonlit dome disdains
> All that man is,
> All mere complexities,
> The fury and the mire of human veins.
> ("Byzantium")

Off rhyme   *See* **Slant rhyme.**

O. Henry ending   *See* **Trick ending**.

Old English   The language spoken by inhabitants of England in the five centuries prior to the Norman Invasion in 1066. During those years, groups from what is now Denmark and northern Germany migrated to England and began to convert to the native Christianity but kept their language, a Germanic tongue differing from **Modern English** both in lexicon and grammar. In Old English, nouns and adjectives are inflected to indicate gender, case, and number, and the syntax often places the verb at the end of a sentence and prepositions after the object, not before. Although many words of common usage today derive from Old English, including those of grammatical function—articles, prepositions, conjunctions, etc.—and those of ordinary experience—*bird, man, good, hard, cold, water, summer*, etc.—to us Old English appears a wholly foreign language. The major extant literary work of Old English is the martial epic *Beowulf* (ca. eighth century), and much Old English literature is heroic and elegiac in theme and character. But in the monasteries during these centuries, learning thrived and produced important studies of Christianity and translations from Latin.

Omniscient narrator   [awm–NISH–unt] An omniscient narrator is one who has the ability to move freely through the consciousness of any character and from setting to setting and time to time. With complete knowledge of the internal and external events in a story, the omniscient narrator can appear indistinguishable from the author, as no discrepancies arise between the knowledge the narrator possesses and the knowledge readers acquire over the course of the narrative. (*See also* **Narrator**, **Nonparticipant narrator**.)

Onomatopoeia   [AW–no–MAW–toe–PEE–uh] A literary device in which a thing or action is represented by the word that imitates the sound associated with it (e.g., *crash, bang, pitter-patter*). Rarely does a word echo precisely an actual nonverbal sound—a real crash doesn't sound the same as the word *crash*—but the phonetic resemblance may be close enough to provide a feel for the sounds it describes. In William Carlos Williams's "The Great Figure" (1921), the final lines contain three examples:

> Among the rain
> and lights
> I saw the figure 5
> in gold
> on a red
> firetruck
> moving
> tense
> unheeded
> to gong *clangs*

siren *howls*
and wheels *rumbling*
through the dark city.

Another example comes from "The Bells" (1849) by Edgar Allan Poe, who considered the sound of poetry an essential part of its meaning.

To the tintinabulation that so musically wells
From the bells, bells, bells, bells
Bells, bells, bells—
From the jingling and the tinkling of the bells.

Because of its unification of sound and sense, onomatopoeia has been a tricky subject for literary theorists and linguists. Some believe that language is an entirely arbitrary system, that there is no natural connection between a particular sound and its meaning or referent. Others claim that some words do, in fact, grow out of a natural connection to things; and that literary language, particularly onomatopoeic language, is where the connection becomes explicit.

Open *dénouement* [DAY-new-mawn] One of the two conventional types of *dénouement* or resolution. In open *dénouement*, the author ends a narrative with loose ends and unresolved matters, provoking readers to speculate on the significance of what has come before and what will happen after the work has ended. In Thomas Pynchon's *The Crying of Lot 49* (1960), for instance, the protagonist Oedipa Maas undergoes a series of mysterious adventures that culminate in an auction that promises to reveal the truth of it all. But the novel ends just before the auction begins. (*See also* **Closed *dénouement*.**)

Open form Verse that has no set scheme—no regular meter, rhyme, or stanzaic pattern. (*See also* **Free verse.**)

Oral tradition The corpus of stories, songs, **folk tales, myths,** and rituals within a culture that are transmitted by word of mouth from one generation to another. In societies without writing, oral tradition serves as a fund of cultural memory, the repository of narratives and heroes that embody the culture's values and beliefs. Works in oral tradition have no single author, but are learned and disseminated by priest-figures, singers, and other individuals charged with maintaining the heritage. Others in the culture experience oral tradition as a kind of communal bond, tying them to each other and to the past of their own nation or community. Before ancient Greek epics were recorded in script, for example, they were passed down by traveling bards who performed them for local audiences and gave them a more or less fixed narrative form.

Orchestra In classical Greek theater architecture, a circular, level performance space at the base of a horseshoe-shaped amphitheater, where twelve to fifteen young, masked, male chorus members sang and danced the odes interspersed between dramatic episodes making up the classical Greek play. In today's standard theater spaces, the orchestra comprises the ground floor seats near the front of the stage.

Ottava rima [o–TAW–vuh REE–muh] Verse composed of stanzas measuring eight lines with a rhyme scheme of *abababcc*. The form developed in Renaissance Italy in the works of Boccaccio, Ariosto, and Tasso, and was adopted freely by later English Renaissance poets Thomas Wyatt, Sir Philip Sidney, Edmund Spenser, and others. Well-suited to lengthy narrative, *ottava rima* was most often used in serious poetry, but in English literature it reached its full potential in the satirical masterpiece of Lord Byron, *Don Juan* (1819-24). The following stanza on Don Juan's father nicely displays the comic potential of the form (note the joke in the final couplet.):

> He was a mortal of the careless kind,
> With no great love for learning, or the learned,
> Who chose to go where'er he had a mind,
> And never·dreamed his lady was concerned;
> The world, as usual, wickedly inclined
> To see a kingdom or a house o'erturned
> Whispered he had a mistress, some said *two*,
> But for domestic quarrels *one* will do.
> (I.xix)

Overstatement Also called hyperbole, overstatement is exaggeration used to emphasize a point. A basic tool of **irony**, it deliberately opens a discrepancy between the description and the thing described. In Mark Twain's *Pudd'nhead Wilson* (1894), for example, the character Judge Driscoll is hailed as "the President of the Freethinkers' Society," a seemingly impressive office, until we read the latter part of the sentence: "and Pudd'nhead Wilson was the other member." The overstatement of the former is undercut by the latter, mocking the pretensions of the title.

Oxymoron [OX–ee–MOR–on] A figure of speech taken from the Greek *oxys* "sharp" + *moros* "foolish." An oxymoron is a flat contradiction in terms, such as the description of Christ's birth in Richard Crashaw's "In the Holy Nativity of Our Lord God" (1646): "In spite of Darkness, it was Day." Oxymorons appear often in Greek, Petrarchan, and Elizabethan love poetry, in which a lover tries to impart the simultaneous pains and joys of his passion, as in Horace's famous *Odi et amo* ("I hate and I love").

Pantomime Acting on the stage without speech, using only posture, gesture, bodily movement, and exaggerated facial expressions to mimic actions and express feelings. Originally, in ancient Rome, a pantomime was a performer who played all the parts single-handedly, but today the term applies mainly to children's entertainments, the plots taken from common tales such as Cinderella and Jack and the Bean Stalk. (*See also* **Mime**.)

Parable A brief narrative that teaches a moral. The parables found in Christian literature, such as "The Prodigal Son" (Luke 15:11–32), are classic examples of the form. In parables, unlike fables (where the moral is explicitly stated within the narrative), the moral meanings are implicit and can often be interpreted in several ways. A form of **didactic literature**, the parable stimulates readers to reflect upon their beliefs and values and gain a higher understanding of the situation the parable addresses. Modern parables can be found in the works of Franz Kafka and Jorge Luis Borges.

Paradox A statement that at first appears self-contradictory, but that on reflection reveals some deeper sense. For example, in Holy Sonnet 14 (1633), John Donne makes a plea to God that paradoxically mingles destruction and creation:

> Batter my heart, three-personed God; for You
> As yet but knock, breathe, shine, and seek to mend;
> That I may rise and stand, o'erthrow me, and bend
> Your force to break, blow, burn, and make me new.

Here, paradox compels readers to think differently about the relation of God to men and women. In this it serves an intellectual function: to adjust the beliefs and values according to which the paradox first appeared contradictory.

Parallelism A side-by-side arrangement of words, phrases, clauses, or sentences for purposes of comparison, contrast, or other relation. For example, in discussing the genesis of one of his plots, novelist Henry James recalls:

> Long had I turned it over, standing off from it, yet coming back to it; convinced of what might be done with it, yet seeing the theme as formidable.
>
> ("Preface" to *The Wings of the Dove*; 1908)

Parallelism is a concise way of organizing ideas, of demonstrating their balance, complementarity, or opposition. Orators use it as an effective strategy in public speech, as in Abraham Lincoln's sentence in the "Gettysburg Address" (1863):

> The world will little note, nor long remember what we say here, but it can never forget what they did here.

Paraphrase The restatement in our own words of what we understand a literary work to say. A paraphrase is similar to a summary, although not as brief or simple; and it addresses not simply **plot** and **character** summations but their thematic significance as well. Because it treats the content of the work and leaves the form largely unexamined, paraphrase is but a partial understanding of the work, best considered a useful tool in commencing an interpretation. Indeed, as soon as we devise a paraphrase of a work of literature, we discover elements in the work that complicate it. In "The Heresy of Paraphrase" (1947), critic Cleanth Brooks maintains that "paraphrase is not the real core of meaning which constitutes the essence of the poem. . . . Indeed, whatever statement we may seize upon as incorporating the 'meaning' of the poem, immediately the imagery and the rhythm seem to set up tensions with it, warping and twisting it, qualifying and revising it."

Parody   A mocking imitation of a literary work or style, usually for comic purposes. A parody typically exaggerates distinctive features of the original, mixing high and low materials to deflate the original source. Parody is related to **burlesque,** but while burlesque bluntly distorts the original, parody plays more lightly within the style and subject matter of the original. The following lines from Samuel Butler's *Hudibras* (1663), describing the main character, are a burlesque of grand descriptions of heroes and of the tedious arguments of logicians:

> He was in *Logick* a great Critick,
> Profoundly skill'd in Analytick.
> He could distinguish and divide
> A Hair 'twixt *South* and *South-West* side:
> On either which he would dispute,
> Confute, change hands, and still confute.
> He'd undertake to prove by force
> Of Argument, a Man's no Horse.
>> (I.i.65–72)

Lewis Carroll's "The White Knight's Song" (1871), though, uses a lighter touch to parody William Wordsworth's "Resolution and Independence" (1807) and the latter's solemn conversation with an aged leech-gatherer:

> I saw an aged, aged man,
>> A-sitting on a gate.
> "Who are you, aged man?" I said.
>> "And how is it you live?"
> And his answer trickled through my head
>> Like water through a sieve.
>
> He said "I look for butterflies
>> That sleep among the wheat;
> I make them into mutton-pies,
>> And sell them in the street."

Participant narrator   A **narrator** that is a character within a story. Often the term is reserved for a participant who is neither the protagonist nor a central figure of the action. Rather, the participant narrator is close enough to be implicated in the events, but distant enough to provide an outside perspective upon them. In Nathaniel Hawthorne's *The Blithedale Romance* (1852), for instance, narrator Miles Coverdale is one of the idealists who join a utopian community; and although he is not one of the main agents in the drama, they include him in their affairs, and all of their actions are colored by his observations. (*See also* **First-person narrator**.)

Pastoral   An idealized rendition of rural life, in which shepherds muse upon love and time, nature is tranquil and idyllic, and the verse or prose is fluid and lovely. The pastoral dates back to ancient Greece and Rome, with Theocritus (third century B.C.E.) and Virgil (first century C.E.) establishing subject matters and conventions. In English literature, the pastoral is a familiar theme from the Renaissance through the nineteenth century. Sir Philip Sidney's *Arcadia* (1590), a pastoral romance mixing prose and poetry, and Edmund Spenser's *The Shepheardes Calendar* (1579), twelve pastoral conversations in archaic language, established the centrality of the genre, and some of the most famous poems of the subsequent three hundred years contain pastoral motifs. John Milton's "Lycidas" (1637) is a pastoral elegy for a deceased fellow student at Cambridge that bears the customary heightened language, natural imagery, and reflective tone:

> Yet once more, O ye laurels, and once more
> Ye myrtles brown, with ivy never sere,
> I come to pluck your berries harsh and crude,
> And with forced fingers rude,
> Shatter your leaves before the mellowing year.
> Bitter constraint, and sad occasion dear,
> Compels me to disturb your season due;
> For Lycidas is dead, dead ere his prime,
> Young Lycidas, and hath not left his peer.

Pentameter   [pen–TAM–uh–ter] A verse meter consisting of five metrical feet, or five primary stresses, per line. In English, the most common form of pentameter is iambic. Examples:

> The first is prone to vice, the last to rage. (Anne Bradstreet)

> The curfew tolls the knell of parting day . . . (Thomas Gray)

> When I have fears that I may cease to be . . . (John Keats)

Peripeteia   [PAIR–uh–puh–TEE–uh] Anglicized as *peripety*, Greek for "sudden change," the term was applied by Aristotle to **tragedy** to signify a reversal of fortune. In the plotting, a sudden change of circumstance or a new piece of information brings catastrophe to the protagonist. The play's peripety occurs usually when a certain result is expected and instead its opposite effect is produced, often through the unwitting actions of the hero. For example, at the beginning of *Oedipus*, Oedipus expects to discover the identity of the murderer of Laius. However, after the Corinthian messenger informs Oedipus that he was adopted, the hero's intent widens to encompass the search for his true parentage, and that search produces the knowledge that he killed his father and married his mother.

In **comedy**, the change produces the opposite reversal. Peripety restores a character to good fortune, when a moment in which the worst that can happen is suddenly turned into happy circumstance. In Shakespeare's *The Merchant of Venice* (1596–97), Shylock is just about to stab Antonio in the chest in order to extract the pound of flesh owed to him when Portia raises an objection: the debt says nothing about blood. If Shylock draws blood, then he is guilty of murder (Antonio will die). Portia's announcement suddenly inverts the course of events. Shylock is stripped of his claims, Antonio is given a portion of his estate, and the romantic entanglements of the lovers in the play begin to be resolved. (*See also* **Cosmic irony.**)

Persona Latin for *mask*. A figure imagined by an author to be the speaker of a poem, story, or novel. A persona is the voice of the work, not a character in it. We sense the "personality" of the persona in the language he or she uses to describe the characters and events, the values and opinions that lie in the persona's judgments, the sympathies he or she feels. In John Keats's "Ode on a Grecian Urn" (1820), the narrator never appears as a character in the poem, but the language and thoughts expressed mark him as a meditative figure sensitive to aesthetic forms and romantic passions, acutely aware of time and loss. (*See also* **Mask.**)

Personification A figure of speech in which a thing, an animal, or an abstraction is endowed with human characteristics. Personification allows an author to dramatize the nonhuman world in human terms, as in these lines from Jean Toomer's "Georgia Dusk" (1923), which project human attitudes upon a Southern twilight:

> The sky, lazily disdaining to pursue
>   The setting sun, too indolent to hold
>   A lengthened tournament for flashing gold,
> Passively darkens for night's barbecue . . .

Personification may produce effects as simple as an entertaining description whereby natural and abstract things acquire a "personality" and become imaginary elements in a story. Or, it may play a more complex role—for instance, in a satire that gives animals human traits in order to criticize those very traits, in reflecting ironically on human society by giving it the mask of an animal habitat (as in George Orwell's *Animal Farm*, 1946).

Petrarchan sonnet *See* **Italian sonnet.**

Picaresque [PIK–uh–resk] A narrative, usually a novel told in the first-person voice, that presents the life and adventures of a likable rogue (*picaro*, in

Spanish) who is at odds with respectable society. Loosely plotted, with adventures unfolding in discrete episodes, the picaresque is part adventure story, part **satire**, and part **realism**. The protagonist wanders through the world engaging all classes of persons, relying on his or her wits to survive, falling into awkward and difficult situations that reveal all the comic and vicious aspects of human nature. But although characters are greedy, dishonest, and lustful, and the picaro enjoys staging their misfortune (and often suffers along with them), the picaresque tends more toward light and **low comedy** than toward bitter satire. The form was popular in Europe in the seventeenth and eighteenth centuries, leading examples including *Lazarillo de Tormes* (Anonymous, 1553), *The Adventurous Simplicissimus* (Hans von Grimmelshausen, 1669), and *Tom Jones* (Henry Fielding, 1749).

Picture-frame stage Developed in sixteenth-century Italian playhouses, the picture-frame stage held the action within a proscenium arch, a gateway standing in front of the scenery (as the etymology of *pro-scenium* indicates). The proscenium framed painted scene panels (receding into the middle distance) designed to give the illusion of three-dimensional perspective. Only one seat in the auditorium, reserved for the theater's royal patron or sponsor, enjoyed the complete perspectivist illusion. The raised and framed stage separated actors from the audience and the world of the play from the real world of the auditorium. Picture-frame stages became the norm throughout Europe and England up into the twentieth century. The illusion of the self-contained stage-world was perfected in the mid-nineteenth century with the **box set** and "fourth wall" staging conventions.

Play *See* **Drama**.

Play review A critical account of a performance, providing the basic facts of the production, a brief plot summary, and an evaluation (with adequate rationale) of the chief elements of performance, including the acting, the direction, scene and light design, and the script, especially if the play is new or unfamiliar. Play reviews aren't a species of scholarship—they are first-time assessments, written while the play is in active performance. But in researching dramas from the past, an important resource is, precisely, the first reviews it garnered. There, one witnesses how the play met contemporary tastes, what people at the time thought of it, and how it matched or mismatched prevailing dramatic conventions.

Plot One of the most important critical terms in literary studies, *plot* names the particular arrangement of actions, events, and situations in a narrative. Aristotle considered it the most crucial element in dramatic compositions ("the first principle, and, as it were, the soul of a tragedy"), and later commentators from Renaissance and seventeenth-century theorists of drama to early-twentieth-century theorists of the novel have evaluated their respective genres upon conceptions of plot. To all of them, plot is not merely the sequence of events in the story, but the artistic pattern formed by its parts, including the **exposition, complication, climax,** and *dénouement*. In Homer's *Odyssey*, the story is comprised of the perilous adventures Odysseus has on his long journey homeward to Ithaca. The plot is the organization of those adventures as they fall within the overarching structure of the journey. Because Odysseus' adventures stand independently as complete episodes and could be rearranged with no disruption of the overall pattern of the journey, Aristotle considered the epic to have an **episodic plot**, really a loose collection of discrete stories with the same characters. In Sophocles' *Oedipus*, on the other hand, the plot has a tighter, more causal structure, preferred by Aristotle as the working of necessity through the chaos of human events. The story portrays King Oedipus speaking to different figures about his past and present as he searches for the cause of the plague in Thebes. The plot is structured like an investigation, and each moment leads inexorably toward the final revelation. The order of the exchanges cannot be altered.

How an author chooses to construct the plot determines the way the reader experiences the story. Manipulating a plot, therefore, can be the author's most important labor. With heavily-coded plots such as that of the detective story, the author's talent lies in how skillfully he or she varies the conventions without violating the implicit requirements of the genre. For the critic, abstracting the plot from the story allows for a comparison and contrast of different works. In studying detective novels, critics may proceed by juxtaposing plots, examining how authors follow and diverge from standard patterns. In Roman Polanski's film *Chinatown* (1974), the plot begins in a routine way: a woman enters an office to hire a detective for a case. But later the plot takes a sudden turn when we discover that the woman who hired him was pretending to be someone else. Without the preexisting convention of "client-hires-detective-and-story-begins," the turn wouldn't have such an intriguing effect. (*See also* **Dénouement, Falling action, Rising action.**)

Poetic diction Strictly speaking, *poetic diction* signifies any language deemed suitable for verse, but the term generally refers to elevated language intended for poetry rather than common use. Poetic diction often denotes the ornate language used in literary periods, such as the **Augustan Age,** when authors employed a highly specialized vocabulary for their verse. In "The Enthusiast, or, The Lover of Nature" (1748), Joseph Warton employs heightened epithets and flowery diction typical of the idiom: birds are referred to as "green-rob'd Dryads" and "choristers of Air," apples as "ruddy orbs / Betwixt the green leaves," and ancient poets as "Fair Nature's friends." Today we consider such terms excessive and bathetic; and Romantic poets such as William Wordsworth considered poetic diction of this kind artificial and hackneyed, while Modernist poets such as

Ezra Pound had no patience for a language that had become so conventionalized. But in earlier eras of literature, the inventions of poetic diction were themselves part of the essence and pleasure of poetry, and should be understood as a mode of expression with different aims than, say, representation of the poetic self. (*See also* **Diction**.)

Poetics   The theory and principles of literary expression. To study the poetics of a poet is to determine the assumptions and habits that inform the verse. That means finding in the work a preference for certain verse forms, levels of diction, subjects, and structures, as well as an attitude toward tradition and a theory of poetry's social, political, religious, or experiential purposes. Added together and explained as a general approach to literature, they constitute a poetics, a kind of creative/conceptual core from which the poems issue. As such, the study of poetics is analytical, not evaluative or ethical. That is, poetics sets out to explain the values and motives of the work, breaking it down into internal parts (themes, language, plots, etc.) but not deciding the external merit of them. The poetics of Walt Whitman's *Leaves of Grass* (1855–92), for example, includes the processes by which his democratic vision of America is converted into such practices as his expansive catalogue sequences, but it doesn't follow up with an assessment of catalogue verse *per se* or of Whitman's democratic vision itself, except insofar as one is a reflection of the other.

Point of view   The perspective from which a story is told. Many years ago, critic Percy Lubbock defined point of view as "the relation in which the narrator stands to the story." There are many types of point of view, including **first-person narrator** (a story in which the narrator is a participant in the action) and **third-person narrator** (in which the narrator is a nonparticipant). Each one produces a different relationship of narrator to story, and hence a different story. A **participant narrator** offers the ambiguous point of view of someone involved in the action but who is not the protagonist. An **omniscient narrator** provides a God's-eye perspective on things, encouraging our trust in the rendition, while an **unreliable narrator** leads us to suspect the account. In each case, an adjustment in point of view forces an adjustment in our interpretation of the action. For example, Melville's *Moby-Dick* (1851) opens with a famous introduction, "Call Me Ishmael," a phrase that wavers between casual salutation and oracular pronouncement, and embodies the curious role the narrator will play in the narrative to come. In the beginning of the novel, Ishmael's point of view is that of a young, somewhat naïve seaman experiencing the rigors of whaling and reflecting metaphysically upon the meaning of life. As the novel progresses, though, Ishmael's presence fades and Ahab's obsessive pursuit of the white whale predominates. And yet, at the end, after Moby-Dick has swamped the Pequod and the smaller boats, only one man survives, Ishmael, whose voice comes back to us as a somber witness to the bizarre drama. (*See also* **Narrator**.)

Portmanteau word [PORT–man–toe] An artificial word that combines parts of other words to express some combination of their qualities. Sometimes portmanteau words prove so useful that they become part of the standard language—for example, *smog* from *smoke* and *fog*, and *brunch* from *breakfast* and *lunch*.

Postcolonialism Inspired by the fall of European colonial governments in the Third World following World War II, postcolonialism is the political and cultural analysis of societies freed from colonial rule. The endeavor has obvious relevance to the traditional work of history, but because of the strangeness of the colonial situation, postcolonialism also bears upon general issues of race, class, education, the West, and capitalism. Colonialism was not just a simple suppression and exploitation of native peoples. Though inspired by economic motives (European governments and businesses coveted the natural resources of other lands), colonialism also entailed imposing the colonists' language and culture upon the local populace. The attempt to Westernize indigenous peoples resulted in a series of social complexities. Because of the difficulty of controlling the local situation by themselves, colonizers cultivated a group of individuals from the indigenous population to serve as administrators, teachers, and police officers, thus creating a distinct class of people racially and historically tied to those on whom they exercise the colonizer's will. The colonizer's language hovered over the colony as an official language hated as a language of tyranny, yet prized as a language of education, success, and authority. The colonizer's race was equally hated and admired, as was his military might.

These complexities make for fruitful subjects of study, and they become even more significant in the wake of the colonizer's departure. As colonies gained their independence, the political and economic power of the colonizer disappeared, but the cultural influence remained. English is still spoken in India, French in the Ivory Coast. From the vantage point of the politically-liberated but culturally-influenced native peoples, postcolonialists interpret literature and art as a fraught expression. In analyzing literature and artworks produced in postcolonial settings, they expound controversial debates over race, miscegenation, complicity, and ethnocentrism. In this way, postcolonialism focuses on the text, but has a larger ambition: to impart the experience through the eyes of the colonized individual, not the eyes of the colonizer. To postcolonial critics, this is a final act of liberation from the colonizer.

Postmodernism Originally a movement in the arts in the 1950s and 1960s, postmodernism is now a broad, ill-defined cultural movement whose import includes a host of aesthetic tastes, artistic practices, philosophical beliefs, and social behaviors. People use the term to describe things as various as Frank Gehry's Guggenheim Museum in Bilbao, Spain, French **deconstruction**, advertisements showing famed sculptural figures wearing sunglasses, and media stunts. To encapsulate these diverse expressions into a coherent definition is impossible, but one can determine certain common aspects:

A skepticism toward models of truth, value, and history: Postmodernists disbelieve in overarching structures of time and space and in abstract epistemological conceptions. They regard those who posit large-scale social progress or decline, supernatural forces guiding human history, and laws of human thought as naïve and earnest, as exemplars of a "master narrative" that doesn't stand up. Against them, postmodernists adopt a relativist approach to belief. Claiming that all truths are relative to history and place and that all values are relative to a culture, postmodernists respond with ironic works of art and skeptical interpretations of reason and its institutions (the University, the Church, etc.).

An irreverence toward artistic tradition: Postmodernists disbelieve in temporal and generic categories of art. They mix the ancient with the modern, the high with the low. They work with materials from **mass culture** as well as from high culture, and favor tactics of **parody** and **kitsch** (kitsch is the conversion of works of art and important events in history into popular forms, as in Hollywood versions of the Roman Empire).

An emphasis on contemporary political and technological world processes: Postmodernists believe that the world is no longer governed by traditional authorities—that is, by governments, organizations of science and education, religious institutions, etc. Instead, they argue that multinational capitalism, cybertechnology, media, consumerism, and globalization are the working forces of the world today. Hence, postmodern artists and critics like Thomas Pynchon and Jean Baudrillard speculate upon shadowy powers orchestrating the society, but operating beneath the notice of ordinary citizens. What people take to be the reality of things, they suggest, is, in fact, but a surface phenomenon. (Baudrillard considers Disneyland to be the most "real" place in the United States.)

Wavering between these impulses, postmodernism is sometimes a political critique, other times an aesthetic diversion. Sometimes it seems playful, other times serious, and while it mocks the aesthetic and social boundaries set by tradition, in its best practitioners it displays a deep knowledge of the tradition. Whether this coy, fugitive movement adds up to an enduring legacy remains to be seen.

Print culture A culture that depends primarily on the printed word—in books, magazines, and newspapers—to distribute and preserve information, history, and knowledge. The category has been important in fields of anthropology, in which researchers have found that literate societies—those functioning through the written word—differ fundamentally from preliterate societies, which have only an oral culture (maintained through **oral tradition**). Scholars of print culture highlight the importance of the material nature of print—for instance, contrasting the way knowledge spread in a society whose writing circulated primarily in manuscript versus the way it spread in a society whose writing circulated primarily in mass publications. They regard the advent of the modern book form in the fourteenth and fifteenth centuries as a momentous threshold in the course of Western civilization. In recent decades, new computer technology has created a new sense of print culture. Scholars in communications and media studies have distinguished traditional print culture from a culture whose information is shared and preserved electronically, claiming that we now inhabit an Electronic or Digital Age. Although print exists in both books and Web sites, the electronic medium incorporates means of processing and consuming it that, scholars suggest, have altered the nature of information and produced novel forms of reading and understanding.

Projective verse A theory of poetry developed by American poet Charles Olson in the mid-twentieth century. Example:

> the motion
>
> not verbal
>
>> the newt
>
>> less active
>
>>> than I: the fire pink
>
>> not me
>
>>> (the words
>
>>> not me
>
>>>> not my nature
>
>>>> I
>
>>>>> Not even honor
>
>>>>> anything . . .

("The Motion"; 1954)

Olson believed that poets should compose as if they were an object placed among other objects in the world, not as subjects imposing an order or meaning upon the world. Against the Romantic and impressionist impulses to set the experience of the poet at the center of things, Olson's poets "project" themselves into a situation and write as but one part of it, suppressing the urge to conceptualize things or to let one's ego shape the composition. To that end—assuming that such projections are possible—poets allow the realities around and within them (the nonego elements) to dictate the verse—for instance, heeding their own breathing and using it, rather than standard meter and form, as a rhythmic guide. (*See also* **Open form.**)

Proscenium arch [pro–SEE–nee–um] Separating the auditorium from the raised stage and the world of the play, a proscenium arch is the architectural frame or gateway that stands in front of the scenery (as the etymology of *proscenium* indicates) in traditional European theaters from the sixteenth century on. (*See also* **Picture-frame stage.**)

Prose poem Poetic language printed in prose paragraphs, but displaying the careful attention to sound, imagery, and figurative language characteristic of poetry. While some prose achieves poetic status by virtue of its lyricism, sonority, figurative language, etc., prose poetry goes further in constituting itself *as* poetry, but without the visible appearance of verse. Although prose poems date back to the Old Testament Psalms, the form comes into its own as a recognizable subgenre in France in the mid-nineteenth century. In the volume of prose poems entitled *Paris Spleen* (1869), French poet Charles Baudelaire speaks of "poetic prose, musical, without rhythm and without rhyme, supple and rugged enough to adapt itself to the lyrical impulses of the soul." Arthur Rimbaud became a master of the prose poem in his *Les Illuminations* (1886):

> Seen enough. The vision met itself in every kind of air.
> Had enough. Noises of cities in the evening, in the sunlight,
>   and forever.
> Known enough. The haltings of life. Oh! Noises and Visions!
> Departure in new affection and sound.
>   ("Departure"; 1886)

Prosody [PRAW–suh–dee] The study of metrical and rhythmic structures in poetry and prose. Prosody covers the sounds of words, the accents of syllables, verse lengths, metrical conventions, rhyme—in sum, any element of language that contributes to verbal rhythms. Although the practices of prosody apply to language of any kind (linguists, for example, study the phonetic features of speech in part by quantifying intensity, duration, and pitch), in literary studies prosody usually focuses on poetry. The prosody of prose entails analyzing one structure (the sentence), but because of the structural complexities of verse, whereby line patterns, stanza breaks, poetic license, rhyme, and other formal properties interrupt and complicate the articulation of ordinary speech, prosody of poetry must account for a host of idiosyncratic sounds and cadences. The simplest prosodic exercise is **scansion**, the charting of stresses and pauses—an essential task in the understanding of poetry—while more ambitious efforts try to relate poetic rhythms to music, dance, and other cultural activities.

Protagonist From the Greek word meaning "first actor" or "first combatant," a protagonist is the central character in a literary work. The protagonist usually initiates the main action of the story, often in conflict with the antagonist. In Victor Hugo's novel *Les Miserables* (1862), we have a classic pairing of protagonist and antagonist: Jean Valjean, the former convict trying to live virtuously and help others, and Monsieur Javert, an inspector who hounds Valjean for years until a crisis of conscience leads him to suicide. (*See also* **Antagonist**.)

Proverb A brief saying encapsulating homespun wisdom. Proverbs have an ancient history, and the range of proverbs found in the Old Testament:

> The fear of the Lord is the beginning of wisdom . . .

in Erasmus's *Adagia* (1500):

> Between friends all is common.
>
> Well begun is half done.

in William Blake's *The Marriage of Heaven and Hell* (1793):

> The road of excess leads to the palace of wisdom.
>
> Always be ready to speak your mind, and a base man will avoid you.

and in Wallace Stevens's *Adagia* (ca. 1940):

> War is the periodical failure of politics.
>
> The death of one god is the death of all.

evince the enduring popularity of the proverb. As the examples show, its pithy form makes it useful for comic and satiric purposes, and its memorableness makes it an effective didactic tool. (*See also* **Didactic literature**.)

Psalms Sacred songs, usually referring to the 150 Hebrew poems collected in the Old Testament. Formally, the psalm is marked by symmetrical patterns, refrains, and repetitions. For example, Psalm 8 begins and ends with the phrase, "O Lord our Lord, how excellent *is* thy name in all the earth!" In content, psalms often involve praise or supplication, as in Psalm 10:

> Why standest thou afar off, O Lord? *why* hidest *thyself* in times of trouble?

and Psalm 22:

> My God, my God, why hast thou forsaken me?

Psychological criticism   The practice of analyzing literature in terms of the nature of literary genius, the psyche of a particular artist, and the psychic content of fictional elements, especially characters. Such approaches, proponents argue, disclose the underlying motivations and meanings of a literary work and lay bare the process of its creation. Although psychological elements have appeared in literary criticism for centuries, not until the work of Sigmund Freud does psychological criticism become a distinct and systematic school of thought. In keeping with his theory of human nature, Freud tied literary expression to wish fulfillment, infant sexuality, the unconscious, and repression, extending the meanings of language and symbols to their reflection of unconscious fears and desires. He also derived many psychoanalytic theories from literary sources: narcissism from the myth of Narcissus, the Oedipus Complex from the Oedipus story, *Hamlet* (1601), and Fyodor Dostoyevsky's *The Brothers Karamazov* (1879–80).

A pioneering instance of psychoanalytical criticism is Freud's brief essay, "Creative Writers and Day-dreaming" (1908). Here Freud explains the attraction of certain works of literature: they provide "compromise formations" by which repressed and taboo desires are expressed in sublimated forms, that is, forms that in one way or another bypass the shame and guilt the direct expression of those desires evokes. Popular works of literature are like collective fantasies, and it is the genius of the artist to discover plots, characters, etc., in which fantasies are realized and through which readers experience troublesome desires in pleasurable ways. In the make-believe space of literature, readers share the freedom of repressed wishes (for instance, a story in which a youth cleverly undermines an authority's command), but once the story ends they return to the restraints of social life. What would be upsetting in real life is pleasurable in fantasy life. Although the interpretation of literature as bits of fantasy yielding vicarious pleasure often yields predictable interpretations and foregone Freudian conclusions, handled judiciously psychological criticism sometimes provides explanations of creativity and the power of certain works that other schools of criticism cannot.

Since Freud's time, psychological criticism has become at once more eclectic and less formulaic. Carl Gustav Jung's **mythological criticism** was an early rival of Freudian thinking, and, more recently, **reader-response criticism** has drawn attention to the psychological mechanisms at work in the reader. The work of French psychoanalyst Jacques Lacan has been tremendously influential in Anglo-American literary theory since the late-Sixties, in part because Lacan set the acquisition of language at the center of psychic development, thus making every work of literature a psychically-meaningful statement.

Opposition to psychological criticism has come from many sides. The decline of Freud's reputation among clinicians and professional psychologists has hampered the prestige of Freudian interpretation, and the many instances of reductive, simplistic conversions of complex texts into routine psychic problems has annoyed literary critics sensitive to historical contexts and formal traits. Despite the attacks, however, psychological criticism of literature is bound to continue as long as psychology thrives as an academic discipline and a professional field. (*See also* **Literary theory**.)

Pulp fiction   A type of formulaic and hastily-produced fiction originally distributed in cheap mass circulation magazines. The term *pulp* refers to the inexpensive wood-pulp paper developed in the mid-nineteenth century on which these magazines were printed. Most pulp fiction journals printed melodramatic genre pieces—westerns, science fiction, romance, horror, adventure tales, and crime stories.

Pun   A play on words in which one word is substituted for another similar or identical sound, but of very different meaning. Shakespeare, a chronic punster, plays on his own name in Sonnet 135 (1609):

> Whoever hath her wish, thou hast thy Will,
> And Will to boot, and Will in overplus . . .

In *Romeo and Juliet* (1596) as Mercutio lies dying from a stab wound, Romeo assures him "the hurt cannot be much." Mercutio replies with a pun on "grave": "No, 'tis not so deep as a well, nor so wide as a church-door. But 'tis enough, 'twill serve. Ask for me to-morrow, and you shall find me a grave man" (III.i). In *Hamlet* (1601) when Claudius calls him into the light, Hamlet replies, "I am too much i' th' sun" (I.ii.67), a not-so-subtle remark upon his sense of filial responsibility. Although Shakespeare and other canonical writers indulge in puns, many critics have found it an inferior practice. Eighteenth-century critic Samuel Johnson considered punning Shakespeare's chief defect, and nineteenth-century essayist Charles Lamb called a pun a "pistol let off at the ear; not a feather to tickle the intellect"—that is, a blunt and easy joke.

Purgation   *See Katharsis.*

Quantitative meter   A meter constructed on the principle of vowel length rather than stress. Such quantities are difficult to hear in English, whose meters are based upon a syllable's intensity, not its duration. Classical Greek and Latin poetry is scanned in quantitative meters. (*See also* **Accentual meter**.)

Quatrain   A stanza consisting of four lines—for example, the **ballad stanza**. The quatrain is the most common stanza form used in English-language poetry.

Rap   A popular style of music that emerged in the 1980s, in which lyrics are spoken or chanted over a steady beat, usually sampled or prerecorded. Rap lyrics are almost always rhymed and jarringly repetitive, articulating crude phrases over a heavy, syncopated rhythm. Originally an African American form, rap is now international, a popular poetry that mingles adolescent protest, street slang, and irreverence:

> With vice I hold the mike device
> With force I keep it away of course
> And I'm keepin' you from sleepin'
> And on the stage I rage
> And I'm rollin'
> To the poor, I pour it on in metaphors
> No bluffin', it's nothin'
> We ain't did before.
> (Public Enemy, "Prophets of Rage"; 1988)

Reader-response criticism   The practice of analyzing a literary work by describing what happens in the reader's mind as he or she assimilates the text. A school of criticism popular in the Seventies and Eighties, reader-response criticism assumes that no literary text exists independently of readers' interpretations, and that there is no single fixed interpretation of any literary work. Reading is a transaction of text and mind, the latter a subjectivity bringing dispositions, memories, habits, tastes, and beliefs to bear upon all its experiences. Because no two readers read alike, reader-response criticism recognizes the inevitable plurality of readings, treating reading as a creative process just as writing is a creative process. When an idiosyncratic interpretation comes along, David Bleich maintains, it reveals "not an error, but an important form of individuated perception created by the particular biases of the reader." As Oscar Wilde remarked in the preface to *The Picture of Dorian Gray* (1891), "It is the spectator, and not life, that art really mirrors."

Reader-response criticism invokes common experience to back up its premises. A book one read as an adolescent often fails to impress the same reader many years later. The character one initially emulated now seems less admirable, while another character formerly disliked seems sympathetic. Likewise, the same book may appear entirely different to people of different backgrounds and cultures. A suburban teenager is likely to interpret a text quite differently than a middle-aged Native American. While other schools of criticism try to arbitrate these differences by appealing to the evidence of the text, reader-response critics preserve these differences, indeed, treating them as fundamental aspects of the text. The difficulty with such an approach, of course, is that it resists the selection of one interpretation over another—which is a necessary act in disciplinary settings (classrooms, editorial offices, etc.). In leveling interpretations to, precisely, "reader response," reader response criticism takes away the criteria of judgment that teachers, scholars, and editors need in order to carry out their work of grading, peer review, and manuscript acceptance.

Realism   An attempt to reproduce faithfully the surface appearance of life, especially that of ordinary people in everyday situations. As a literary term, *realism* has two meanings, one general, the other historical. In a general sense, realism refers to the representation of characters, events, and settings in ways that the spectator will consider plausible. The setting is common and the characters are consistent, recognizable types. This sort of realism does not necessarily depend on elaborate factual description or documentation but more on the author's ability to draft plots and characters within a conventional framework of social, economic, and psychological reality. Fantastical and supernatural plots and unusual personages are excluded, as are strange situations and extreme emotional states. What happens in the narrative should be the kind of thing that happens in real life.

In a historical sense, Realism (usually capitalized) refers to a movement in nineteenth-century European and American literature and theater that rejected the idealism, elitism, and romanticism of earlier verse dramas and prose fiction in an attempt to represent life truthfully. Realist literature customarily focused on the middle class (and occasionally the working class) rather than the aristocracy, and it invoked social customs and economic detail to create an accurate description of ordinary human behavior. It considered **romance** mere escapism, and eschewed **sentimentality** as a phony intensification of ordinary circumstances to teary levels. Realism began in France with Honoré de Balzac, Stendhal, Gustave Flaubert, and Guy de Maupassant, and then spread throughout the world. Other major Realists include Leo Tolstoy, William Dean Howells, Anton Chekhov, and Thomas Hardy.

Critics of Realism judged it both tedious and limited. "Why read a book portraying real life when you can observe real life by riding a train?" they asked, and writer Ambroise Bierce defined realism as "The art of depicting nature as seen by toads." But Howells insisted that the effort to put ordinary life and people into literature wasn't as simple as it seemed. A character in his realist novel *The Rise of Silas Lapham* (1885) declares:

> Commonplace? The commonplace is just that light, impalpable, aerial essence which they've never got into their confounded books yet. The novelist who could interpret the common feelings of commonplace people would have the answer to "the riddle of the painful earth" on his tongue.

Recognition   In the plotting of tragedy, the moment of recognition occurs when ignorance gives way to knowledge, illusion to disillusion. As described in Aristotle's *Poetics*, this is usually a disclosure of blood ties or kinship between persons involved in grave actions and consequent suffering. According to Aristotle, the ideal moment of recognition coincides with *peripeteia* or reversal of fortune. The classic example takes place in *Oedipus*, when Oedipus discovers that he had unwittingly and inadvertently killed his own father when defending himself at the crossroads, and that he later married his own mother when assuming the Theban throne. A less structured moment of recognition occurs in the *Star Wars* films when Luke Skywalker and Princess Lea learn they are siblings, and comedic recognition takes place in Henry Fielding's *Tom Jones* (1749), when Tom is revealed as Squire Allworthy's illegitimate nephew and is saved from the gallows. Such turnabouts, Aristotle argued, should emerge from the internal contents of the action, not from external agents such as the *deus ex machina*. (*See also* **Hamartia, Katharsis.**)

Refrain   A word, phrase, line, or stanza repeated at intervals in a song or poem. The chorus of popular songs, when all the musicians in the group voice recurring lines ("His soul is marching on," "John Brown's Body"), is a version of refrain. A refrain may appear as a consistent part of the verse, as in Edmund Spenser's "Prothalamion" (1596), a poem written in 18-line stanzas whose final line is "Sweete Themmes runne softly, till I end my song." The lines:

> With my sharp heel I three times mark the ground,
> And turn me thrice around, around around . . .

appear in John Gay's "Thursday; Or, The Spell" (from *The Shepherd's Week*, 1714) at the end of each verse paragraph, although the paragraphs have inconsistent lengths. Additionally, a refrain need not appear in the same position, but may be a line echoed at numerous but random points in the poem, as in Section II of T. S. Eliot's *The Waste Land* (1922), in which a barman cries out four separate times, "HURRY UP PLEASE ITS TIME."

Regionalism   The literary representation of a specific locale that incorporates the particulars of geography, custom, history, folklore, and speech into the work. In regional narratives, the locale plays a crucial role in the presentation and progression of a story that could not be moved to another setting without artistic loss. Usually, regional narratives take place at some distance from the literary capital of a culture, often in small towns or rural areas. Part of the significance of regional literature lies in its representation of, precisely, a region—the landscape, the weather, the atmosphere, the lingo, the people. That is, the work stands not only as a fictional creation with interesting characters, but also as a representation of a real place, often one with a colorful heritage and unique culture. Prominent examples of American regionalism are Kate Chopin's Louisiana, Willa Cather's Western plains, William Faulkner's Yoknapatawpha County (Missippippi), and (an urban example) Raymond Chandler's Los Angeles. (*See also* **Local color.**)

Resolution The final part of a narrative, the concluding action that follows the climax. Resolutions play a structural role in the plot in that they mark a period of reflection upon the preceding events, a determination of their consequences. There is little further action, and no new knowledge is introduced. At the end of Shakespeare's *Othello* (1604), for instance, after Othello has killed Desdemona and tried to kill Iago, Lodovico cries out:

> O thou Othello that wert once so good,
> Fall'n in the practice of a damned slave,
> What shall be said of thee?
>   (V.ii)

The summary question is a sign of resolution. Although Othello stabs himself moments later, the tensions of the plot have been settled: Iago is exposed as a liar, Desdemona as virtuous, Cassio as loyal, and Othello as a dupe. All is clear, and Othello has fallen. Now it is time to ponder the significance of his error. (*See also* **Conclusion**, **Dénouement**.)

Restoration Period In English literary history, the period following the restoration of Charles II to the throne in 1660 and extending to 1700 (even though Charles died in 1685). Having spent much of his youth in exile in France while the Puritan Commonwealth governed England—his father Charles I was executed; he barely escaped capture—Charles returned to the throne bringing Continental literary tastes and sexual mores with him. Among the social changes the restored monarchy wrought was the reopening of the theaters, which the Puritans had shut down because they believed drama was impious and sinful. The success of the theaters led to the emergence of Restoration Comedy, a **comedy of manners** genre that emphasized sexual gamesmanship, urbane wit, and loose morality. The novelist Henry Thackeray termed it "That miserable, rouged, tawdry, sparkling, hollow-hearted comedy of the Restoration," but despite its perceived whimsy, Restoration Comedy has delighted audiences from its inception to our own time.

Alongside the revived stage during the Restoration was a fresh outburst of satire, its leading lights being John Dryden and John Wilmot, Earl of Rochester. Rochester's "Impromptu on Charles II" (pub. 1707) imparts well the biting satiric tenor of the age:

> God bless our good and gracious King,
>   Whose promise none relies on;
> Who never said a foolish thing,
>   Nor ever did a wise one.

Literature was centered on London life and the British Court—Dryden's great poem "Absalom and Achitophel" (1681) is a clever study of challenges to Charles's sovereignty by one of his sons—and the era signaled a new public literature geared toward active theatergoers and an increasing middle-class readership.

Retrospect   *See* **Flashback**.

Reversal   *See* **Peripeteia**.

Rhetoric   The art of eloquence and persuasion. As a discipline of study, rhetoric dates back to ancient Greek civilization and was employed in areas ranging from the training of lawyers to the assessment of a politician's moral nature. Since Aristotle, scholars have broken rhetoric up into three parts: *logos*, the logical content of a verbal expression; *ethos*, the character of the speaker as derived from the words and the speaker's reputation; and *pathos*, the emotional appeal of the words. Because of the power of the latter two—rhetoric often succeeds not by its logic but by its ethical and emotional pull—rhetorical analysis usually concentrates upon aspects of language that are the least based upon reasoning: **anecdotes**, logical fallacies, **figures of speech**, **rhythms**, and intonations. Rhetoricians in ancient times composed manuals of composition instructing readers in verbal techniques of persuasion such as the skillful employment of **irony**. The biographer Plutarch reports that the great orator Demosthenes improved his voice by placing pebbles in his mouth while practicing his speeches. Renaissance and seventeenth-century rhetoricians compiled taxonomies of figures of speech, and twentieth-century scholars interpreted rhetoric as a complex social behavior involving speaker, audience, situation, and language. Today's theorists of rhetoric seek to dispel the analysis of rhetoric as an ornamental "dress" for an abstract content, a known meaning that is cloaked in persuasive stories and clever metaphors. Instead, they insist, all verbal behavior has a rhetorical side that is often just as functional to the significance of a statement as is the knowledge it "contains."

Rhyme, Rime   Two or more words that contain an identical or similar vowel sound, usually accented, with following consonant sounds (if any) identical as well: *queue* and *stew, prairie schooner* and *piano tuner, stayed in school* and *played in school*. Such repetitions, be they **internal rhyme** (in the middle of a line) or **end rhyme** (at the end of consecutive lines), produce an organization of rhythm and meaning. In effect, two words or phrases that rhyme become linked, and the lines in which they appear fall into a discrete unit. The **heroic couplet** is a clear instance, for the rhyme sets the verse into two-line pieces and makes each pair incline toward a discrete statement:

> Some have for wits, then poets passed,
> Turned critics next, and proved plain fools at last.
> Some neither can for wits nor critics pass,
> As heavy mules are neither horse nor ass.
> (Alexander Pope, *An Essay on Criticism*, ll. 36–39; 1711)

Skillful rhymes are surprising and varied. For instance, the rhyme of noun with noun is less effective than rhyme of noun and verb, and a rhyme made of two abstract ideas (say, *suspension* with *dimension*) or of two overtly connected things (*cherubim* and *seraphim*) sounds easy and glib. The two rhyming words must differ enough grammatically and semantically to make an interesting conjunction, and yet not so much that the rhyme appears strained. This decorum of rhyme has a secondary aspect in that it provides opportunities for writers to mismatch words and ideas for ironic effect. Lord Byron's rumination in *Don Juan* (1819–24) on his young hero's lovestruck condition relies on **doggerel** rhymes to work its humor:

> Young Juan wandered by the glassy brooks,
>   Thinking unutterable things; he threw
> Himself at length within the leafy nooks
>   Where the wild branch of the cork forest grew;
> There poets find materials for their books,
>   And every now and then we read them through,
> So that their plan and prosody are eligible,
> Unless, like Wordsworth, they prove unintelligible.
>   (I.xc)

The words *eligible* and *unintelligible* form an unimaginative coupling, as if Byron wrote them off the top of his head. And yet the triviality of the rhyme manages to underscore the jab at Wordsworth. Indecorous rhyme may also serve serious purposes, as in "The Love Song of J. Alfred Prufrock" (1915), when T. S. Eliot rhymes the profound with the trivial to impart Prufrock's wavering temperament:

> I grow old . . . I grow old . . .
> I shall wear the bottoms of my trousers rolled.
>   (T. S. Eliot, "The Love Song of J. Alfred Prufrock"; 1915)

(*See also* **Consonance, Exact rhyme, Eye rhyme, Slant rhyme.**)

Rhyme scheme, Rime scheme   The pattern of rhyme in an individual poem or a fixed form. A rhyme scheme is transcribed with small letters representing each end rhyme —*a* for the first rhyme, *b* for the second, and so on. The rhyme scheme of a stanza of **common meter**, for example, is notated as *abab* and is a fundamental structuring mechanism of the form.

Rhythm   The pattern of stresses and pauses in a poem. A fixed and recurring rhythm establishes the **meter**, while the pace of the rhythm and the strength of the beats help determine the **tone** of the work. (*See also* **Prosody.**)

Rising action   That part of the play or narrative in which events start moving toward a climax. In the rising action the protagonist typically begins to engage the complications of the plot and speed it to decisive moments. In *Hamlet* (1601), the rising action develops as the conflict between Hamlet and Claudius comes to a head, with Hamlet succeeding in controlling the course of events. Because the mainspring of the play's first half is the mystery of Claudius's guilt, the rising action reaches its height when Hamlet proves the king's guilt by the device of the play within a play (III.ii—the "mousetrap" scene). Sometimes, however, the rising action is precipitated unintentionally by a character. In Jean-Baptiste Racine's *Phèdre* (1677), the play's **conflict** lies in the forbidden love that Phèdre, wife of the absent Thésée, feels for her stepson Hyppolytus. In an awkward encounter, Phèdre discloses her passion to Hyppolytus and he recoils in shock. The action "rises" and moves swiftly to its conclusion. Rebuffed, Phèdre tells her returning husband Thésée that his son has violated her. Refusing to deny the charge, Hyppolytus is banished by his father and soon killed by a monster sent by Neptune. Phèdre takes her own life, and the play ends. (*See also* **Falling action.**)

Rising meter   A meter whose movement rises from an unstressed syllable (or syllables) to a stressed syllable (for-*get*, De-*troit*, by the *car*, inter-*act*). Iambic and anapestic are examples of rising meter, rhythms that gain strength in the latter part of the metrical feet. It is important to remember, however, that the "rise" applies only to force of pronunciation, not to the meaning or tone imparted by the words. (*See also* **Meter.**)

Romance   In broad terms, romance is a narrative that employs exotic adventure and lofty emotion rather than realistic depiction of character and action. In the romance (out of which most popular genre fictions developed) people, ideas, and events are depicted in fanciful, idealized ways—heroes are very brave, villains are very villainous, beliefs and feelings are all-powerful—and plots incorporate mysterious figures and extraordinary forces. Romance originated in medieval tales in both prose and verse such as those based on Arthurian legends (for example, the *Morte d'Arthur* [1485] borrows from romance narratives), stories that presented chivalric tales of kings, knights, ladies, and the passions that overcome them. Love (both licit and illicit) is the central **motivation**, and how characters respond to it is the central **conflict**. Weaving Christian doctrine with heroic subject matters, medieval romances follow what today we recognize as familiar **motifs**: an Arthurian knight searching for the Holy Grail, young lovers separated by bizarre circumstance and finally reunited, a hero or heroine's virtue tested, carnal love subordinated to or displacing Christian love. Elements of medieval romance have continued to modern times in works such as Sir Walter Scott's *Ivanhoe* (1820), Lord Tennyson's *Idylls of the King* (1859–85), Walker Percy's *Lancelot* (1977), and the *Star Wars* films, but in general, modern romances curtail the idealized characters and supernatural settings. On one hand, as in Nathaniel Hawthorne's *The House of the Seven Gables* (1851), the symbolic quests and elevated characters of earlier, chivalric romances are skillfully adapted to more realistic and morally-complex conditions. On the other hand, in popular romance novels and movies, love plots are simplified into formulaic patterns, and their resolution turns upon not a difficult moral test but a sentimental assertion of feeling or a physically-difficult but morally-simple triumph over an antagonist. (*See also* **Realism**.)

Romantic comedy   A type of comic drama in which the plot focuses on one or more pairs of young lovers who overcome difficulties—an unapproving parent, a class difference, their own pride—to achieve a happy ending, usually marriage. Whereas other types of drama often involve the same kinds of conflicts and characters, romantic comedy maintains them as largely circumstantial, as utterly human creations, not the result of fate or moral law. For example, Oliver Goldsmith's *She Stoops to Conquer* (1773) ends with the joyous marriage of two couples. Leading up to their union, however, is a series of mistaken identities, parental interference, and class conflicts, those due to the trickery, obstinacy, and prejudices of the characters. Many of Shakespeare's comedies are romantic in conception, as in *A Midsummer Night's Dream* (1595), *As You Like It* (1598), and *Twelfth Night* (1600), where lovers, clowns, young women in disguise, dukes, and divided siblings frolic in fanciful realms hoping to win the devotion of a beloved. Never do the hindrances appear anything more than the result of human frailty and misconceptions. Because the consequences of them are comical, we laugh at them, knowing that an adjustment in the social scene (for instance, a change in a character's attitude, the introduction of an authority figure) may eventually overcome them. (*See also* **Comedy**, **Sentimentality**.)

Romantic Period   In English literary history, the Romantic Period covers the years starting with the French Revolution in 1789 and ending in the early 1830s with the deaths of Samuel Taylor Coleridge and Sir Walter Scott and the passage of the Reform Bill in Parliament. As traditionally understood, the Romantic Period is dominated by six poets: William Blake, William Wordsworth, Coleridge, Lord Byron, Percy Bysshe Shelley, and John Keats. Broader treatments include the political writers William Godwin and Mary Wollstonecraft, novelists Sir Walter Scott, Jane Austen, and Mary Shelley, and essayists William Hazlitt and Charles Lamb.

   As a European movement encompassing the arts, philosophy, cosmology, politics, and the social sciences, the term *romanticism* is applied to a loose collection of ideas about human nature, modern society, political systems, and artistic practice, plus, of course, the artworks that embody them. In the nineteenth century, the shadow of Romanticism hung over novelists, poets, thinkers, critics, and social theorists as an astonishing "burst of creative activity," as Victorian writer Matthew Arnold put it. During the twentieth century, critics and historians of ideas debated the meaning and value of Romanticism at length, and dozens of definitions, eulogies, and vilifications of the movement appeared. In a famous essay "On the Discrimination of Romanticisms" (1924), historian of ideas A. O. Lovejoy observed that Romanticism has been credited with the French Revolution, the Return to a State of Nature, the philosophies of Hegel and Nietzsche, Ralph Waldo Emerson's transcendentalism, Oscar Wilde's aestheticism, and so on. His survey showed that sometimes romanticism is defined in historical terms, tied to historical events such as the storming of the Bastille; other times, Romanticism is cast as a psychology of human nature that focuses on the individual self. Other conceptions in terms of aesthetics, politics, and philosophy are equally prevalent, and to explain them all is to uncover contradictions and generalities in the -ism that will not be resolved. A basic catalogue of Romantic notions includes:

1. An insistence on the value of nature, as opposed to the value of rationality and scientific inquiry: Romanticism posits a vision of nature and spirit shrouded in sublime mystery and therapeutic power. Whereas modern science demystifies nature as material elements following laws of physics and chemistry, romantic writers regard nature as a life-giving source of mystical joy and moral nobility. Blake dismisses "The Atoms of Democritus / And Newton's Particles of light" ("Mock On, Mock On, Voltaire, Rousseau," ca. 1800) as impoverished visions of existence, while Wordsworth counsels:

    > . . . move along these shades
    > In gentleness of heart; with gentle hand
    > Touch—for there is a spirit in the woods.
    > ("Nutting"; 1800)

2. An emphasis on the individual ego: Romantic figures postulate their own private being as a special entity transcending the normal run of humanity. Lord Byron's title character Manfred asserts his own personal drama against the vast workings of the universe:

    > I disdained to mingle with
    > A herd, though to be a leader—and of wolves.
    > The lion is alone, and so am I.
    > (*Manfred*, III.i; 1817)

3. On the other hand, Romanticism is a sensibility of pure imagination, an attitude rendered clearly in the letters of Keats. There, Keats imagines the poetic temper as the opposite of egotism, whereby the poet is able to imagine himself or herself as another existence: "because [the poet] has no Identity—he is continually in for—and filling some other body." To have a life of sensations rather than of thoughts is the height of inspiration.

4. In aesthetics, Romanticism takes the solitary creative imagination as the source of art. Art is primarily an expression of one person's vision and experience, and tradition and authority are to be subordinated to the real lives of individuals and the transcendent scope of the artist.

5. In politics, Romanticism insists upon an egalitarian vision of society, despite its elevation of the artist-figure. The central political event of Romanticism is the French Revolution, which Romantics hailed as the downfall of aristocracy and the promise of democratic reform. It went along with what is, according to the early-twentieth-century critic/poet T. E. Hulme, a fundamental romantic tenet: "man was by nature good, that it was only bad laws and customs that suppressed him. Remove all these and the infinite possibilities of man would have a chance" ("Romanticism and Classicism"; 1924).

Rondel [ron–DEL] A French late-medieval verse form that became popular in English poetry in the late-nineteenth century. The rondel has had slight variations in structure over the centuries, but generally it is a thirteen- or fourteen-line poem consisting of three stanzas built on two rhymes (one feminine, one masculine) and linked by a refrain. H. Austin Dobson's "The Wanderer" (1880) is a strictly-observed example:

Love comes back to his vacant dwelling,—	a	
The old, old Love that we knew of yore!	b	(a two-line refrain)
We see him stand by the open door,	b	
With his great eyes sad, and his bosom swelling.	a	
He makes as though in our arms repelling	a	
He fain would lie as he lay before;—	b	
Love comes back to his vacant dwelling—	a	
The old, old Love that we knew of yore!	b	(lines 1–2 repeat)
Ah! Who shall help us from over-spelling	a	
That sweet forgotten, hidden lore?	b	
E'en as we doubt in our hearts once more,	b	
With a rush of tears to our eyelids welling,	a	
Love comes back to his vacant dwelling.	a	(line 1 repeats)

Round character A term coined by English novelist E. M. Forster to describe a complex character who is presented in depth and detail in a narrative. While **flat characters** remain constant, round characters change significantly during the course of a narrative. In Kate Chopin's novel *The Awakening* (1899), Edna Pontellier develops from a subservient wife and mother into an independent woman free to explore her sexuality and her artistic talents. Her husband remains the same throughout the novel, an obtuse and insensitive patriarch. She is round, he is flat. In one scene, just after they have quarreled about the care of their children, the narration probes her feelings in depth, but maintains a surface vision of him.

> An indescribable oppression, which seemed to generate in some unfamiliar part of her consciousness, filled her whole being with a vague anguish. It was like a shadow, like a mist passing across her soul's summer day. It was strange and unfamiliar; it was a mood. . . .
> The following morning Mr. Pontellier was up in good time to take the rockaway which was to convey him to the steamer at the wharf. He was returning to the city to his business, and they would not see him again at the Island till the coming Saturday. He had regained his composure, which seemed to have been somewhat impaired the night before.

(*See also* **Characterization**.)

Sarcasm   A simple, often nasty or bitter form of **irony** in which the ironic statement is designed to mock its target by blunt exaggeration or understatement, or by contemptuous imitation. Sarcasm implies blank disrespect, as if the target of sarcasm were hardly worth the effort of ridicule (hence the bluntness). Because of its "low" nature, sarcasm is unsuited to high, heroic genres such as **epic** and **tragedy**, and is more common in **burlesque**, caricature, etc. In serious works of literature, sarcasm thrives generally as the outlook of a minor character, or as a brief expression of disgust that the reader has come to share in the course of the work. For example, in Ernest Hemingway's novel *The Sun Also Rises* (1926), Jake Barnes and Brett Ashley seem to love each other, but Jake has been rendered impotent by a war wound and Brett engages in a series of love affairs. At the end of the novel, Jake and Brett drive through the streets in a taxi and Brett whispers to him, "Oh, Jake, we could have had such a damned good time together." By now, Jake is repulsed by the whole situation, and even wonders whether Brett only loves him because she can't have him. The final line of the novel is his sarcastic rejoinder: "Yes. . . . Isn't it pretty to think so?"

Satire   A genre using derisive humor to mock human pretense and vice, or to censure social and political follies and incompetence. Satire has been practiced for millennia, from the ancient Greeks to the great age of English satire (late-seventeenth and early-eighteenth centuries) to our own time, and it remains a constant tool of moral judgment. The tone of satire ranges from detached amusement to unremitting contempt, depending on the anger with which satirists regard their subject. It is the art of the ridiculous, blending criticism and humor with varying degrees of spite and mischief, **irony** being its chief tool.

The moment we read the opening lines from John Dryden's *Absalom and Achitophel* (1681), we know we are in the realm of satiric commentary:

> In pious times, ere priestcraft did begin,
> Before polygamy was made a sin;
> When man on many multiplied his kind,
> Ere one to one was cursedly confin'd . . .

Each line contains a sly sally. First, Dryden implies that piety preceded priestcraft, and that the latter undermines the former; second, polygamy is said to be *made* a sin, as if in a natural world polygamy is just as upright as monogamy; third, marriage is asserted to be a "curse."

The lines are irreverent and witty, but satirists often claim a moral basis for their mockery, puncturing vanity, greed, and other moral traits in the name of reform and elevation. In Book III of Jonathan Swift's *Gulliver's Travels* (1726), Gulliver visits a fantasy city in the clouds presided over by scientists and mathematicians who revere rational calculation and deductive reasoning. The narrative is satiric in that, however brilliant they are, the residents are so abstract in their thought that they can't concentrate upon what lies before their eyes, and they neglect the concrete needs of human contact. They require a servant to tap them when someone speaks to them, else they remain absorbed in their mental ruminations.

Swift's satire is bitter and endless, and few of his characters escape his withering scrutiny. Other works of satire are more comic, with the bearers of vices exposed and punished over the course of the plot. In Aristophanes's *The Clouds* (423 B.C.E.), a man whose son has burdened him with debt attends a school of philosophy thinking that learning the arts of logic will improve his son's morals and help the father outwit his creditors. What follows is a cutting and hilarious portrayal of sophistry, the direct object of the attack being the teacher Socrates, a figure quite distinct from the sage hero of Plato's dialogues. Socrates's instruction fails with the father, but succeeds with the son, who learns to justify any evil (including his debts) with specious reasoning and threatens to beat his mother. That is the sum of Socratic education. The play ends with the father taking revenge by burning the school to the ground.

What makes these works satiric is that beneath the literary features of **plot**, **character**, **setting**, and so on, is a moral design. They entertain, but they also impart an instruction, or at least a message, regarding the human condition. True, the pleasure they give may originate in malice, and the targets of satire feel its sting (the people of whom Alexander Pope drew mocking portraits never forgave him), but the rage behind satire is usually attributable to the respect satirists have for the ideals their subjects have violated.

Satyr play [SAY–ter] A type of comic play in ancient Greece commonly performed after the tragedies at the City Dionysia, the principal civic and religious festival of Athens. The playwrights winning the right to stage their works in the festival wrote three tragedies and one satyr play to form the traditional tetralogy, or group of four. The structure of a satyr play was similar to the structure of tragedy. Its subject matter, treated in **burlesque**, was drawn from myth or the epic cycles, and its **chorus** was composed of satyrs (half-human and half-horse or half-goat) under the leadership of Silenus, the adoptive father of Dionysius. Rascals and revelers, satyrs represented wild versions of humanity, opposing the values of civilized men. Euripides's *Cyclops* (ca. 450 B.C.E.) is the only complete surviving example of the genre.

Scansion [SCAN–shen] A method of **prosody** that measures rhythms in a poem, scansion separates the metrical feet, counts the syllables, marks the accented ones, and indicates the pauses. Taking the line of verse,

/ / / / / (stresses marked with /)
Since you ask, most days I cannot remember . . .
(Anne Sexton, "Wanting to Die"; 1964)

scansion marks eleven syllables, a feminine ending, one pause, etc. Scansion is a basic feature of any description of a poem, revealing a poet's handling of **rhythm**, verse length, and sound. It trains the ear, making explicit the cadences that they register implicitly as they sound out the lines.

Scene In drama, the term *scene* denotes two things. First, the scene is the physical setting of the play, drawn, painted, or modeled three-dimensionally. Second, the scene is the subdivision of **acts** in a play, in which no change of place or time occurs. There is no universal convention as to what constitutes a scene, and the practice differs by playwright and period. Usually, though, a scene represents a single dramatic action that helps fill out the **dramatic situation** or build up the **climax** (through its own subclimax). Scenes often end in the entrance or exit of a major character. So-called "French scenes," for example, are marked by the entrance of a new character that changes the subject matter and shifts the direction of the story as a part of the progressive unfolding of the **plot**.

Selective omniscience [awm–NISH–ints] The point of view that has the capacity to know everything that transpires in a narrative, but chooses to see them through the eyes of a single character. The narrator of Henry James's novel *The Portrait of a Lady* (1881), for example, focuses upon a single character, Isabel Archer, rendering her first impressions and private thoughts with detail and nuance. Although the novel maintains a third-person distance toward Isabel and follows other characters at times, the narration remains centered on her perspective. (*See also* **Narrator, Point of view.**)

Semantics Semantics is the study of meaning, usually the province of linguists and philosophers of language. As applied to literary study, semantics ponders the difference between the denotative and connotative meanings of words, the influence of context on those meanings, and how they function in fiction and poetry. Critic I. A. Richards drew an important semantic distinction when he divides meaning into four kinds (*Practical Criticism*, 1929). First, he names "sense"—the thing we wish to say; second comes "feeling"—the attitude we take toward the sense; third is "tone"—the attitude we have toward our audience; and fourth is "intention"—the effect we wish to promote. Richards's point is that sometimes one meaning stands out, sometimes another. In a scientific treatise, which requires objectivity, sense is emphasized and feeling suppressed, for lab reports and the like are supposed to be contributions to knowledge, not expressions of opinion. But in poetry, Richards argued, the opposite is the case. Feeling takes priority: "many, if not most, of the statements in poetry are there *as a means* to the manipulation and expression of feelings and attitudes." Hence the semantics of poetry tend to highlight the emotional "coloring" of the words, not the literal, referential aspects of them. (*See also* **Hermeneutics**.)

Semiotics As opposed to **semantics**, which studies meanings (that is, the things which signs signify), semiotics examines the signs themselves—their structure, their mode of signification, their interrelations, etc. Conceived in the late-nineteenth century by American philosopher Charles Sanders Peirce, semiotics expands the analysis of signs beyond verbal signs alone to include any phenomenon that points toward some meaning or other object. A high temperature may be treated as the sign of a disease, the relationship between sign and meaning being a causal one. Or, a flag may be treated as the sign of a nation, the relationship being one in which a recognized authority stipulated at a certain historical moment that the flag represent the sovereign power of the State. It is the signifying surface that counts, and the way in which it functions in a signifying system (such as the system of symptoms and their medical diagnosis). The work of semiotics involves cataloguing signs by their operations, determining the relation between a sign and its meaning, and extrapolating the rules by which a sign system works.

Sentimental comedy In eighteenth-century English theater, a genre developing out of the middle-class reaction against the immoral situations and indecent language of Restoration comedy. Eliciting neither laughter nor ridicule, sentimental comedies, such as Sir Richard Steele's *The Conscious Lovers* (1722), tried to inculcate noble feelings by depicting trials bravely suffered by sympathetic characters that are rescued and rewarded. Inspired by the Enlightenment belief in the essential moral goodness of human nature, sentimental comedies sought to arouse the audience's finer sentiments with the sight of virtue in distress, villains chastened by their own vice, and conflicts resolved through a simple assertion of love, generosity, faith, and sympathy. Contemporary writer Oliver Goldsmith regarded it as a simplistic, formulaic genre:

It is only sufficient to raise the characters a little; to deck out the hero with a riband, or give the heroine a title; then to put an insipid dialogue, without character or humour, into their mouths, give them mighty good hearts, very fine clothes, furnish a new set of scenes, make a pathetic scene or two, with a sprinkling of tender melancholy conversation through the whole . . . ("Essay on the Theatre; or, A Comparison between Sentimental and Laughing Comedy"; 1773)

(*See also* **Comedy, Sentimentality.**)

Sentimentality A literary work that tries to convey the finer emotions but fails to provide sufficient grounds within the work for them. In a typical sentimental plot, human conflicts are resolved not through the inner workings and interactions of the force in conflict—say, two friends in love with the same woman—but through the invocation of a standard emotion external to the plot—in this case, fraternal devotion—one putatively honored by the characters, the author, and the reader-audience. The real ingredients of the conflict—the rivalry of desires—is never authentically engaged. Instead, it is dissipated by an assertion of conventional sentiment. For this reason, many writers and critics have found something false about sentimentality. Poet Wallace Stevens remarked, "Sentimentality is the failure of feeling," and novelist D. H. Lawrence said, "Sentimentalism is the working off on yourself of feelings you haven't really got."

Sestet A poem, stanza, or unit of six lines of verse. The term usually applies to **Italian sonnets** to indicate the final six-line section of the poem, as distinct from the **octave** (the first eight lines). Other than the sonnet, British and American writers have infrequently opted for a six-line stanza structure. Elizabeth Bishop's "The Moose" (1976) is an interesting example, with twenty-eight sestet stanzas in a curious rhyme scheme *abcbdc*:

> From narrow provinces
> of fish and bread and tea,
> home of the long tides
> where the bay leaves the sea
> twice a day and takes
> the herrings long rides,
>
> where if the river
> enters or retreats
> in a wall of brown foam
> depends on if it meets
> the bay coming in,
> the bay not at home . . .

Sestina [ses–TEE–nuh] A complex verse form ("song of sixes"), in which six end words are repeated in a prescribed order through six stanzas. A sestina ends with an **envoy** of three lines in which all six words appear, making a total of thirty-nine lines. Originally composed by French and Italian poets, and occasionally adopted by English Renaissance writers (for example, Sir Philip Sidney's "Ye Goat-herd Gods," 1593), the sestina has become a popular modern form in English. For example, even though Diane Wakoski, in "Sestina to the Common Glass of Beer: I Do Not Drink Beer" (1976), creates irregular verse lengths, she follows the six-line/three-line envoy structure and sticks with the endings *sun*, *histories*, *perspective*, *daffodils*, *flashing*, and *beer*.

Setting   The time and place of a literary work. Most narrative works have identifiable settings, but the locale becomes important when it seems to acquire a more than circumstantial significance. In the opening of Joseph Conrad's story "The Secret Sharer" (1912), the description of the seascape is extensive enough to make the setting an independent element:

> On my right hand there were lines of fishing stakes resembling a mysterious system of half-submerged bamboo fences, incomprehensible in its division of the domain of tropical fishes, and crazy of aspect as if abandoned forever by some nomad tribe of fishermen now gone to the other end of the ocean; for there was no sign of human habitation as far as the eye could reach. To the left a group of barren eyelets suggesting ruins of stone walls . . .

The description continues for a long paragraph until it ends with "And then I was left alone with my ship, anchored in the Gulf of Siam." The vast detail establishes a relation between the narrator and the setting, specifically, the loneliness he feels and the emptiness of the seascape.

Setting may entail not only the physical environment of the work, but also the social, psychological, or spiritual state of the participants, if the latter prove to have a shaping effect on the former. For example, in Edgar Allan Poe's "The Fall of the House of Usher" (1839), the mental state of Roderick Usher is so intensely melancholic and morbid that it seems to emanate across the landscape. The first sentence goes: "During the whole of a dull, dark, and soundless day in the autumn of the year, when the clouds hung oppressively low in the heavens, I had been passing alone, on horseback, through a singularly dreary tract of country; and at length found myself, as the shades of the evening drew on, within view of the melancholy House of Usher." The description appears entirely physical, until the narrator enters the house and finds Usher wildly depressed, his mood spreading gloom and disquiet through the house and surrounding countryside. (*See also* **Regionalism**.)

Shakespearean sonnet   *See* **English sonnet**.

Short story   A prose narrative too brief to be published in a separate volume, as novellas and novels frequently are. The short story is a focused narrative that presents one or two main characters involved in a single compelling action. One of the originators of the modern short story, Edgar Allan Poe, made the concentration of the short story an essential component of the reading experience:

> in almost all classes of composition, the unity of effect or impression is a point of the greatest importance. It is clear, moreover, that this unity cannot be thoroughly preserved in productions whose perusal cannot be completed at one sitting . . .
> (Review of Nathaniel Hawthorne's *Twice-Told Tales*; 1842)

So, he concluded, the short prose narrative must entail no more than two hours of reading time. This requires the writer to establish **character** and **setting** with economy, and to speed the **plot** toward its **climax**. Although the short story has precursors in the ancient genres of **fable** and **parable**, its modern form begins in the nineteenth century and has proven one of the most popular literary genres of our time.

Simile   A major **figure of speech**, a simile is a comparison of two ostensibly unlike things, indicated by some connective, usually *like, as,* or *than.* An effective simile draws two things together, positing a resemblance that elucidates each thing in a fresh way. For example:

> The clouds were low and hairy in the skies,
> Like locks blown forward in the gleam of eyes . . .
> (Robert Frost, "Once by the Pacific"; 1928)

Unlike **metaphor, metonymy,** and **synecdoche,** however, which condense unlike things into a single verbal unit, simile often expands the comparison by elaborating the figurative side of the pairing. In another poem by Frost, "The Silken Tent" (1942), a simile begins with the first line:

> She is as in a field a silken tent
> At midday when a sunny summer breeze
> Has dried the dew and all its ropes relent,
> So that in guys it gently sways at ease . . .

For another ten lines Frost details the figurative "tent" side of the description, the central pole, the cords, the breeze, and the pinnacle, but says nothing literal about "She." Such extended comparisons, "epic similes," date back to Homer and are a basic technique epic poets use to achieve the grandiloquence of heroic verse.

Situational irony   *See* **Irony.**

Skene   [SKEE–nee] In classical Greek drama of the fifth century B.C.E., the temporary wooden stage building in which actors switched masks and costumes when changing roles. Its facade, with double center doors and possibly two side doors, served as the setting for action taking place before a palace, temple, cave, or other interior space.

Sketch   A short, static, descriptive composition. Either fictional or nonfictional, a sketch usually delineates a person or place with a minimum of narrative, providing a kind of snapshot of a person or place. The informality and transience of the sketch are neatly rendered in the prefatory note to Washington Irving's *Sketch Book of Geoffrey Crayon, Gent.* (1819–23):

> I have wandered through different countries and witnessed many of the shifting scenes of life. I cannot say I have studied them with the eye of a philosopher, but rather with the sauntering gaze with which humble lovers of the picturesque stroll from the window of one print shop to another; caught sometimes by the delineation of beauty, sometimes by the distortions of caricature and sometimes by the loveliness of landscape.

Slack syllable   An unstressed syllable in a line of verse. (*See also* **Prosody**, **Rhythm**.)

Slant rhyme   A rhyme in which the final consonant sounds are the same but the vowel sounds are different, as in letter and litter, bone and bean, priestess and justice. Slant rhyme may also be called *near rhyme*, *off rhyme*, or *imperfect rhyme*. Although slant rhyme fails to reach a complete rhyming sound, it should not be considered a flaw. Sometimes poets deliberately miss a perfect rhyme for reasons of effect or meaning, as in Stanza 6 of Hart Crane's "The Broken Tower" (1932):

> My word I poured. But was it cognate, scored
> Of that tribunal monarch of the air
> Whose thigh embronzes earth, strikes crystal Word
> In wounds pledged once to hope—cleft to despair?

Lines 2 and 4 make a perfect rhyme, lines 1 and 3 a slant rhyme. (*See also* **Consonance**.)

Slapstick comedy   A kind of **farce**, featuring pratfalls, pie throwing, fisticuffs, and other boisterous action. It takes its name originally from the stick carried by the *commedia dell'arte*'s main servant type, Harlequin, who slapped other characters with it.

Sociological criticism   The application of sociological methods to literary works. This entails studying empirically the social conditions in which the work was written and received. "Art is not created in a vacuum," critic Wilbur Scott observed, "it is the work not simply of a person, but of an author fixed in time and space, answering a community of which he is an important because articulate part." Adopting the premise that all art is socially-embedded, sociological critics explore such phenomena as the demographics of different readerships, the social influences on writers, the modes of publication prevailing at a given time, and the social status of different genres. Many sociologists have a Marxist orientation that leads them to emphasize the writer's financial position and the class relations represented in the literary work. The Hungarian philosopher Georg Lukacs maintained that art was class-based—that is, that it implicitly or explicitly expressed class structures and interests—and studied the **novel** in terms of bourgeois society. Others focus on social trends, such as the economic function of authorship and the changing relations of high and low culture. What ties sociologists of literature together is their belief that literary works are the result of social forces, that the forms and contents of art are explicable as direct and indirect representations of specific social factors. To study a Dickens novel, they would say, one must study the labor conditions of mid-nineteenth-century England. A sociological view of Shakespeare might look at the professional position of Elizabethan playwrights and actors, or at the varied tastes of Elizabethan theatergoers.

Handled judiciously (with sound empirical study of social forces), sociological criticism illuminates social, political, and economic dimensions of literature that other approaches overlook. It is hard to imagine a full understanding of any artwork that lacked a sociological element. But there is a danger in letting sociological criticism claim the entire meaning of art. In reducing the artwork to social influences, it downplays the aesthetic features of the work. Lukacs believed that all art is political in one way or another. Those works that appear apolitical only seem so because they enact the tacit politics of the time. But this assumption only holds if one reduces all forms of experience to political grounds. Many find religious, emotional, intellectual, and other meanings in literature and resist the conversion of them all into political values. Moreover, in converting the artwork into a social statement, critics sometimes proceed to turn criticism into a litmus test: those works that represent good social forces are good, those that represent bad forces are bad. Today's political correctness measures works of literature by their alignment with notions of social justice. Years ago sociological critics in the Soviet Union rated Jack London superior to William Faulkner, Ernest Hemingway, Edith Wharton, and Henry James, because he illustrated communist principles more clearly. London was America's first major working-class writer, but slighting other authors for lacking his sensitivities doesn't help us to understand *their* work. Nor does it tell us (entirely) why people of different classes and politics have enjoyed London's and the others' work for several generations. (*See also* **Literary theory.**)

Soliloquy [so–LIL–o–kwee] In drama, a speech by a character alone onstage in which he or she utters his or her thoughts aloud. The soliloquy is a crucial part of drama, as it imparts a character's inner life and private motivations. For example, Act I, Scene II of Shakespeare's *King Lear* (1605) opens with Edmund standing alone with a letter in hand. He announces, "Thou, Nature, art my goddess; to thy law / My services are bound." He continues for another twenty lines, spewing his resentment at being born a bastard until the entrance of his father ends his speech.

Sonnet   From the Italian *sonnetto* ("little song"), the sonnet is a traditional and widely-used verse form, especially popular for love poetry. A fixed form of four-teen lines, traditionally written in iambic pentameter, sonnets may be divided into an **octave** (the first eight lines) and a **sestet** (the final six lines) or into three **quatrains** and a **couplet**, the former an **Italian sonnet**, the latter an **English sonnet**. The poem turns—that is, shifts in focus or mood—after, re-spectively, the eighth line or the twelfth line. Within this structure, poets work variations. William Wordsworth's "The World Is Too Much with Us" (1807) turns in the middle of the ninth line, running the octet an extra two feet with "It moves us not." William Butler Yeats's "Leda and the Swan" (1924) has two turns, one at the traditional point after the eighth line and one in the middle of the eleventh line. Robert Graves's "Spoils" (1955) changes the structure of the sonnet entirely, breaking it up into two seven-line stanzas, one addressing the "spoils of war," the other the "spoils of love." The high point in English literary history for the sonnet occurred during the **Elizabethan Period**, when major writers composed lengthy sonnet cycles to their beloved. Sir Philip Sidney's *Astrophel and Stella* (1591) runs to 108 poems; Edmund Spenser's *Amoretti* (1595) to 89; Samuel Daniel's *Delia* (1592) to 60; Michael Drayton's *Amours* (1594) to 51 and his *Idea* (1619) to 63; and Shakespeare's sonnets (published in 1609 but some written as early as the 1580s) to 154.

Spenserian stanza   The stanza of Edmund Spenser's epic poem *The Faerie Queene* (1590). Nine lines long and predominantly iambic, with the first eight measuring five feet and the last six feet (rhyme scheme: *ababbcbcc*), the Spenserian stanza has the advantage of being long enough to contain a single thought or image, yet short and flexible enough to allow a narrative to flow through it. The opening of Canto I of *The Faerie Queene* (1590) displays the stanza's combination of storytelling and lyric structure:

> A gentle knight was pricking on the plain,
> Y-clad in mighty arms and silver shield,
> Wherein old dents of deep wounds did remain,
> The cruel marks of many a bloody field;
> Yet arms till that time did he never wield.
> His angry steed did chide his foaming bit,
> As much disdaining to the curb to yield.
> Full jolly knight he seemed and fair did sit,
> As one for knightly jousts and fierce encounters fit.

Spondee [SPAWN–dee] A metrical foot of verse containing two stressed sylla-bles. No English meters are spondaic, and the foot appears only as an exception, often for emphasis. In Dylan Thomas' "Do Not Go Gentle into That Good Night" (1951), for example, the first line of several stanzas begins with a spondee: "Good men, the last wave by . . . ," "Wise men who caught . . . ," and "Grave men, near death . . ."

Stage business Nonverbal action that engages the attention of an audience. Common to forms of **realism** in drama, stage business is a subtle means of re-vealing the inner thoughts and feelings of a character without resorting to solil-oquy. At the beginning of Arthur Miller's *Death of a Salesman* (1949), the **anti-hero** Willy Loman enters the stage hauling two large sample cases. As he moves across the stage, the text says, "his exhaustion is apparent." He opens the door and steps into a kitchen, drops his bags, rubs his palms, then sighs while a flute plays.

Stanza From the Italian, meaning "stopping-place" or "room." A unit of two or more lines of verse with space breaks before and after, the stanza is poetry's equivalent to the paragraph in prose. It is a basic organizational principle of verse, the definitive feature of many forms, such as **ballad**, *ottava rima*, and **sestina**.

Static character *See* **Flat character**.

Stock character A stereotypical character that occurs frequently in literature. Examples of stock characters are the mad scientist, the battle-scarred veteran, and the strong-but-silent cowboy. Some genres rely on stock characters for plot development and **setting**. The hard-boiled detective story, for instance, seems incomplete without a *femme fatale*, a stodgy cop, a doltish thug, and a loyal "girl Friday." (*See also* **Archetype**.)

Stream-of-consciousness Not a specific technique, but a type of modern nar-ration that employs various literary devices, especially interior monologue, in an attempt to duplicate the subjective and associative nature of human con-sciousness. To capture the "stream" of perceptions, memories, and thoughts, writers compose ungrammatical sentences and shapeless paragraphs, leap from present to past, and disregard conventions of storytelling. In William Faulkner's *The Sound and the Fury* (1929), just before Quentin Compson commits suicide, we get his final ruminations in all their rambling incoherence:

> Just by imagining the clump it seemed to me that I could hear
> whispers secret surges smell the beating of hot blood under wild
> unsecret flesh watching against red eyelids the swine untethered
> in pairs rushing coupled into the sea and he we must just stay
> awake and see evil done for a little while its not always and i it
> doesnt have to be . . .

The flow continues without punctuation for two pages, rendering Quentin's wavering mind putatively without writerly organization. (*See also* **First person narrator.**)

Stress An emphasis or **accent** placed on a syllable in speech. Clear pronunciation of polysyllabic words depends on the correct placement of stress. For instance, *de*-sert and de-*sert* are two different words and parts of speech, depending on their stress. The same is true of *con*-tract and con-*tract*, *re*-cord and re-*cord*. In English-language poetry (with the exception of certain experimental forms and the rare case of **syllabic verse**), stress is the basic unit of meter. Except for **spondee**, each metrical foot has one stress. (*See also* **Meter, Prosody.**)

Style The distinctive forms and uses of language in a literary work, an author's corpus, or an historical epoch. Style is the sum of **diction, imagery**, syntax, grammar, punctuation, and figurative language, and stylistics is the formal study of it. A stylistic analysis of Hemingway's short story collection *In Our Time* (1925), for example, would detail the clipped, declarative sentences, extensive dialogue, simple diction, lack of subordinate conjunctions, infrequent metaphors, and so on:

> Nick looked down into the pool from the bridge. It was a hot day. A kingfisher flew up the stream. It was a long time since Nick had looked into a stream and seen trout. They were very satisfactory.
> ("Big Two-Hearted River: Part 1")

A stylistic analysis might focus on the flat **prosody** and repetitive **diction** of the passage, and then be extended comparatively to other Hemingway works and to modernist fiction in general. In emphasizing the verbal features of literature, stylistics treats style as more or less distinct from content, while admitting that neither exists entirely without the other. **Poetic diction** is a style, as is **stream-of-consciousness** narration. In some stylistic criticism, style is treated as ornamentation—a kind of external dress of thoughts, ideas, emotions, and things—an approach typical of rhetorical conceptions of literature. In other cases, style is treated as expression—a kind of organic extension of thoughts, etc.—an approach typical of Romantic conceptions of literature. The first raises questions of **decorum**, the second questions of subjectivity. Style rhetorically understood invokes the concepts "high" and "low," "correct" and "incorrect," relating sentence structure, diction, and figures of speech to the subject matter and the aims of the author. Style subjectively understood invokes terms such as "Renaissance" and "Miltonic," relating stylistic features to one or more recognized authors.

Sublime In classical literature (as in Longinus' treatise "On the Sublime," ca. 300 C.E.), the sublime marks moments of lofty passion and drama, elevated thoughts and expressions. An episode in Virgil's *Aeneid*—when Aeneas encounters the rejected Dido in the underworld (she committed suicide after he left her), and she turns from him in silence as he weeps—is an instance of sublimity. As in this affecting example, sublimity isn't merely a rhetorical construct; it must have genuine emotional power behind it. Other sublime moments: when King Lear enters the stage bearing the body of Cordelia; when Milton's Satan spies upon the innocent Eve in the Garden; when Wordsworth describes the "light of setting suns" in "Tintern Abbey" (1798); the conclusion of the short story "The Dead" (1915), when James Joyce presents a vision of snow and death encompassing all of Ireland.

Sublimity also has an epistemological meaning, one articulated by German philosopher Immanuel Kant. In *Critique of Judgment* (1790), Kant explained sublimity as an experience in which the perceptual powers seem to break down or appear inadequate to take in the phenomena at hand. Standing at the foot of a majestic mountain, gazing across a vast ocean, listening to an overpowering symphony—these are moments that prove too "big" for our eyes and ears to take in. We feel awe and, according to Kant, must adjust our minds, activating a higher mental faculty (what he termed "reason") to comprehend the phenomenon. We are drawn to such experiences not only because the objects (oceans, waterfalls, high art, etc.) are beautiful and profound in themselves, but also because they activate our minds to more capacious understandings.

Subplot   *See* **Double plot.**

Surrealism   An early twentieth-century European movement in art and literature that tries to model creation according to the irrational dictates of the unconscious mind. Founded by the French poet André Breton, Surrealism sought to reach a higher plane of reality by abandoning logic for the seemingly absurd connections made in dreams and other unconscious mental activities. It aims, Breton declared, "to uproot thought from an increasingly cruel state of thralldom, to steer it back onto the path of total comprehension, return it to its original purity." But to do so requires the destruction of standard ways of seeing and thinking. A phrase about poetry in a letter by precursor Arthur Rimbaud became a motto: "the reasoned disorder of all the senses." Surrealists set this effort against ordinary modes of communication, which, they believed, were bound by bourgeois social restraints and norms of rationality. A human expression that bypassed filters of modern convention might yield works closer to our psychic needs and more in tune with the reality underlying political and social systems. Indeed, to its practitioners, to conceive surreal poems and paintings was to commit both an aesthetic and a political act. Allied to the French Communist Party and supportive of native rebellions against French colonial power, Surrealism presented itself as a critique of Western society and sought to foment revolution in the streets, not only in the salons and the classrooms. In one of his manifestoes, Breton wrote, "The simplest Surrealist act consists of dashing down into the street, pistol in hand, and firing blindly, as fast as you can pull the trigger." The political efforts failed, but as an artistic movement

Surrealism profoundly influenced practices in literature and the arts. Its impact may be measured by the extraordinary talents it attracted: Salvador Dalí, Louis Aragon, Max Ernst, Joan Miró, Paul Éluard, Georges Bataille, and Alberto Giacometti. Éluard's poem "Woman in Love" (1924) exemplifies surrealist imagery and theme:

> She is standing on my eyelids
> And her hair is in mine,
> She has the shape of my hands,
> She has the color of my eyes,
> In my shadow she is engulfed
> Like a stone in the sky.
>
> She always has open eyes
> And does not let me sleep.
> Her dreams in broad daylight
> Make suns evaporate,
> Make me laugh, cry and laugh,
> Speak having nothing to say.

Suspense   Anxiety created in readers and audiences by the author's handling of plot. When the outcome of events is unclear, the author's suspension of resolution intensifies our interest, particularly if the plot involves characters for whom we feel sympathy. For example, detective stories seek to create suspense by supplying enough clues to keep readers engaged with the detection, but delaying the full revelation of truth until the end, often adding an unexpected plot twist. Suspense is also created when the fate of a character is known to us but not to the character, as in the case of mythical figures, such as Oedipus, and historical figures, such as Shakespeare's Richard III. The suspense results not from the **plot**, but from our anticipation of how and when the character will meet his or her inevitable fate.

Syllabic verse   A verse form in which the poet establishes a pattern of a certain number of syllables to a line. That is, the syllable count matters more than the **stress** count (most English meter is stress-based). Syllabic verse is the most common meter in Romance languages such as Italian, French, and Spanish; it is less common in English because English has a stronger force of accent in its pronunciation. Syllabic verse appears, however, in several Modernist works, most conspicuously those of Marianne Moore. Moore eschews regular meter and rhyme, letting the verse lines flow solely by the counterpoint of accented and unaccented syllables:

> Fuzzless through slender crescent leaves
> of green or blue or
> both, in the Chinese style, the four

pairs half-moon leaf-mosaic turns
out to the sun the sprinkled blush
    of puce-American-Beauty pink
    applied to beeswax gray by the
uninquiring brush
    of mercantile bookbinding.
        ("Nine Nectarines"; 1935)

(*See also* **Accentual verse, Meter, Prosody.**)

Symbol   A person, place, or thing in a narrative that suggests meanings beyond
its literal sense. Symbol is related to **allegory**, but it works more complexly. In
an allegory an object has a single additional significance, one largely determined
by convention. When an allegory appears in a work, it usually has a one-to-one
relationship to an abstract entity, the relationship recognizable to readers and
audiences familiar with the cultural context of the work. A character named
"Christian," a plot in which a power-mad politician is exposed as corrupt, a setting of carnal delights—each serves as an allegory for set ideas and values.

By contrast, a symbol bears multiple suggestions and associations. It is unique
to the work, not common to a culture. In Herman Melville's *Moby-Dick* (1851),
for example, the great white whale accrues powerful and mysterious meanings as
the narrative progresses. It had never before appeared in literature, and no single
interpretation of the whale exhausts its possibilities. Moreover, the symbol
cannot be repeated in any other work and still retain its symbolic aspect, for once
it is repeated it becomes conventionalized. This is what leads many critics to elevate symbol over allegory: allegory seems like a mechanical translation of abstractions into forms; symbol seems like a glimpse into a higher truth. Samuel Taylor
Coleridge even attributes to the symbol a metaphysical value, for it

> is characterized by . . . the translucence of the eternal through and in
> the temporal. It always partakes of the reality which it renders intelli-
> gible; and while it enunciates the whole, abides itself as a living part
> in that unity of which it is the representative.
>   (*The Statesman's Manual*; 1816)

Symbolic act   An action whose significance goes well beyond the concrete act
itself. In literature, symbolic acts often involve a primal or unconscious ritual
element such as rebirth, purification, forgiveness, vengeance, or initiation. A
powerful instance occurs in Samuel Taylor Coleridge's "Rime of the Ancient
Mariner" (1798), when the solitary mariner stranded on a ship gazes into the
water at the snakes and blesses them "unawares." At that moment the albatross
around his neck (which he'd earlier killed for no reason) falls into the sea and
he is freed. The unconscious blessing becomes a symbolic act, a sign that grace
has descended upon the mariner and expiated his former sin. In Ernest Hem-

ingway's short story "Big Two-Hearted River, Parts I and II" (1925), we have a less metaphysical example. Nick Adams sets out to camp in the woods near his home after returning from service in World War I. He fishes, cooks breakfast, makes his bed, and so on, but he does it so deliberately, so meticulously, that it becomes clear the whole endeavor is a deep psychological process of purification and recovery. Each task turns into a symbolic act in Nick's attempt to reconstruct his war-torn psyche. (*See also* **Symbol**.)

Symbolist movement   An international literary movement that originated with nineteenth-century French poets Charles Baudelaire, Arthur Rimbaud, and Paul Verlaine. In their practice, symbolists aspired to make poetry achieve the condition of music. Seeking to excite and bewitch readers, they preferred evocation and suggestion to direct statement and exposition. Poets should act as seers who look beyond the mundane aspects of the everyday world to capture visions of a higher reality in a language of hypnotic power. Verlaine's "Endless Sameness" (1872) strives for a haunting effect through clipped images and verbal melody:

> Dans l'interminable
> Ennui de la plaine
> La neige incertaine
> Luit comme du sable.
>
> Le ciel est de cuivre
> Sans lueur aucune.
> On croirait voir vivre
> Et mourir la lune.
>
> In the interminable
> Weariness of the land
> The uncertain snow
> Shines like the sand.
>
> The sky is of copper,
> Its light is a swoon,
> I seem to see living
> And dying the moon

Symbolists influenced modernist writers all across Europe and North and South America, and together they constitute one of the most important movements in Western literary history. But symbolism is also significant on a theoretical level, and many twentieth-century critics have explored symbolism for its conception of the **semantics** of poetic language. What has been particularly noteworthy has been the way in which symbolists contrast the ordinary speech of prose with the heightened idiom of poetry. The symbolist poet-essayist Paul Valèry drew an analogy between prose/poetry and walking/dancing. Prose is like walking in that it has a concrete purpose apart from the walking itself—that is, to reach a destination. When one arrives at the goal, the walking ends and is forgotten. Prose is like walking in that it has an outside purpose—that is, to communicate a message—and when the message has been understood, the language of prose dissipates. Dancing is different. Dancing has no external purpose. The joy, grace, and beauty of dancing are embedded in the dancing itself. When the dance is over, it lingers as a remembered experience. One recalls the form, the movement, the execution. Similarly, poetry (in a symbolist sense) has no extrinsic message, no extra-linguistic content. It has a meaning, of course, but the meaning is tied to the poetic form itself. Once the poetry has ended, like dance it sticks in the mind in its formal state. One recalls the words, the sounds, the rhythm. For symbolists such as Valèry, this is the essence of poetry: it resists conversion from its material form (the exact words) into an abstract meaning or value. When we translate the language of a poem into different words, although the latter may have roughly the same meaning, we are unsatisfied and return to the original. (*See also* **Aestheticism, Aesthetics**.).

Synecdoche   [sin–EK–doe–kee] A figure of speech in which a significant part of a thing stands for the whole of it or vice versa. Substituting *wheels* for *car* or *rhyme* for *poetry* are examples of synecdoche, as are "All *hands* on deck" and "One hundred *head* of cattle." William Blake forms a synecdoche with "tongue" in the opening lines of "The Chimney Sweeper" (1789):

> When my mother died I was very young,
> And my father sold me while yet my tongue,
> Could scarcely cry weep weep weep weep . . . [the child means
>   "sweep," but his lisp yields "weep"]

(*See also* **Metonymy**.)

Synopsis   A brief summary or outline of a story or dramatic work. (*See also* **Paraphrase**.)

Tactile imagery   Imagery that refers to the sense of touch. For instance:

> I am the hounded slave, I wince at the bite of the dogs,
> Hell and despair are upon me, crack and again crack the
>   marksmen,
> I clutch at the rails of the fence, my gore dribs, thinn'd with the
>   ooze of my skin . . .
>   (Walt Whitman, "Song of Myself," ll. 838–40; 1855)

(*See also* **Imagery**.)

Tale   A word originating from the Old English *talu*, or "speech," a tale is a short, anonymous narrative without a complex plot or three-dimensional characters. An ancient form of narrative found in **folklore** and **oral tradition**, tales present basic stories with simple **motivations**, their literary power stemming from supernatural elements, twists of fate, and comic or tragic outcomes. A tale differs from a **short story** by its tendency to linear plotting and **flat** and **stock characters**, a distinction that British writer A. E. Coppard attributes to the fact that a story is something that is written and a tale is something that is told. The ambition of a tale is usually similar to that of a yarn: a concentrated revelation of the marvelous, comical, and ironic, rather than the careful representation of the everyday world.

Tall tale   A humorous short narrative that provides a wildly exaggerated version of events. Originally an oral form, the tall tale assumes that its audience knows the narrator is distorting the events. The form is often associated with the American frontier, as in the case of Paul Bunyan—mighty lumberjack said to have cleared the States of Iowa and Kansas and to have dug the Mississippi River—and of Davy Crockett, who rode an alligator up Niagara Falls. (*See also* **Tale**.)

Tercet   [TUR–set] A group of three lines of verse, usually all ending in the same rhyme. Sometimes tercets form the consistent stanza unit of a poem, as in *terza rima*, and in poems such as Robert Frost's "Provide, Provide" (1934), which is composed of three-line stanzas rhyming *aaa*. Often, though, tercets appear as exceptional moments in poems written generally in other forms. For example, Alexander Pope's *Essay on Criticism* (1711) is written in **heroic couplets**, but sprinkled in the verse are several tercets:

> Music resembles poetry, in each
> Are nameless graces which no methods teach,
> And which a master hand alone can reach.
>   (ll. 143–45)

Terminal refrain   A refrain that appears at the end of each stanza in a song or poem. The most famous example in American poetry is the "Nevermore" that concludes most of the stanzas in Edgar Allan Poe's "The Raven" (1845). Each stanza of Edmund Spenser's *Epithalamion* (1595) ends (with slight variations in wording) with the line "That all the woods may answer and your Eccho ring," and the four stanzas of John Skelton's "Mannerly Margery Milk and Ale" (1523) end:

> Gup, Christian Clout, gup, Jack of the Vale!
> With Mannerly Margery milk and ale.

(*See also* **Refrain**.)

Terza rima [TAIR–tza REE–muh] A verse form made up of three-line stanzas that are connected by an overlapping rhyme scheme (*aba, bcb, cdc, ded*, etc.). Dante employs *terza rima* in *The Divine Comedy* (1314–21):

> I cannot well remember in my mind
> How I came thither, so was I immersed
> In sleep, when the true way I left behind.
> But when my footsteps had attained the first
> Slope of a hill, at the end of that drear vale
> Which with much terror my spirit pierced,
> I looked up, and beheld its shoulders pale
> Already in clothing of that planet's light
> Which guideth men on all roads without fail.

In a modern instance, Robert Frost chooses it for "Acquainted with the Night" (1928), whose first stanzas are:

> I have been one acquainted with the night.
> I have walked out in rain—and back in rain.
> I have outwalked the furthest city light.
>
> I have looked down the saddest city lane,
> I have passed by the watchman on his beat
> And dropped my eyes, unwilling to explain.

The "rain" rhyme (line 2) is taken up by the first and third lines of the following stanza, the "beat" rhyme is taken up by the first and third lines of the following stanza, and so on.

Tetrameter [tet–RAM–uh–ter] A verse meter consisting of four metrical feet, or four primary stresses, per line. Example:

> Had we but world enough, and time,
> This coyness, lady, were no crime . . .
>   (Andrew Marvell, "To His Coy Mistress"; 1681)

Textual criticism A traditional form of literary study that includes scholarly editing, annotation, attributing authorship, and compiling bibliographies. A historical practice, textual criticism follows a work through different manuscript and published versions, searches for grounds for choosing one variant over another, and produces standard editions of authors' complete works. It is a laborious procedure involving long periods in archives, poring through manuscripts and successive editions. But without textual criticism the extant texts available for study would be less reliable and contextualized, and the speculative interpretations of literary criticism and theory would have less empirical backing.

Theater of the absurd A postwar European genre of drama depicting the grotesquely comic plight of human beings thrown by accident into an irrational and meaningless world. The critic Martin Esslin coined the term to characterize plays by writers such as Samuel Beckett, Jean Genet, and Eugene Ionesco. Samuel Beckett's *Waiting for Godot* (1955), considered to be the prime example of the absurd, features in two nearly identical acts two tramps waiting almost without hope on a country road for an unidentified person, Godot. "Nothing happens, nobody comes, nobody goes, it's awful," one of them cries, perhaps echoing the unspoken thoughts of an audience confronted by a play that refuses to do anything. There is a hole at the thematic center of the action—pointlessness, empty humor, absurdity—and the faiths and ideals of humankind that might fulfill—God, Goodness, Progress—remain absent.

Theme   The prevailing topic or issue conspicuously running through a literary work. A short didactic work like a fable may have a single obvious theme, but longer works can contain multiple themes. Not all subjects in a work can be considered themes, however, only the central subject or subjects; and one must be wary of identifying the theme of a work of literature with its overall meaning. The theme is an abstraction from the work, and many diverse works address the same theme. The theme of jealousy appears in Seneca's *Medea* (ca. 45 C.E.), Shakespeare's *Othello* (1604), Leo Tolstoy's *Kreutzer Sonata* (1889), and Alain Robbe-Grillet's *La Jalousie* (1957), and it is important to identify jealousy as their main concern. Yet the theme by itself is but a starting point in the comprehension of individual works.

Third-person narrator   A type of narration in which the narrator is a nonparticipant, an objective perspective upon the action. Often, the third-person narrator may be identified with the author, unless the narration attributes an identifiable personality to the narrator "himself." In a third-person narrative the characters are referred to in the third person ("he" or "she") and described objectively, even when the narrator enters their heads and records their inner thoughts and feelings. Third-person narrators are commonly omniscient, but the level of their knowledge varies from total omniscience (the narrator knows everything about the characters and their lives) to **selective omniscience** (the narrator is limited to the perceptions of a single character). (*See also* **Narrator, Point of view.**)

Tone   The attitude toward a subject conveyed in a literary work. No single stylistic device creates tone; it is the net result of various verbal elements that an author brings to the representation. Tone may be mirthful, sarcastic, sad, joyful, and so on, more as an emotional or moral climate, so to speak, than an explicit description. A writer's tone plays an important role in establishing the reader's relationship to the characters or ideas presented in a literary work. Because tone stems from more or less subtle shades of diction and perspective, discussions of tone can tend to be fuzzy and vague; and so it is important to link assertions about tone to the specific language of the text. Take, for example, the opening of Frank Norris's novel *McTeague* (1899):

It was Sunday, and, according to his custom on that day, McTeague took his dinner at two in the afternoon at the car conductors' coffee joint on Polk Street. He had thick gray soup; heavy, underdone meat, very hot, on a cold plate; two kinds of vegetables; and a sort of suet pudding, full of strong butter and sugar. On his way back to his office, one block above, he stopped at Joe Frenna's saloon and bought a pitcher of steam beer. It was his habit to leave the pitcher there on his way to dinner.

The description continues with McTeague reading the paper, sipping his beer, smoking a pipe, and drifting off to sleep, "cropfull, stupid, and warm." The tone is banal and ordinary, and the fixation on McTeague's eating narrows his days to the crudest satisfactions. The words *hot, cold, thick, strong, warm,* and *underdone* reduce the scene to bare appetites, and *custom* and *habit* emphasize the indiscriminate routine of McTeague's life. (*See also* **Atmosphere**.)

Total omniscience   [awm–NISH–ints] A **point of view** in which the narrator knows everything about all of the characters and events in a story. A narrator with total omniscience can move freely from one character to another and from one setting to another. Generally, a totally omniscient narrative is written in the third person. (*See also* **Narrator**.)

Traditional epic   *See* **Folk epic**.

Tragedy   The representation of serious actions which lead to a disastrous end for the **protagonist**. In Aristotle's formulation in the *Poetics*, tragedy is a genre that evokes pity and fear in the audience, but not simply through a plot that culminates in suffering. Several elements besides mere violence, loss, and misfortune are required to bring about a tragic situation. One, the hero must be fundamentally good, for the fall of an evil man would not call for pity or fear. He should be good, though, but not perfect, for we must be able to identify with the hero so that we might feel we share a common world of mischance. Two, the hero must fall because of an unwitting error (the **tragic flaw**) or an unavoidable run-in with fate, not because of an immoral nature or deed. Indeed, in many cases the tragedy lies in the fact that in acting properly the hero brings about his own ruin. For example, as a good king, Oedipus searches for the cause of the plague in Thebes, but even as he begins to sense that he himself is the cause, he does not waver. Finally, the work must conclude the suffering in a way that reconciles the spectators to what they have witnessed. Without some form of resolution, the suffering seems senseless and irrational, and the pity and fear that have been aroused remain unpurged (that is, the *katharsis* must be enabled by something in the action that transcends the specific sufferings portrayed).

These requirements come from Aristotle, but later theorists of tragedy have asserted similarly specific conditions. The early-nineteenth-century German philosopher G. W. F. Hegel proposed that tragedy involve not only a single **hero** and the circumstances of fate, but rather two heroes whose clash brings both to ruin even though their respective motives are justifiable. In Sophocles's *Antigone*, for instance, the action opens in the wake of civil war in Thebes. Two brothers have battled for control of the city, both have been killed, and their uncle, Creon, now reigns. He decrees that one brother be given burial honors, but that the other's corpse remain on the field, dishonored, left as carrion for wild dogs. Anyone attempting to bury the latter shall be put to death. Their sister Antigone can't bear the shame, and she sneaks onto the battle ground to rescue the body. Both sides have their rationale—Creon wishes to reunite Thebes, Antigone wishes to be a loyal sibling—and Hegel interprets each as the representative of larger historical forces (the polis versus the family). But whichever character is right, their commitments can only lead to further bloodshed. That's what makes *Antigone* a tragedy.

Such elaborate and grand ruminations upon tragic works indicate that the genre entails broad questions of human life, freedom, virtue, and failure. On one hand lie the quandaries of fate, on the other the qualities of character, a pairing that applies broadly to human experience. The predicaments of tragic heroes are easily compared (in less extreme forms) to the predicaments of ordinary life, especially when they turn upon a fateful error, a long-forgotten incident, a conflict of personal belief and political expediency. Situations that call for courage in the face of disaster, self-sacrifice for a greater good, moral clarity at the crossroads of competing interests, equanimity despite a frustrating and ironic conjunction of disabling circumstances—all have tragic potential, if the hero behaves with sufficient probity. Tragedy lies in the fact that probity doesn't save him or her from catastrophe.

These are the measures of tragic art, according to Aristotle and his successor-theorists. Ultimate questions of value and existence come into play, and tragedy is conceived as one mode of profound reflection upon the human condition. Even in cases in which Aristotle's, Hegel's, and others' formal strictures have been loosened, the air of tragedy is still felt. We call Shakespeare's *Othello* (1604), *Hamlet* (1601), *King Lear* (1605), and *Macbeth* (1605) tragedies, even though each one violates Aristotle's rules (for example, because Macbeth has intentionally committed thoroughly evil acts, we do not regret his demise). Although each one undergoes crucial tests of fortitude, none of them suffers an ironic conjunction of circumstances. Othello's motives are never justified, nor are Iago's, and Lear's decision to divide his kingdom makes no sense in political or historical terms. Macbeth, not Fate, is the author of his own demise, and Hamlet's demise rests as much in his self-doubts as in his death. Today, although it is best to keep the stricter definitions of tragedy in mind, the genre covers any literary work that moves from a happy situation to an unhappy one, in the process expanding into a rueful commentary upon human life.

Tragic flaw   A fatal weakness or ignorance in the protagonist that brings him or her to a bad end. In some interpretations, the tragic flaw is merely a mistaken judgment; in others, it is a personal failing (not necessarily a moral one). As Aristotle puts it in the *Poetics*: a tragic hero is a "man who is not eminently good and just, yet whose misfortune is brought about not by vice or depravity, but by some error or frailty." Some examples: in Sophocles's *Antigone*, Creon, whose stubborn refusal to allow the burial of his nephew spurs more bloodshed; Shakespeare's Othello, whose jealousy leads him to murder; Racine's Phèdre, whose passion for her son-in-law leads her to accuse him of rape. The idea that the tragic hero's catastrophe is caused by an error in judgment (*hamartia*) applies to many tragedies, but the idea of a protagonist ruined by a tragic flaw is also related to the Greek idea of *hubris* ("outrage"), involving transgressions against moral or divine law. For example, in early Greek tragedies, wealth and position often tempt those who possess them to overstep their bounds, to try to become more than mortal. This is the case with Aeschylus's depiction of the Persian despot Xerxes, whose pride led him to invade Greece, where his army and navy suffered humiliating defeat. (*See also* **Tragedy**.)

Tragic irony   A form of **dramatic irony** that ultimately ends in tragedy. The irony may involve a relation of the character to the universe, whereby circumstances seem to conspire against the character's best efforts to avoid danger or disgrace. Or, tragic irony may lie in the relationship of the character to the audience, as when the audience knows of a character's eventual misfortune before the character does, placing his pre-fall actions and utterances in an ironic light. (*See also* **Tragedy**.)

Tragicomedy   A type of drama that combines elements of both tragedy and comedy. Usually it creates potentially tragic situations that bring the protagonists to the brink of disaster but then ends happily, yet not so much that the tragic potential of the events has entirely disappeared. Tragicomedy can be traced as far back as the Renaissance in plays such as Shakespeare's *Measure for Measure* (1604) and *The Winter's Tale* (1610). When applied to modern plays, it tends to name any plot in which the distinction between comic and tragic experience becomes blurred, as in Anton Chekhov's *The Cherry Orchard* (1900) and Beckett's *Waiting for Godot* (1955), as well as in plays by Harold Pinter and Sam Shepard. (*See also* **Comedy**, **Tragedy**.)

Transferred epithet   A kind of **metonymy** in which the poet attributes some characteristic of a thing to another thing closely associated with it. It usually places an adjective next to a noun in which the connection is not strictly logical (John Milton's "blind mouths" or Hart Crane's "nimble blue plateaus"), but has expressive power.

Trick ending   A surprising and delayed **climax** that depends on a quick reversal of the situation from an unexpected source. The success of a trick ending is relative to the degree in which the reader is surprised but not left incredulous when it occurs. The American writer O. Henry popularized this type of ending, and it is often an element in detective fiction. O. Henry's tale "From the Cabby's Seat" (1904) begins by noting the categorical vision of the New York cabdriver. To him, every person is only a "Fare." Henry then focuses on a cab sitting outside a café where a wedding party is in progress. Among the crowd is the cabby himself, who spots a woman climb aboard. Although drunk and tired, he clambers up, whisks her around the park, takes her to a casino, and waits outside. At the end of the night, he drives her home, but first checks to see if she has the fare of four dollars. She answers, "dear me, no. I've only got a few pennies and a dime or two." He curses, then speeds to a police station. Hauling her inside, he blinks in the bright lights and sobers up in the face of men in blue. He turns to the woman, pauses, then looks at the sergeant. The truth dawns on him, and he introduces her to all as his new bride! (*See also* **Dénouement.**)

Trimeter [TRIM–uh–ter] A verse meter consisting of three metrical feet, or three primary stresses, per line. In the stanzas of Thomas Hardy's "Doom and She" (1902), all verses except the fourth are trimeter lines:

> There dwells a mighty pair—
> Slow, statuesque, intense—
> Amid the vague Immense:
> None can their chronicle declare,
> Nor why they be, nor whence.

Triolet [TREE–uh–lay] A lyric form of eight rhymed lines derived from the French. The two opening lines are repeated according to a set pattern. Many triolets are playful, but Robert Bridges' "Triolet" (1873) opts for a sad theme:

When first we met we did not guess	*a*	
That Love would prove so hard a master;	*b*	
Of more than common friendliness	*a*	
When first we met we did not guess.	*a*	(repeat line 1)
Who could foretell this sore distress	*a*	
This irretrievable disaster	*b*	
When first we met?—We did not guess	*a*	(repeat line 1)
That love would prove so hard a master.	*b*	(repeat line 2)

Trochee [TRO–kee] A metrical foot in which a stressed syllable is followed by an unstressed syllable, as in the words *sum*-mer and *chor*-us. The trochaic meter is often associated with children's songs and magic spells in English, such as the witches' chant in Shakespeare's *Macbeth* (1605):

> Double, double, toil and trouble;
> Fire burn and cauldron bubble . . .

Eye of newt, and toe of frog,
Wool of bat, and tongue of dog,
Adder's fork, and blindworm's sting,
Lizard's leg, and howlet's wing . . .
    (IV.i. 10–17)

Troubadours [TROO–buh–doors] The minstrels of the late Middle Ages. Originally, troubadours were lyric poets living in southern France and northern Italy who sang to aristocratic audiences of chivalry and love, heartache and beauty. The lyric "*Ab lo temps qe fai refrescar*" by Cercamon (twelfth century) is a typical effort:

> You hear me sing of her and I
> have no skill to tell you her loveliness.
> Her glance kills, the beauty of its directness does, her
> color's fresh, skin white, white without blemish, no
>   she wears no makeup.
> And they can say no hard word of her, so
> fine, clear as an emerald, is her excellence.

Understatement An ironic figure of speech that deliberately describes something as less than it really is. Often it suits comic motives—for example, when one says of a glutton, "He enjoys his food, doesn't he?" But understatement can also be poignant, as in the last stanza of William Wordsworth's "She Dwelt among th'Untrodden Ways" (1800), about a deceased woman or girl (note the understatement on "difference"):

> She lived unknown, and few could know,
> When Lucy ceased to be;
> But she is in her grave and Oh,
> The difference to me.

(*See also* **Overstatement**.)

Unities The three formal qualities recommended by Italian and French Renaissance literary critics to unify a plot in order to give it a cohesive and complete integrity. Good plots, they insisted, honored the three unities of action, time, and place. The action in neoclassical drama was patterned by strict cause and effect and generic consistency (genres are not to be mixed), the time to occur within a 24-hour period, and the setting to remain in one unchanging locale. Although Renaissance theorists cited Aristotle as an authority, in the *Poetics* Aristotle urged only the unity of plot, with events in a cause-and-effect relationship from beginning to middle to end forming a coherent whole. Moreover, to Aristotle, the so-called "unity of time" in the *Poetics* relates to performance time, not the time represented in the action. Because the dramatic competitions in ancient Greece took place during daylight in an outdoor theater, the three linked plays making a tragic trilogy, plus the concluding **satyr play**, had to be short enough to be performed within the period from sunrise to sunset. The *Poetics* never touches on unity of place, and indeed the action of many Greek plays occurs in several locales, though set changes would have been minimal if considered at all. But Renaissance and neoclassical critics on the Continent nevertheless asserted the artistic excellence of the unities, and elevated the condensed, well-crafted, focused **plot, setting**, and **time** as the highest dramatic art. But the unities never enjoyed such popularity in England. Shakespeare and his Elizabethan contemporaries violate all three unities consistently in their plays, and the authoritative critical voice of the eighteenth century, Samuel Johnson, mocked the unities as false conventions untrue to the mixed, haphazard nature of real life.

Unreliable narrator   A **narrator** who, intentionally or unintentionally, relates events in a subjective or distorted manner. The author usually provides some indication early on in such stories that the narrator is not to be completely trusted. The narrator of Fyodor Dostoevsky's *Notes from Underground* (1864) wallows in enraged resentment at mistreatment by society, yet relishes his own abasement. He says of his own "notes":

> Such confessions as I intend to make are never printed nor given to other people to read. Anyway, I am not strong-minded enough for that, and I don't see why I should be.

Nevertheless, a few paragraphs earlier he blurts:

> "I swear to you, gentlemen, there is not one thing, not one word of what I have written, that I really believe."

This is unreliability emphasized to the point of becoming a central issue in the work. (*See also* **Point of view**.)

Verbal irony   A statement in which the speaker or writer states the opposite of what is really meant. For example, a friend might comment, "How graceful you are!" after you trip clumsily on a stair. As opposed to **cosmic irony**, which involves the workings of life and fate, and **dramatic irony**, which involves the different perspectives of dramatic characters and audience members, verbal irony is strictly a phenomenon of language, of words saying one thing and meaning another. (*See also* **Sarcasm**.)

Verisimilitude   [VAIR–uh–sim–ILL–i–tude] The quality in a literary work of appearing true to life. In fiction, verisimilitude is usually achieved by careful use of realistic detail in description, **characterization**, and **dialogue**. For example, in his novel exposing conditions in the Chicago meatpacking industry, Upton Sinclair depicts a group of visitors encountering the bloody work first-hand:

> At the same instant the ear was assailed by a most terrifying shriek; the visitors started in alarm, the women turned pale and shrank back. The shriek was followed by another, louder and yet more agonizing— for once started on that journey, the hog never came back; at the top of the wheel he was shunted off upon a trolley, and went sailing down the room. And meantime another was swung up, and then another, and another, until there was a double line of them, each dangling by a foot and kicking in frenzy—and squealing.
> (*The Jungle*; 1906)

The calm brutality of the scene heightens its verisimilitude, and Sinclair's novel was powerful enough to bring about Federal investigations into food quality standards in subsequent years. (*See also* **Realism**.)

Verse   From the Latin *versum*, "to turn." Verse has two major meanings. First, it refers to any single line of poetry. Second, it refers to any composition in lines of more or less regular rhythm, in contrast to prose.

Vers libre   [vair LEE–bruh] *See* **Free verse**.

Villanelle   [VILL–uh–nel] A **fixed form** developed by French courtly poets of the Middle Ages in imitation of Italian folk song. A villanelle consists of six stanzas (five **tercets**, one **quatrain**) containing two rhymes, with two lines repeated in a prescribed pattern. For example, Edwin Arlington Robinson's "Villanelle of Change" (1891):

Since Persia fell at Marathon,	*a*
The yellow years have gathered fast:	*b*
Long centuries have come and gone.	*a*
And yet (they say) the place will don	*a*
A phantom fury of the past,	*b*
Since Persia fell at Marathon;	*a* (repeat line 1)
And as of old, when Helicon	*a*
Trembled and swayed with rapture vast	*b*
(Long centuries have come and gone),	*a* (repeat line 3)
This ancient plain, when night comes on,	*a*
Shakes to a ghostly battle-blast,	*b*
Since Persia fell at Marathon.	*a* (repeat line 1)

But into soundless Acheron	a	
The glory of Greek shame was cast:	b	
Long centuries have come and gone,	a	(repeat line 3)

The suns of Hellas have all shone,	a	
The first has fallen to the last:—	b	
Since Persia fell at Marathon,	a	(repeat line 1)
Long centuries have come and gone.	a	(repeat line 3)

Visual imagery   A word or sequence of words that emphasizes the visual appearance of things. For example, two stanzas from Wallace Stevens's "A Study of Two Pears" (1942):

II
They are yellow forms
Composed of curves
Bulging toward the base.
They are touched red.

III
They are not flat surfaces
Having curved outlines.
They are round
Tapering toward the top.

Text Credits

Barth, John. Excerpt from "Lost in the Funhouse," copyright © 1967 by The Atlantic Monthly Company, from *Lost in the Funhouse* by John Barth. Reprinted by permission of Doubleday, a division of Random House, Inc.

Basho, Matsuo. Haiku from *Haiku for People*, at http://www.toyomasu.com/haiku/#basho.

Beckett, Samuel. *Waiting for Godot* (New York: Grove Press, 1954).

Bishop, Elizabeth. Excerpt from "The Moose" from *The Complete Poems 1927–1979* by Elizabeth Bishop. Copyright © 1979, 1983 by Alice Helen Methfessel. Reprinted by permission of Farrar, Straus and Giroux, LLC.

Cercamon. "Ab lo temps qe fai refrescar" from *Proensa: An Anthology of Troubadour Poetry*, selected and translated by Paul Blackburn. Copyright © 1978 by Joan Blackburn. Reprinted by permission of the University of California Press.

Crane, Hart. Lines from "The Broken Tower," from *Complete Poems of Hart Crane* by Hart Crane, edited by Marc Simon. Copyright 1933, 1958, 1966 by Liveright Publishing Corporation. Copyright © 1986 by Marc Simon. Used by permission of Liveright Publishing Corporation.

Cummings, E. E. Line from "my father moved through dooms of love," Copyright 1940, © 1968, 1991 by the Trustees for the E. E. Cummings Trust, from *Complete Poems: 1904–1962* by E. E. Cummings, edited by George J. Firmage. Used by permission of Liveright Publishing Corporation.

Cummings, E. E. "l(a." Copyright © 1958, 1986, 1991 by the Trustees for the E. E. Cummings Trust, from *Complete Poems: 1904–1962* by E. E. Cummings, edited by George J. Firmage. Used by permission of Liveright Publishing Corporation.

Dante. Excerpt from *The Divine Comedy*. From *The Portable Dante: The Divine Comedy*, complete, trans. Laurence Binyon (New York: Viking Press, 1947).

Dickinson, Emily. Lines from "Mine – by the Right of the White Election!" and line from "I felt a Funeral, in my Brain." Reprinted by permission of the publishers and the Trustees of Amherst College from *The Poems of Emily Dickinson*, Thomas H. Johnson, ed., Cambridge, Mass.: The Belknap Press of Harvard University Press, Copyright © 1951, 1955, 1979 by the President and Fellows of Harvard College.

Dostoevsky, Fyodor. "Notes from Underground" from *White Nights and Other Stories*, trans. Constance Garnett (London: Heinemann, 1918).

Eliot, T. S. Lines from "The Love Song of J. Alfred Prufrock," *Poetry: A Magazine of Verse*, June 1915. Reprinted by permission of Faber and Faber Ltd.

Eliot, T. S. Excerpts from "Tradition and the Individual Talent," *The Egoist* (1919). Reprinted by permission of Faber and Faber Ltd.

Eliot, T. S. Lines from *The Waste Land* by T. S. Eliot (1922). Reprinted by permission of Faber and Faber Ltd.

Eliot, T. S. Excerpt from "The Hollow Men" in *Collected Poems 1909–1962* by T. S. Eliot, copyright 1936 by Harcourt, Inc., copyright © 1964, 1963 by T. S. Eliot, reprinted by permission of Harcourt, Inc., and Faber and Faber Ltd.

Éluard, Paul. "Woman in Love" from *Paul Éluard: Selected Poems*, selected and translated by Gilbert Bowen. Copyright © 1988 by John Calder Ltd. Reprinted by permission of Calder Publications Ltd.

Faulkner, William. *The Sound and the Fury* (New York: Cape & Smith, 1929; New York: Random House, new, corrected edition, 1984).

Frost, Robert. Excerpts from "Desert Places," "Once by the Pacific," "The Silken Tent," and "Acquainted with the Night" from *The Poetry of Robert Frost*, edited by Edward Connery Lathem. Copyright 1964, 1970 by Lesley Frost Ballantine, copyright 1936, 1942, 1956 by Robert Frost, copyright 1928, 1969 by Henry Holt and Company. Reprinted by permission of Henry Holt and Company, LLC.

Verlaine, Paul. "Endless Sameness" from *Paul Verlaine: His Absinthe-Tinted Song, a Monograph on the Poet, with Selections from his Work*, ed. and trans. Bergen Applegate (Chicago: R. F. Seymour, The Alderbrink Press, 1916).

Williams, William Carlos. Lines from "The Rose (The rose is obsolete)," "The Yachts," and "Spring and All" from *Collected Poems: 1909–1939*, Volume I, copyright © 1938 by New Directions Publishing Corp. Reprinted by permission of New Directions Publishing Corp.

Williams, William Carlos. Lines from "The Dance (In Brueghel's)" from *Collected Poems 1939–1962*, Volume II, copyright © 1944 by William Carlos Williams. Reprinted by permission of New Directions Publishing Corp.

Yeats, William Butler. Lines from "Byzantium." Reprinted with the permission of Scribner, an imprint of Simon & Schuster Adult Publishing Group, from *The Collected Works of W. B. Yeats, Volume I: The Poems, Revised*, edited by Richard J. Finneran. Copyright © 1933 by The Macmillan Company; copyright renewed © 1961 by Bertha Georgie Yeats.